It's Not Just
MUMBO JUMBO

IT'S NOT JUST MUMBO JUMBO

The 7 Steps That Will Change Your Life

CHARLEY LAW

First published in 2025 by
Phoenix Mind Ltd, in partnership with Whitefox Publishing Ltd

9 8 7 6 5 4 3 2 1

www.wearewhitefox.com

Copyright © Phoenix Mind Ltd, 2025

EU GPSR Authorised Representative
LOGOS EUROPE, 9 rue Nicolas Poussin, 17000, LA ROCHELLE, France
E-mail: Contact@logoseurope.eu

ISBN 9781916797987 | eBook ISBN 9781916797994 | Audiobook ISBN 9781918191158

Phoenix Mind Ltd asserts the moral right to be identified as the author of this work.

Extract from *The Power of Now* reproduced with permission of Hodder and Stoughton and New World Library via PLSclear.

From *The Book You Wish Your Parents Had Read (and Your Children Will Be Glad That You Did)* by Philippa Perry published by Penguin Life. Copyright © Philippa Perry 2019. Reprinted by permission of Penguin Books Limited.

Excerpt(s) from REINVENTING YOUR LIFE: HOW TO BREAK FREE FROM NEGATIVE LIFE PATTERNS by Jeffrey E. Young and Janet S. Klosko, copyright © 1993 by Jeffrey E. Young and Janet S. Klosko. Used by permission of Dutton, an imprint of Penguin Publishing Group, a division of Penguin Random House LLC. All rights reserved.

Excerpt(s) from THE FOUR AGREEMENTS: A PRACTICAL GUIDE TO PERSONAL FREEDOM by Don Miguel Ruiz with Janet Mills, copyright © 1997 by Miguel Angel Ruiz, M.D., and Janet Mills. Used by permission of Amber-Allen Publishing, an imprint of Penguin Publishing Group, a division of Penguin Random House LLC. All rights reserved.

Excerpt(s) from THE CHIMP PARADOX: THE MIND MANAGEMENT PROGRAM TO HELP YOU ACHIEVE SUCCESS, CONFIDENCE, AND HAPPINESS by Steve Peters, copyright © 2011 by Steve Peters. Used by permission of Tarcher, an imprint of Penguin Publishing Group, a division of Penguin Random House LLC. All rights reserved.

From ATTACHED: Are You Anxious, Avoidant or Secure? by Dr Amir Levine and Rachel Heller, first published in the UK in 2011 by Rodale, and in 2019 by Bluebird, an imprint of Pan Macmillan, a division of Macmillan Publishers International Limited. Reproduced by permission of Macmillan Publishers International Limited, Copyright © Amir Levine and Rachel Heller 2010.

All rights reserved. No part of this publication may be reproduced, stored in a retrieval system or transmitted in any form or by any means, electronic, mechanical, photocopying, recording or otherwise, without prior written permission of the author.

While every effort has been made to trace the owners of copyright material reproduced herein, the author would like to apologise for any omissions and will be pleased to incorporate missing acknowledgements in any future editions.

All photographs and illustrations in this book © Phoenix Mind Ltd, unless otherwise stated.

Designed and typeset by Siulen Design
Cover design by Extract Studios
Project management by Whitefox Publishing

Dedicated to my parents.
Thank you for everything.

CONTENTS

Introduction	9
Step 1 – Desire	13
Step 2 – The Body Baseline	57
Step 3 – The Essentials	79
Step 4 – Know Thyself	145
Step 5 – Responsibility in Action	237
Step 6 – Clarity	309
Step 7 – Consistency	387
Resources & Bibliography	439

A Note to the Reader

This book draws from real experiences and events, told as truthfully as memory allows. To protect privacy and confidentiality, some locations and identifying details have been changed. Some individuals are composite characters representing patterns across multiple relationships. Certain scenes have been compressed or re-imagined while preserving their essential truth.

The heart of this story remains true: these are the lessons, struggles and transformations as I lived and understood them.

This book is shared for general informational purposes and should not be considered professional, medical or therapeutic advice.

INTRODUCTION

If you had met me in my late twenties, you would have seen the high-flying job, the series of models hanging off my arm, the money flying out of my wallet. You would have seen someone apparently very successful and ambitious, always chasing the next bonus, the next exciting date, the next exotic holiday, the next moment worthy of documenting on an Instagram account that might have seemed almost designed to generate feelings of envy.

But you wouldn't have really been meeting me.

You wouldn't have seen someone who was always stressed, always in a hurry, always working, always cutting corners. Someone for whom nothing was ever enough. Someone who was never really satisfied. Someone who could never really relax.

If only I could just get the right girl, just make enough money, just buy that house, just get into shape, then surely, I told myself, I would finally be able to relax and start enjoying life.

I managed to hide all of this stuff, and I did it so well that I even managed to hide it from myself – for a while, at least.

The truth was I always had one foot in the past and one foot in the future, but I was pissing in the present. And when I tripped, I found myself sitting in that puddle.

This book is the story of what I did next, though it needs to start while I was still mid-piss. You'll see why. Sometimes you can only appreciate how far you've come by looking all the way back, even when it hurts to do so.

If you've picked up this book because you're interested in self-help, you are already a few steps further down the road than I was when I started on this journey. I was the typical cynical Brit who once would have dismissed all of this as 'mumbo jumbo', and consequently wary of taking the wrong steps through the minefield of self-help, being bombarded by online gurus who weren't necessarily really trying to help, but had spotted a good money-making scheme. When I most needed guidance, I had no idea who to trust or where to turn.

As I began navigating the minefield and started to see how transformative and life-changing some of these practices can be, I also became more aware of the people around me quietly struggling with a lot of the same things I was overcoming within myself. But I knew many of them, especially some of my mates, were unlikely to ever get into a lot of this stuff.

'Piss off, Charley, have another half shandy and stop boring us with all this mumbo jumbo.'

And so that's when I went all in, for myself and for everyone else out there who could benefit from it – even if they didn't know it yet. I was determined to demystify the 'mumbo jumbo'. I made it my mission to dive even deeper into self-help and self-improvement. I became like an investigative journalist uncovering the most effective books, teachers, theories, courses, therapies and retreats. I needed to figure out what actually worked, putting myself through experiences from the sublime to the absurd with an open mind, so that I could write this book for you, distilling all the key ingredients, the essential pieces to the puzzle, into the most practical, digestible, no-nonsense roadmap possible.

There is no hiding from my privilege, but I've come to realise that a lot of our emotional struggles, urges and desires – the search for happiness, peace, success, energy, balance, clarity and direction – are often universal, irrespective of where we're from, who we are or what we have. Money of course helps solve our money problems, but to feel happy, fulfilled and loved can cut through all things material.

In this book I hope to synthesise the best of everything I discovered so that in the shortest amount of time and by spending the least amount of money, you can create a better life for yourself too.

STEP 1
DESIRE

> "Your desire to change must be greater than your desire to stay the same."
>
> UNKNOWN

MIAMI HEAT

'You must be Charley.'

I had been sitting patiently in the Philippe Starck-designed lobby of the apartment building, waiting for Pablo to arrive. Fitted with oversized chandeliers, a white marble floor and art deco furniture, the space was vast, with gigantic golden eggs and purple mirrors towering up to the high ceilings. I watched as fashion models ambled by in their chic designer outfits – effortlessly cool.

Must be an event happening, I presumed.

Pablo was mid-forties, with a fresh black tee, stubble, relaxed vibe, and a vape. Hopefully he was about to become my landlord.

With my pasty English skin and collection of luggage he must have had no problem spotting me among this crowd.

'Let's head upstairs, shall we? Here, I'll give you a hand.'

We headed up to the twenty-seventh floor and rolled in through the front door.

'So here we are.' He tried to gauge my reaction. It was hard not to be drawn straight to the spectacular view of Miami Beach through the wall of sheer glass barely separating us from the royal blue sky and midday sun.

'That's Alton Road – look, you can just see the towers at Sunset Harbour.'

I tried to hold my composure, paying attention to the sales patter while trying to quickly scan my new home. It was even better in real life. Neatly furnished, chic but homely. A nice kitchenette-cum-sitting room, decent double bedroom and spacious bathroom – the perfect bachelor pad.

'So, what do you do, Charley?'

'Commodity trader – I do a lot of business in South America, hence why–'

'No way – I'm Chilean. We trade a lot of copper.'

'Nice! I'm in iron ore and coal, we should chat.'

He stayed cool – as if he had conversations like this every day.

I tried not to show him how thoroughly chuffed I was. I wanted him to believe I was in his league too, that I belonged here.

'This is the heater-cooler system, I just keep it on five. So, who do you work with?'

I knew he was trying to sus out whether I was for real.

I listed off some contacts, and eventually one name registered.

Relief, I was legit.

'So, what are your plans here, Charley?'

'Working mainly – a lot easier to travel to where I need to go than damn London. Hopefully meet some nice chicks too.' I gave him a cheeky grin; I knew he was on board.

He chuckled. 'Nobody really works here, man, you'll see.'

I dismissed that. Not me. I was a grafter.

'I'm gonna be up in Wellington a bit too.'

'Polo? Palm Beach?' he replied attentively.

'Yeah.'

Now he knew I rode. Good. I wondered whether I should mention the polo ponies I owned back in the UK, whether he would be impressed.

'Ah, nice – I have some friends up there. I'll have to introduce you. BIG showjumping family.' Maybe he was the name-dropper, brown-noser type. Or maybe he belonged and thought I did too.

'Have you got a car?'

'Er, no, not yet, need to sort that out.'

He took another drag of his vape. 'Well, I have a spare G-Wagon. It would make sense – it's downstairs in the parking bay and I barely use it. Fully licensed, automatic tolls, insured.'

'Honestly, Pablo, that would be amazing – how much?'

'Charley, we can figure something out – let me speak to my girlfriend... Here's the number for the porter downstairs. All the post is delivered to your locker at reception, I'll show you... Listen, you should come join me at Soho tonight – I'll introduce you to some friends.'

He was talking about Soho Beach House; one of the hottest tickets in town. Maybe he knew some models.

'Are you a member?'

'Still waiting for my application to be approved,' I replied.

I didn't tell him I'd been on the waiting list for nearly two years now.

'Don't worry about that – we'll sort it. I know who to speak to.' He gave me a wink.

I liked the way he rolled.

We pinballed off each other. I couldn't wait to immerse myself into Miami life.

'Let's head back downstairs – I think that's everything.'

'Pablo, by the way, what's happening here today?'

'What do you mean?'

'You know – all the guys and girls downstairs, models, fashionistas.'

He took a moment to look me properly in the eye this time and smiled. 'Charley, there's nothing happening today, it's just like any other day. Welcome to the Icon South Beach, my friend.'

I'd really hit the jackpot with my apartment block.

I hoped Pablo thought I was joking, and that I knew all along this is just what life in the Icon South Beach was like. That this was me – the commodity trader, the wannabe playboy, the South American jet-setter. The hustle, the English charm – that all came so naturally to me. I was good at living on my wits and, best of all, it made me feel good.

As far as I – or, perhaps more importantly at this moment, Pablo – was concerned, I had made it. I had become the person I'd always wanted to be – independent, successful, admired.

Little did I know – soon the dream would be over.

And not just over, but smashed to smithereens.

'The bigger the ego
the bigger the fall.'

RYAN HOLIDAY,
THE EGO IS THE ENEMY

MISS MEXICO

Settling in for my dose of late morning vitamin D by the pool. Cabana, cream and coconut water. The phone rings. It's one of my port agents.

'Charley, the minister just died, they're refusing to load the vessel, everything is chaos – you better get down here ASAP.'

By 4 p.m. I was boarding the American Airlines flight south. I was like a duck to water.

I had two ships anchored off the pacific coast of Mexico waiting to load. I'd already prepaid a few million for the cargo and more to get both vessels into position. If I couldn't get them loaded it would be a disaster; I'd be finished.

'*Siguiente.*'

Next.

I crossed the yellow line and made my way towards the customs officer squashed in her little booth. She glanced up and gave me that look. The customs hall at Mexico City International Airport AKA Aeropuerto Benito Juárez was big, bright and airy. I'd dressed low key in my blue button-down Oxford, dark blazer and Converse, but I still liked how much attention I got from everyone. The general advice was not to travel to where I was going unless it was essential – too much crime and instability. There were very few tourists and even fewer Brits like me coming to do business. Handing her my passport I tried to make eye contact, but her chin stayed firmly glued to her chest.

She begins the performance; leisurely flicking through the inked-up pages, doing her best to exert maximum authority and ensure I'm made to feel as uncomfortable as is humanly possible.

It was a well-known routine. I was acutely aware of how different I looked to everyone else, how the multiple entry stamps piqued their interest, and how they might take me to the detention centre. To interrogate me about what I was doing there so frequently. The rush of adrenaline was a kick.

'Hablas Espanol.'

'Si, pero un poquito,' I lied – I spoke more than a little, but I needed to play dumb in case things got tricky.

She drilled me with the standard questions but in the end gave up and reached for the industrial-sized stamp while creasing through the pages with her index finger.

Clunk.

Siguiente.

Next.

I was through – to another world, a far cry from Sloane Square, Kings Road pubs, my private school posse and of course the high life in Miami Beach.

I walked briskly through the sliding doors into the arrivals lounge and kept moving between the sea of poachers sizing me up to make some cash.

'Taxi'

'*Cambio*' [Exchange]

'Hotel'

'Cellular'

It was like a computer game, I was the avatar dropping into the scene with dollar bills spinning over my head. I kept going – I knew exactly what my next steps were.

I needed to get local currency. The airport exchange rates were terrible – I made my way along the concourse down to exit 14A where luckily, I spotted a familiar face.

Stepping outside into the burning afternoon sun, my fair skin soaking it up like blotting paper. The traffic smoked past and I inhaled that familiar blend of old cigarettes, diesel engines, sweat, street food and open drains. It was good to be back.

With my pockets full of pesos, I headed back into the air conditioning, I was ready. Converting from dollars, everything was ridiculously cheap. I felt like Richard Pryor in Brewster's Millions. I couldn't spend it fast enough – meals, bars, clubs, travel. It was like Monopoly money.

It was time for the next leg of my journey – the hour or so flight from the capital to the Pacific Coast. The port town was an industrial heartland, it's where my ships were waiting to load, and I was like the gringo straight out of the eighties action movie.

Bugger, my flight was delayed by two hours.

That would probably mean three or four – it was pretty standard. I took a few seconds to adjust my expectations – a crucial skill every successful trader needs to learn quickly. I changed my mindset from: I'm about to get on a plane to reach my destination, to: I'm spending part of my day here, just like I would at home. It was the only way I could manage the constant uncertainty. I tried to avoid feeling transitory, instead I would tell myself this is where I belong. I became as fluid on the inside as my environment on the outside.

I went upstairs and sunk my teeth into a freshly cooked gordita – the charred corn bread was golden brown on the outside and still steaming, white and fluffy on the inside, packed with melted butter, moist white cheese and shredded chicken. Juices squirted onto my paper plate. It was warm and savoury, proper local food. I washed it down with a swig of cold beer.

I began flicking through my Nokia. I was feeling needy for company – the country relaxed me; the humidity, the slower pace, the easy-going vibe, there was less pressure to be a certain way. I text Cata and Lucía the same message:

'Hola, mi amor! Tengo una surprisa – estoy llegando esta noche!'

[Hello, my love! I have a surprise – I'm arriving this evening!]

I had to hedge my bets.

Only Lucía replied. Luckily, I'd fired her the odd message since the last time, keeping her vaguely warm.

'Quiero verte' [I want to see you]

'Te extrano' [I miss you]

'Tengo regalo' [I have a present]

Our texts pinged back and forth. I cut to the chase – if she couldn't make it, I'd move on to the next.

'Dale OK mi amor. Nos vemos en hotel al las dies. Nos vemos pronto. Ciao.'

We had a date.

I went to a convenience store and grabbed some supplies. My mind was already racing ahead to the evening, planning, anticipating. I was an opportunist, always plotting how to satisfy my next fix, excitement, something to make me feel alive. The last thing I could do was sit down and read a book or master my Spanish – the neurons and synapses were jumping around in my head like popcorn.

At last. I was walking up the steps onto the dated Boeing 737.

'*Bienvenido.*'

Everything about the Latin stewardess was exotic: her deep walnut eyes, her glossy make-up, her Arabian perfume, her silk neck scarf, the way she confidently stood there in her fitted pinstripe uniform. She greeted me with a smile (not a hint of remorse for the four-hour delay – you wouldn't expect it though, it was their way).

Think *Mad Men* meets *Narcos*. The eighties cabin was tired and there was a haze against the dim lights – you could hardly see to the back. The thickly padded leather seats were well worn and had quickly filled with a weary mix of local passengers. Suits flying home from business in Ecuador. Students returning from the Embassy with essential papers. Families getting home after a vacation to Miami. Girls nursing their bodies after plastic surgery in the capital.

I shimmied down the narrow isle, eyes peering at me subtly. I found my seat, checked in with Lucía to make sure she wasn't going to flake, rested my temple against the plastic casing around the window and fell asleep.

—

The hotel was a pyramid-like structure with a flat roof. Surrounded by green lawns, water features and palm trees, it rose up in a series of austere contours, concrete walls and grids of mirrored windowpanes. More Soviet military headquarters than a luxury hotel. Still, it was the best hotel in town, a sought-after spot for smart local weddings and business conferences.

I wheeled my Rimowa through the door into the familiar hotel room. It was spacious. Two queen-sized beds. Simple beige, cream and wooden décor. Panoramic views out onto the resort-like pool, then green shrubbery all the way to the port in the distance. From the seventh floor you could just make out one of the Panamax ships leaving the berth. The size of a horizontal skyscraper, she was sitting deep in the water, with her hull fully laden with ore.

I switched off the AC and proceeded to unpack my belongings. I laid out my toiletries in the bathroom, my shoes beside the armchair, my clothes in the wardrobe, the dirty laundry in the plastic bag by the door for collection. I swept the desk clear of hotel memorabilia, shoved it all into the left drawer and laid out my operations centre neatly in the clear space. Laptop, note pad, phones, chargers, battery packs and adaptors all linked up. Cash, passport, cigarettes and sunglasses in the right-hand drawer. It grounded me; it was like dropping my anchor among the choppy currents of travel. It was my way of enduring the constant change – it gave me just enough stability to function.

My Nokia lit up and chimed a text.

'Estoy en camino amor' [I'm en route]

She was on her way. It was 11 p.m., bang on what I called Mexican time – everyone and everything usually ran an hour or so late. I'd timed it perfectly. A shot of adrenaline hit my bloodstream.

Eager not to create a scene I hurried down to the foyer and awaited her arrival.

Smoking a cigarette, I paced up and down casually trying to hide my anticipation. It was dark and the crickets were out, I slowly inhaled the smooth, sweet smoke deep into my lungs. I wasn't really a smoker back home, but smoking felt different out here. It felt natural.

SUVs and Toyota Hiluxes cruised by picking up and depositing guests. Fifteen minutes later a little Clio hatchback with blacked-out windows pulled up. I knew it was her.

I stayed by the sliding doors. As she got out the back seat, she peered up and smiled briefly, then walked over to me with her head bowed discreetly.

'Hola, mi amor.' We embraced each other. She was shy and excited. We

both wanted to navigate the lobby as quickly as possible so intuitively kept moving and picked up the pace as we strode through the atrium, past reception. Her platform heels echoed against the marble floor. I walked close to her and whispered small talk, making it look like we knew each other better than we did. We were quiet but the receptionist surely heard my heart pounding. I tried to catch his eye and nod to head off any judgement – he didn't even look up.

The elevator doors slid closed. Finally, we were alone.

I could breathe. My shoulders dropped and I looked at her properly for the first time.

Lucía was in her early thirties and brunette, 'morocha' as they'd describe that deep dark brown hair of hers, scraped back into a ponytail. Her face was pretty with a button nose, soft eyes and shallow, neatly groomed brows. There was a thin scar as long as my little finger stretching down the side of her temple to her cheek bone. It was barely visible, but the bright flickering strobe light in the elevator helped me catch a glimpse glistening through the extra layers of make-up.

Her freshly conditioned hair and sweet vanilla pink perfume filled the air between us. It reminded me of those pheromone-enhancing aromas the girls piled on in strip clubs.

I placed my hands on her hips admiringly.

'*Que guappa,*' [How beautiful] I said with a hit of Latino passion.

She'd made an effort but kept it casual. Her round silicon breasts were straining against her fresh white tank top – her toned brown arms glowing in contrast.

'*Te extrano mucho, Lucía.*' [I missed you a lot, Lucia.]

She smiled.

The door clunked shut. The room was now nice and humid. Less chance of a chill uncovering any nervy shivers. The TV was tactfully switched to VH1 and playing some upbeat Latino vibes.

'*Quieres algo para tomar?*' [Would you like something to drink?]

Defaulting back into being a polite Brit, the momentum paused.

Tu? [You?]

We looked at each other – trying to gauge what the other was thinking, just like any other second date.

'Whisky con Coca Cola?' I jumped in with a local favorite.

'*Dale, mi amor – wikkey con cola entonces!*' [OK, my love – whisky and Coke it is!] She said it with naughty spice and playfulness. It felt like this was unfamiliar fun to her.

I pulled her up from off the bed and held her tight as we checked each other out in the floor-length mirror.

'*Ay, Papi,*' she squeaked.

I felt powerful, masculine and alive – everything I tended to suppress back home, where I had been brought up to do as I was told and rarely expressed myself. Here there was no one to judge. Here I could be anyone I wanted to be.

We were promptly interrupted by a knock. '*Servicio.*'

The drinks had arrived. I grabbed a few pesos from the drawer and ran over to make the exchange in the doorway so the porter couldn't see her.

'Salud!' We clunked glasses and stood there practically naked, moving to the music and sipping the quenching, moreish nectar from our ice-cold tumblers.

She could see how excited I was. She put her drink down and beckoned me closer. '*Veni, veni*' [come come]. Her voice was lower and softer now.

After she left, I stood there, looking out onto the night sky across the rust jungle of factories, refineries, cranes and conveyors. It was hard to see where the yellow safety lights ended, and the stars began. I guess if I'd stopped to think about it – I would have felt pretty empty, maybe allow a hollow ache to creep in – but the reality was I never gave it a chance, I was straight back to business. I reached for my phone, checked my emails, refreshed my WhatsApp and then headed to bed.

EL FANTASMA

It took me twenty-four hours to play catch up – things were moving fast. I hadn't been in a situation like this before, having to salvage a deal that seemed to be on the verge of collapse.

'Charley, my friend, they're trying to cancel the contracts. Everything's in chaos.'

If I couldn't get these two ships loaded, everything I'd built was about to go up in smoke. I'd be ruined.

It was time to meet my supplier.

I fired off a WhatsApp:

'Rafael. Need to meet urgently. Pls let me know availability soonest.'

'Yes OK – tomorrow morning 8 a.m. breakfast at your hotel.'

'OK see you there – thank you.'

He was a man of few words.

The next morning I'd just polished off my breakfast at the hotel. It was nearly 9 a.m. – *where was he?*

Late. They all were, but Rafael especially. He was impossible to track down. It was normal to sometimes wait two or three hours to meet *El Fantasma* [The Ghost].

I sent a chaser.

'Sorry, Charley, I'm still in Guadalajara. Could you come here?'

Really, Rafael? Good of you to let me know.

He was the quiet, sophisticated one, trusted by those at the highest levels. He was a brain who enjoyed his Vacheron Constantine timepieces and Scabal suits.

'Listen, Rafael, don't worry. I'm going to fly to Guadalajara ASAP. I'll get there by this afternoon, please wait for me because we need to talk.'

All I cared about was getting the job done – whatever it took.

'OK fine, I'll see you this afternoon at 3 p.m. in my office.'

Boom. It was still on.

I couldn't afford to risk the usual commercial flight delays so I chartered a jet to get me there in good time. I checked out of the hotel and headed to the local airport.

'Sorry, Señor Law – your plane is delayed; we're checking to see what the issue is.'

You're joking?

I waited nearly one and a half painstaking hours but eventually it arrived. Refuelling problems apparently.

They escorted me along the baking tarmac to the jet and I clambered in – I knew I was cutting it fine, I kept checking my watch and playing the timings through in my head.

'Hello – you must be Charley.'

I looked up. *What the hell?! This guy is making himself comfortable in my plane.*

'Hi, I'm Mauro – Pedro's cousin, he said you wouldn't mind giving me a lift!'

Pedro was one of my fixers who'd sorted the plane. Cheeky bugger. I wasn't in the mood for small talk, but it turned out he was a Spanish teacher, so I asked him to give me a trial lesson during the flight. Always taking the opportunity, always trying to make progress.

We landed in Guadalajara, and just as I was hurrying out of the terminal building to find the driver, I got through to Rafael. It was already 3 p.m.

'Rafael, I'm just jumping in a cab – be with you shortly.'

'Sorry, Charley – I've already left, I have to catch a flight.'

Jesus, you have GOT to be joking.

I cursed under my breath.

Out of the corner of my eye I saw a familiar face.

'Señor Law! Good to see you!'

It was Rafael's pilot Santiago – he was at the kiosk preparing his flight log.

I'd been on Rafael's jet before – big burly guy – we got on well.

'Señor Law, are you coming with us?'

I made a double take – I didn't know if he was flying to Tokyo or Trinidad and Tobago. But I hung up the phone and didn't hesitate.

'Si, Santiago, I'm coming with you.' I handed him my passport for the flight log.

By the time Rafael pitched up to his plane I was sitting in the cream and mahogany clad cabin sipping on a cold gin and tonic. He paused in the doorway looking up at me in surprise.

'*Que loco*,' he said as he gave me a wry smile. He looked calm and composed.

We took off in the Dassault Falcon and the two of us sat there opposite each other nattering away at 30,000ft.

Would you believe it, less than forty-five minutes later we touched down back at the port where I'd just come from – of all the places.

We shook hands and parted ways – I knew he'd help, I knew I'd get the job done, he always did what he said.

Every few weeks, I'd travel to Central or Latin America on another mission critical. Always last minute, always a mission to sort another crisis, always alone, always the same ritual. This was my new normal. I'd pack like a military operative. The currencies, the phones, the sim cards, the battery packs, the backup medicines. It was a rite of passage, a journey to another world, another 'me'.

I was *Carlos Ley*, the man who could make things happen. And for a while I loved it. I even started believing he was me.

BACK TO BLIGHTY

'Crispin works for Glencore – he's running Africa.'

I was back in London for a few weeks.

I'd hit the gym hard and was on my way to get a protein shake after our Saturday morning HIIT class with my buddy Pete. He was looking like one of the instructors in his bottle-green military vest hanging over his built torso, in perfect keeping with the trendy Kensington gym. I was in my off the shelf Nike.

'Crispin – hey, bud! What are you doing here?' They gave each other a big man hug, Pete making a scene still pumped and glowing after the session.

'When did you get back from Geneva?' he said admiringly. 'Crispin this is my buddy Charley; we were at Edinburgh Uni together.'

I shimmied over to say hello, trying not to look too hard. A slimmer more sophisticated version of Heath Ledger was standing there, relaxed shoulders, still, poised, confident and content. Charcoal grey cashmere sweater with a bright white tee just showing, navy blue immaculately fitted jeans, and chic white trainers. He reached out his hand with a friendly smile as if to say *good on you for working out, I did mine at 5 a.m.*

Crispin was better than me in every department. Even the way he wore his Audemars Piguet and his silver bracelet (skinny) told the story of someone who didn't need to try. Unlike me, it all just came naturally to him, or so it appeared.

'Congratulations on the new role,' I said, trying to level up.

'I've done some stuff with you guys in the past – I know Justin Hagman' – (I'd spoken to him once) – 'he's running coal now, isn't he?'

'Oh yes, Justin used to be my boss, great guy – actually he's on the metals desk,' said Crispin.

'Oh yeah, it was the metals desk,' I said quickly and agreeingly.

'So what are you up to, Charley?'

I eagerly launched into my elevator pitch. I went on and on, trying to compensate for the feeling of inferiority. Colombia this, Mexico that... I wanted him to get to see a bit of Carlos Ley.

Crispin was a Master of the Universe. Was I trying to seek his approval? Words were spraying out of my mouth in the hope of eliciting a response. I lost his gaze momentarily as a leggy nine walked past and gave him a familiar smile. He politely reciprocated and then returned his attention to me. I was still talking.

'Crispin!' a familiar voice interrupted – it was Jason the gym owner.

Everyone knew Jason. I stood there while he greeted the group. I felt gun-shy, a deer in the headlights. I'd just blurted out a speech and was waiting for what I craved – the appreciation, the admiration. He was better-looking than me, more successful, better dressed and more popular – I hated it. My insecurity grew. I was surrounded by people who all seemed to have one up on me, no matter what I said or did.

'Guys, great to see you all – I have to run.' I hurried out the door before anyone got a whiff of my self-consciousness.

TOWIE

I'd decided to pull out all the stops to celebrate my thirtieth birthday.

One hundred and fifty people.

Marquee.

Our family home where I grew up in Sussex.

The theme of the party was TOWIE (*The Only Way is Essex*) – think reality TV but a double dose of fake tan, fake eye lashes and fake breasts. The show was my guilty pleasure.

My father wasn't there – still banned from the house after the divorce. At the time, I didn't dwell on it. I judged his choices in the way a son thinks he understands, not realising how much more there was to the story, or how deeply it might have hurt him.

'Charley, your first guest is arriving,' my mother shouted up the stairs.

I peered out of the top floor window and saw my friend Katie walking up the drive.

Shit.

Back to the bathroom mirror simultaneously trying to fix my hair over my thinning crown, fussing over my freshly sprayed fake tan and trying to second-guess how well my purple polo shirt (top button done up), skinny black jeans and patent leather loafers would go down – *what would they all think?*

'Hey, Katie! You look amazing!' We air hugged trying not to smudge each other. She'd gone all out. Wedges, hoop earrings, fake eye lashes and ridiculous make-up and tan.

My older brother Matthew suddenly appeared in a bright pink suit – fresh off the plane from Singapore where he'd co-founded a successful media tech business with offices across Asia and over 130 people on the payroll. He'd got measured up just for the occasion and it looked amazing – like a real boss.

The guests began to appear around the yew hedge into the rose garden by the dozen. Polo friends, uni friends, Sussex friends and even Peruvian friends... Yup, even one of my suppliers pitched up with his wife. Champagne and canapes were being dished out to the beat of the band.

'Charley! So good to see you – it's been ages – this is awesome.'

I barely had a chance to greet them before I could feel the next couple hovering to say hello. *Shit*, the music is too quiet – the band is too far away. *Shit*, is it going to rain? *Shit*, what does everyone think of my outfit – maybe I'm underdressed? *Shit*, no one's talking to Gonzalo and Alejandra.

'Dinner's served – please make your way to the marquee, everybody.' Jerry and Graham, our neighbours, were loving playing their role as Essex security slash master of ceremonies.

We all squelched across the sodden lawn towards the main event – it had been raining for months. I hovered around the entrance waiting for the reactions – the mixologist, the decorations, the Sugar Hut night club. *Were they impressed?*

Eventually I took my seat at the top table with friends and family. Katie on my left, Flora on my right. For a split second I felt like I could breathe – I was home at my round table.

'Good evening, everyone.'

That familiar eruption of jeering and anticipation as Matthew took to the mic in his bright pink suit. I could see he was nervous – in my mind the spotlight was back on me – *I hope he does a good job – I hope he makes me look good.*

He launched into it, racing through the words on his wad of A4 sheets of paper. He stumbled slightly. A joke fell flat. Someone coughed. Oh God, I thought, it wasn't coming across so well. *What would they think?*

Matthew had come all the way from his home in Singapore just to be there for me – barely twenty-four hours. But I was selfish and all I could think about was myself, it was automatic.

The night unwound into cocktails, shots, dancing and chats. I just remember bouncing between different huddles, not really engaging, not really letting go. I was like the maître d', playing a role, always moving on in search of something better but not really knowing what.

Before I could blink it was already 1 a.m., the music had stopped and most people had gone home. I was standing in the hallway alone with Claudia, one of the women I was hoping to hook up with. We had met on holiday in Mustique and had been on a few dates. I needed to salvage something from the evening, just a quick cheeky snog would be enough.

'This was so much fun – thank you. Let's do something in London soon.'

She took charge, leant in for a split-second peck on my lips, swivelled round and rushed outside to hop into her taxi.

I stood there stunned. It was all over.

Months of work and now a hollow feeling inside. Alone again.

Could I dance like nobody was watching? Let my hair down? Of course not, I was stressed as hell. I barely danced at all; I was far too self-conscious and paranoid of what everybody was thinking. I was performing, pleasing and chasing some sort of elixir.

A COLOMBIAN CRISIS

Months passed.

More flights.

More close shaves.

More adrenaline.

Then it happened.

Bogota, Colombia, the restaurant was dripping with models and the owners of Maseratis. Voluptuous bronzed bodies poured into micro dresses teetered on stilettos. It was noisy, the energy was intoxicating; I had some stuff going on, but so did everyone else in town.

I got the message every trader dreads. It was from my port agent in Santa Marta.

'Señor Carlos. Tengo problema con Calidad. Ellas no cargaran tu barco.'

[Señor Charley, I have a problem with the quality. They will not load your ship.]

Shit.

I was loading a coal shipment in Santa Marta, the Colombian coal terminal on the Caribbean coast. This was a problem because bad quality and delayed loading could mean that I'd lose the sale I'd locked in with my Chinese buyers and the market was tanking.

Usually, to mitigate risk where cargos worth tens of millions change hands and to avoid the 'you load my ship first', 'no, you pay me first' situation, Letters of Credit (LCs) are the industry standard. LCs are an official IOU issued from the buyer's bank with conditions to say if you (the seller) load this many tons, at this quality, in this time frame, then the seller can go to their bank and cash the LC. It reduced risk massively. But right now if I didn't complete loading by the agreed latest date of shipment as per the LC, I'd be screwed – the LC would default and the price I'd locked in weeks ago when the market was up would be lost.

I'd be up shit creek without a paddle, as they say – or in this case, without a buyer in a falling market.

I caught the next flight up to Santa Marta the following morning hopeful I'd avoid another disaster, use my charm and somehow put things right like I usually did. But my body and mind weren't functioning as normal, things seemed foggy and slow. I didn't know then what was happening to me. Adrenaline wasn't enough. More Colombian coffee… even that wasn't working.

I did what I could but the coal was high in moisture and a much lower grade quality than what was expected. I knew it as well as everyone at the port. There was no way this coal was going to get loaded and there were no alternatives. I'd worked all the angles. It was surreal – it almost happened in slow motion. The deadline came and went. The buyers reneged. The ship wanted payment. The dominos began to fall. And I felt numb. I'd gotten away with close calls so many times, I started to think I was invincible. But this time round I wasn't so lucky. I'd overleveraged my business and hadn't protected myself enough, this one deal going wrong was enough to wipe me out financially.

All that was left to do was pick up the pieces, suffer the immense losses and head back to Miami to nurse my wounds.

As my domestic commercial jet ascended into the clear blue sky, the port of Santa Marta faded into the distance and the pilot banked hard towards Bogota. Staring out the window, my jittery brain was trying to come to terms with things.

Then I heard a loud BANG, the plane wobbled and I felt a commotion among the passengers. I was sitting on my own in a window seat just over the left wing of the eighties hand-me-down. What the hell was going on? It was obvious no one really knew.

'*Señoras y señores.*'

The captain came onto the tannoy – I couldn't really make out the Spanish, something about engine '*motor*', return '*regreso*', emergency '*emergencia*'. I saw a lot of dark smoke bubbling up from the engine and gliding over the wing – people started to panic. The lady across from me was clutching her prayer beads, men making the sign of a cross between their forehead and chest, some wails and shrieks came from up the front.

For the first time in my life I experienced what it felt like to have no control whatsoever.

I was shitting myself even as I tried to remain cool, calm, collected. The engine must have exploded but it seemed the other one was OK. The plane started to bank as we turned around, the manoeuvre was more aggressive than normal – only adding to the reality. I tried to rationalise the situation, making my own assessment to stay calm. OK, we're heading back, only a few minutes away, one good motor.

But just as I was getting a grip, we were dealt another killer blow, the reassuring murmur of the solo engine all of a sudden fell into an eerie silence. The lights went out and we could only hear the sound of a dashboard alert. For a few seconds it felt like we were just suspended, about to drop out of the sky. No reassuring message from the captain this time. I could even see the stewardesses looking at each other covertly with panic in their eyes. There was a deathly silence in the cabin, the old can of metal just suspended in the air. We were helpless – in the laps of the gods now. What would it feel like if we plummeted to the ground?

No one knew I was on this plane – how long would it take for people back in England to realise what had happened?

You could almost feel how gently the pilots were coaxing her home, like a wounded animal cautiously willing her to stay alive, to keep gliding through the air until we reached safety.

I just sat there alone staring out the window, watching every field, road and rooftop getting closer and hoping that was a good sign, that we were going to land, that we were going to be fine. Everyone on that plane probably felt as alone as I did but I fancied we were all in this together, shallow breathing in unison.

It felt like a lifetime, but then, finally, the wheels touched the runway, and we all gasped for air, the relief. The Colombians all clapped and cheered.

Me? I just sat there. I felt nothing.

I could see fire engines waiting for us. Eventually I peeled my clammy shirt away from the leather seat and got up. I passed the galley where two old ladies were wearing oxygen masks and I got a sheepish goodbye from the crew.

I had no choice but to return to my hotel while I rearranged my flight.

The wheels had well and truly come off my Latin fantasy – no more filling the empty hours with girls, tanning by the pool or long lunches. I was on my own and my mind was racing, playing out the next steps – what was I going to do? How could I get back on track? Where could I get some money to do some more deals?

A few days later, things went from bad to worse. I woke up in my Miami apartment in a deep lethargy – like a hangover that wouldn't let go. Every movement was an effort, as if I was slogging through quicksand.

Why can't I shift this exhaustion?

Why isn't a good night's sleep, an afternoon nap, or a brisk jog sorting me out?

To make matters worse my mind felt like an overloaded computer – freezing, slow, non-reactive. What was usually a high twitch was now like a thick fog. Even just going to the 7/11 felt overwhelming – I couldn't even remember half the things I'd gone to buy. I would just look at the shelves before me, my eyes jittering, unable to process what I was seeing. I'd completely lost my sharpness. I even felt dizzy.

It was scary wondering whether I'd ever get back to how I was before.

What the hell was going on?

When would I feel normal again?

Only a short time ago I thought I had everything, and now, all of a sudden, not only am I on my way to financial ruin, but I was starting to panic that there was something seriously wrong with me.

I felt helpless, confused and disconnected. Suddenly everything seemed a lot more precarious and I had no idea why. I realised I could lose it all – the houses, the cars, the polo ponies. What would everyone think? What would everyone say? I might have been preoccupied by that before, but now that seemed more important than ever.

I was standing in Whole Foods Market and saw my reflection. I had a gold chain hanging around my neck, and too many buttons undone. I was seeing Carlos Ley for the very first time. And he looked like a drug dealer. I felt like an idiot. I didn't belong here. I wasn't on the same level as everyone else living in this upmarket neighbourhood south of fifth on Miami Beach. The fantasy ended in that store. I had finally stepped out of it and was faced with reality.

Back in my apartment, I just stared at the ceiling. I had always prided myself on being a lone wolf but now, sitting on my own, I saw what that really meant – being single, without many friends, distant from my family. And that just made me feel empty. I suppose the hollowness had always been there. It's just that I'd been moving too fast to really notice it.

Suddenly, inexplicably, I was terribly homesick. I wasn't entirely sure what it was. But in many ways home represented stability, support, protection. I certainly didn't have the vocabulary to ask for the help

I needed at that point. I was all over the place. I felt like that plane – damaged, without an engine, running on fumes, rudderless, feeling like I was about to fall out of the sky.

I'm not sure I'd quite hit rock bottom yet. There were still a few more dominos to fall; I was still sparring with denial, looking for an easy way back, hoping I could pull something off. Yet there was no denying this underlying sense of panic that had set in. For the first time since I could remember, I was totally out of control. My mind, my bank account, what everyone would think.

I thought to myself, *shit – I need to do something about all this.*

STEP 1 – DESIRE

You might not be in a moment of personal crisis like I was. You might simply be feeling stuck. You might even be feeling just fine, but you're not quite where you want to be and you just want more – to not have regrets and reach your potential.

Trust me, I get it.

But simply put, if you want to make change, you must first want to make change.

Isn't that the same thing?

No. And here's why.

Everyone wants a better life in some shape or form.

More from a relationship, more success at work, more joy, more peace, more money, more happiness, more fulfilment.

Dreaming, wanting, desiring... However you like to put it, that's not what I'm getting at here. That would be far too easy!

I know you want to change your life.

But do you have the *desire* to change yourself?

A lot of us have moments of inspiration to make big changes in life, but then we let life get in the way. Making any sort of change isn't easy. It requires a lot of time, effort and commitment (which you'll come to see). I know it might not be what you want to hear, but there aren't many quick fixes, it can be uncomfortable at times, you'll be going against your deeply ingrained habits, cravings, daily behaviour patterns, even your identity in some cases. It can require a lot of energy and attention to break away from the gravitational pull of being who you are used to being every day.

And so that is why, if you really want change, if you want your life to be different, you have to have the personal will, the motivation, the *desire* to make change.

In *The Lion Tracker's Guide to Life*, Boyd Varty describes men experiencing a 'disengagement', 'sleepwalking through their lives'. The way out, he says, 'will begin not with a call but with the *desire* to hear the call'.

The world of self-improvement correctly assumes you want a better life, but I seldom came across anyone that helped me with this first critical step – stoking the fire of desire, asking the hard questions:

- *How bothered are you really?*
- *Are you actually willing to feel uncomfortable?*
- *Do you really want to make change?*

It doesn't just happen.

The harsh reality is that if you're just not bothered enough, then you will likely stay where you are and the only thing that will kick you into gear will be a crisis or hitting rock bottom. As the old adage goes, change happens when the pain of staying the same becomes worse than that of making a change.

The good news is I've spent the last decade figuring out how to help you make positive change without needing to wait for things to become unbearable – or worse, the pain of regret as the years slip by. And it is 100 per cent possible: you can change your entire life if you want. You can transform it, become it, live it, and it can happen a lot quicker than you think – you just have to want it badly enough.

Desire is the precursor to change.

Desire serves as a catalyst that propels us to overcome obstacles, embrace discomfort and take action.

If you want to make change and are not sure if you've got what it takes, here's how to *stoke the fire of desire*:

1. Be Honest

Those whispers, those moments of inspiration, your yearning for something better, to end the dissatisfaction, you need to breathe oxygen onto those embers and turn them into a burning fire to be better, to feel better.

Start by being brutally honest with yourself. Take a hard look at your life – really look.

How much longer are you going to avoid what you are capable of doing in order to continue with what you are comfortable doing?

What's the cost going to be down the line of doing nothing or staying the same?

If you're stuck, unhappy or frustrated, it's time to admit it – it's not working.

You don't need that thing to keep happening for you to know it isn't working.

It might seem worse and hurt more when you first acknowledge it, but from this point on, things are going to start feeling better.

Stoke the fire of desire.

2. Believe

The three most powerful words someone can say are *I love you*, but the next most powerful are *I believe in you*.

Sometimes it's hard to see through the fog, to imagine ever getting out of the fog, but I want you to know, from the very fact that you have picked up this book, I don't just think you can – I *know* you can. As Rumi said, 'As you start to walk on the way, the way appears.' You have even more power and potential inside of you than maybe you realise.

Sometimes we're great at giving our friends advice and encouragement, but often don't talk to ourselves in the same way.

Take a breath, be kind to yourself, believe, have faith and take one step at a time.

3. Know Your Why

If you find it hard to make change for yourself, then do it for the person that loves you the most.

Who needs you to be the best version of yourself?

Your wife, husband, son, daughter, mother, father, best friend?

Do it for them. Let the thought of you letting them down or needing to be there for them breathe life onto your embers of desire.

4. Follow a Path

We all know that if something feels super hard, we're less likely to want to do it, or even get started. Who wants to start something you might not be able to finish?

But if we can see the steps, the way through, that the outcome is achievable, we're more likely to want to do it, right?

With a clear blueprint, a guide, it can help dial down resistance and improve your chances of taking the first step and succeeding. You know the juice will be worth the squeeze. You're not thrashing around in the dark not knowing where to start.

The good news is that if you do have the *desire* to make change in your life, I'm going to show you exactly how to make it happen. I've walked this path, and I've built the steps. Read on, and I'll show you the way.

Desire is the driving force behind the journey of personal growth and change.

Stoke the fire of desire:

Be honest.

Believe (I believe in you).

Know your why.

Follow a path.

The path appears when you decide to walk it.

STEP 2

THE BODY BASELINE

> 'In the dance of life, the body leads the mind; take care of the dancer, and the dance shall flow harmoniously.'
>
> UNKNOWN

A BOTTLE-GREEN CARDIGAN

'But what *actually* is it you can feel?'

My mother was sitting opposite me at the kitchen table stirring in her third teaspoon of sugar. The well-used family-size cafetière is in its usual spot by the Aga, filling the air with that familiar smell of Douwe Egberts coffee.

Everything about the scene conspired to make me feel twelve years old again. The Labrador and the two whippets snuggled up on their dog bed. Last week's copies of the *Daily Mail* – Kate and Wills at a food bank – and a pile of *Farmers Weekly* magazines at the end of the oak table. The windowsills cluttered with decades' worth of plants, trinkets, photographs, invitations and thank you cards.

She looked at me, struggling to understand the something she couldn't see.

I tried to explain. Neither of us said what we were really thinking.

Could it be a tumour?

'Charley, you better make an appointment to see Dr Glynne, he can refer you to a specialist.'

Talking to my father didn't cross my mind. I'd pushed him to the edges of my life without even noticing, and right then my mother was the only one I could imagine having this conversation with – and even that felt like more than I wanted.

Miami already seemed like a distant memory. So did Peru, Colombia, Mexico City – all the places where Carlos Ley had had it all. I'd come back to my childhood home in Sussex. I ditched my gold chain and Illesteva shades and was donning an old school navy-blue V-neck sweater with holes in it.

―

'Hello, Charley. Please have a seat.'

I was about to find out if my MRI, blood test and EEG had revealed anything sinister.

Part of me wanted her to find something so I could put my finger on it – medicalise it. I wasn't making it all up. I had a condition.

'Tell me a bit about your lifestyle and your work.'

She was a leading neurologist. Mid-fifties, unassuming in her bottle-green cardi and blouse with kind eyes and a matter-of-fact expression. Cross between a family friend and a university professor. Her office was more library than consulting room.

'It's pretty full on to be honest. I travel a lot, often sixty flights a year. It's stressful, high-pressure situations and constantly on the go.'

I was attempting to paint a picture of a life that didn't really exist for many.

She paused again. Pondering the data on her desk.

'Well, Charley, the good news is all the tests have come back absolutely fine.'

OK. But what did that mean then? What was going on?

'Your symptoms, however, are classic signs of burnout. This high-stress lifestyle needs serious consideration – if you don't make some changes, things could get worse.'

'But what about my work?'

What about the money? I need to figure out a way to get out of the hole I'm in.

'You're on the edge, Charley. If I were you, I'd take a six-month break and reassess.'

What!? That was impossible – everything would fall apart, the missed opportunity.

'I would advise a complete change in lifestyle. Do you know about mindfulness?'

'Sort of,' I said unconvincingly.

'What about meditation and yoga?'

I stayed quiet – my limping mind was still trying to grasp the idea of taking six months off.

How would that even be possible?

But it was more than just clinical advice; it almost felt as if she was talking to me like a son. I hung on to her every word. I was used to brushing off other people's advice, thinking I knew best – but right now I was listening. She spoke to me like a doctor who was also a personal friend. She was cutting through where nobody else could.

It was my turn to sit in silence, contemplating. I massaged my sun-kissed hands still bronzed from Miami. I tried to process what was happening, working through the consequences of this seismic blow.

There wasn't much to debate though. She was right and I had to deal with it.

'Thank you so much. I'll schedule a catch-up in six months.'

Walking outside onto the street it was crisp... the sky was blue but there was a bite in the air. London was still going about its day; black cabs purred past, builders bantering on scaffolding and suits striding back from lunch. But I was in a daze, directionless. A five-minute conversation had smashed me totally off course, taken the wind out of my sails.

What now?

My belly rumbled. Hunger took over. I headed to the deli on the corner. I recalled the smell of the fresh dough and sizzling bacon earlier this morning as I fought off the temptation adhering to my prescribed morning fast.

The juices dripped onto the plate as I was sinking my teeth into a bacon and egg butty when the default survival mechanism I'd resorted to so often over the years as a trader kicked in:

Where does that leave me?

What are the options?

Where's the opportunity?

My hobbling mind began to spark with ideas and scenarios.

Six months sabbatical. Maybe I should go back to Miami and recover in the sun?

That apartment still has six months on the lease.

I'll sell the horses – that should see me through.

I was recalibrating rapidly.

Time to maybe improve myself.

Time to work out, tan, read and explore.

I booked myself on the first flight to Miami to begin my six-month hiatus – even my mother was a little surprised at how quickly I wanted to get away again.

RECOVERY 101

Paul was a man about town in Miami.

We were huddling near our table at the bar – tucking into a few more pisco sours. It was busy that night at Miami Beach House. We were there most Thursdays, it's where all the action was.

'So come on, what's the deal with Jelena, Paul?' I said, observing her as she went to sit back down at the table in her pencil skirt and stilettoes.

'She's lovely – a wellness expert. She's just signed me up. Recently divorced too, Charley.' Paul winked at me – we rejoined the group and got chatting.

'Paul tells me you've just moved to Miami, Charley,' Jelena said with a warm inquisitive smile.

'Yes, well, I'm here for another six months or so; I'd love to come and chat to you sometime, Jelena. I've had to take a bit of time off work – pretty sure I'm just a bit burnt out, nothing you haven't seen before.'

'Sure, Charley. Come to the clinic and we'll take a look at you. Take my number and text me.'

She got up and left for an early night – Kundalini yoga was scheduled for 4 a.m.

A few days later I turned up at her Miami Beach clinic – a white temple stuffed full of rich housewives awaiting their next-gen anti-ageing treatments.

'Hi there, I'm Charley Law – here to see Jelena.'

'Ah yes – Charley,' the receptionist said knowingly. 'Please fill these out over here and Jelena will be with you shortly.'

I was sitting there waiting, remembering what Paul had said about Jelena being divorced, and wondering whether she might have taken a liking to me – or was it strictly just business?

After a few minutes the waiting room quiet was interrupted by a commotion of voices and the strut of confident heels on the hard floor. They appeared at the reception hall, and I got a chance to observe while she said goodbye.

She turned around in her dark-framed glasses – perfectly complimenting her tan, dark brows, red lips and glossy brunette hair. It was as if she'd just stepped off the set of *Dr. 90210*.

'Hey, Charley, great to see you! Come with me.'

Then I'm sitting there in a tiny consulting room in a sort of padded highchair and Jelena is standing next to me – close enough to smell her expensive perfume.

Bloody hell, if only the lads could see me now. I still had it, and at that point I still thought that was a good thing.

I told her my story.

'Jelena, the thing is I just want to feel calmer and more at ease. I want to get my body and mind back to feeling normal again.'

I had an inkling, a niggle, there was another way, that I shouldn't be feeling so frantic about everything – but I was in the dark.

Ever since I could remember I had just let life happen to me. I never stopped to *really* think for myself, to reflect and question *why*. Why I was making certain decisions, why I was the person I was.

I told Jelena about boarding school, home life, friends, the rituals and trappings of British life, my work. How so much of it felt preordained. How there was a path I felt I had to follow without understanding what or who I really was. How I was born to perform, to fit within the social norms of my background, afraid of what people might think if I didn't conform.

Sitting on that padded chair with Jelena next to me in Florida, I felt a sense of lightness.

I expected her to be puzzled by my issues, but instead she was finishing my sentences; she had the words and phrases to describe what I couldn't.

'Like you're trying to get everything sorted before you can start living and enjoying life?'

'Is nothing ever enough?'

Jelena seemed to know exactly what was going on and what I needed.

It felt like there was more to it than just getting back my basic functions, but I was still in the dark. Turns out my nervous system was shot to pieces. I'd been in overdrive for far too long – stuck in fight or flight. But in order to actually heal, change and set myself up on a more sustainable trajectory I was going to need to go deeper – to find answers within myself. But in order to do that, as Boyd Varty puts it in his book, *The Lion Tracker's Guide To Life* – I had to become like a tracker in the bush. 'Track awareness' he calls it, 'how attuned you are to what is around you... you have to learn how your body speaks... you have to follow the inner tracks of your feelings, sensations, and instincts...'

Simply put, if I wanted answers, if I wanted to re-connect with myself and others, I would need to learn how to feel again. To become the tracker, I needed to heal my nervous system, regulate the chaos and find inner harmony.

'We'll get you back on track, Charley – but there's a lot to do and it will take time.'

I left with a list of recommendations:

- Paleo juice cleanse
- The meditation guy's number
- The yoga teacher's number
- *The Power of Now* by Eckhart Tolle
- *The Five-Minute Journal*
- *21-Days of Inspiration* by The Chopra Center

In years to come I'd realise she'd just handed me my starter kit to recovery. But at the time I was still cynical... *Isn't this stuff just a load of mumbo jumbo? Don't I just need some rest and to lay off the booze for a bit?*

Most of my life I'd been scribbling away on my own in a diary beside my bed – frustrated, yearning to be and feel a certain way. Without anyone else to express these thoughts to, it was my only outlet, not that I really paid much attention to the underlying message I was trying to tell myself.

Now, though, all of a sudden, I'd been presented with this new dimension. I had no idea there was so much stuff out there to help with things that I thought were just unique to me.

Turns out this meeting would be the best thing to happen to me at that point – thanks, Paul, thanks, Jelena.

―

'What can I get you guys?'

Day three of my one-week juice cleanse. *God, I'm such a wanker.*

Back in London it would have been a different story. Everything revolved around booze: the pub, the horseracing, the footy, the shooting weekends. *Come on, mate. Your round. Let's get on it.* There was no escaping it.

But Miami Beach was a different story. My Tinder date and I were high on cranberry juice, engaged, sober and letting the conversation go a few notches deeper than usual.

Without really realising it, I was more myself. Unshackled from the cloak of conformity, I found myself talking about emotions, how I felt, in a way that felt radically different to everything I was used to.

It wasn't easy to stick to this juice cleanse for the week. We're talking no caffeine, refined sugar, carbs, processed food, *and definitely* no alcohol. Just a juice for breakfast and dinner, a soup or a salad for lunch, and then enough pills and supplements to open a drug store.

The craving was real.

The first forty-eight hours were the hardest – the cold-turkey phase. Then it got a lot easier.

It was like someone had taken a power washer to my brain and was removing the muck – exposing parts of the fresh, pink, tingling organism. Some of the haze lifted. It felt like there were new cavities that had switched on. It felt like I'd popped NZT-48, the pill from the movie *Limitless*.

Better cognitive function.

Better clarity.

Better concentration.

Better energy.

Better memory.

Less adrenaline.

Less jittery.

Less unease.

Less cravings.

Less anxiety.

A friend told me that fasting was like allowing your insides to heal. I liked that.

What I was doing was more of a cleanse than a straight-up fast. But it had similar effects. Cleansing the body of toxins, reducing inflammation and allowing cells to regenerate. My digestive system hadn't had a break for as long as I could remember. It was a much-needed hard reset.

—

I got into a groove of yoga, running, reading, a better diet, hardly drinking, making time for myself. There's no doubt that being abroad, having fewer distractions and more free time, helped me slow down, explore new ways of doing things and start to recover. I was very fortunate, perhaps even more than I realised at the time, given I was in a position to do this with something of a safety net beneath me – a privilege not everyone might have. If it was still hard for me to even get to this point, then obviously it could be even harder for others. Making that space in your life can feel like a massive first step – until you've taken it, and look back, and realise perhaps it wasn't as painful as you expected.

I wasn't out the woods yet, though.

'Jelena, hi. Have you got a second?'

'Charley, er... Yes, sure. Go ahead.'

She sounded busy – maybe she didn't give everyone her mobile. I cut to the chase.

'A lot of this stuff is helping: the diet, the cleanse, the yoga. I am feeling more myself, but I'm still getting this brain fog. I'm still having trouble remembering stuff – I get a lot of gas and bloating, it doesn't really matter what I eat. I mean, I'm pretty fit, but my stomach is so swollen most of the time it looks like I'm pregnant – that can't be normal, can it?'

She was silent. Pondering. As if surprised that the lifestyle changes hadn't made more of an impact.

'Right. I think we better send you off for a proper look – I want to know what's going on. I'll arrange a consultation with Dr Ortega – he's the best gastroenterologist in Miami.'

And off I went to see the gut doctor.

—

After my gastroscopy (camera down the throat to check my stomach) and a colonoscopy (camera up the bum to check my colon), I'm sitting opposite the young Latin doctor in his office awaiting the verdict.

I could see the faint beads of perspiration where his tanned forehead met his dark slicked-back hair – his core most likely still overheating from his morning workout on the beach. His pecs were pressing against his well-fitted, freshly pressed, sky-blue shirt and of course his flat, washboard stomach gave him the perfect *Men's Health* torso.

I was all ears.

'Right, Charley. Your colon is fine *no* – no issues,' he said in his

Colombian accent.

'Pero, the stomach is a little bit unhappy *no*. A lot of inflammation – very raw. This is classic gastritis and IBS (irritable bowel syndrome). I think what you said about the stress and years of *antibioticos* when you got sick after all those business trips – it's done some damages *no?* We gonna rebuild it though – don't worry, my friend.'

He put me on a course of supplements that included probiotics, magnesium and a bunch of different vitamins, then got Jelena to prescribe me a strict gluten free, lactose free, low FODMAP (fermentable oligosaccharides, disaccharides, monosaccharides and polyols) diet – essentially avoiding everything that might trigger inflammation and giving my gut a chance to recover.

I was relieved. On and off I'd been struggling with my gut for years and finally I had a diagnosis and a clear path to solving the problem.

Dr Tim Spector and Dr Zach Bush were the two standout thought leaders in the gut health space I started to follow. My biggest takeaway was understanding that in just a single gram of the earth's soil there are an array of microorganisms including billions of bacteria. And this rich diversity of tens of thousands of different species shouldn't be too dissimilar to a healthy gut. The gut microbiome, as it's known, is like an exotic garden, home to billions of microorganisms like bacteria, viruses, fungi and more, all contributing to breaking down food to release energy, protecting us against germs and producing vitamins.

But.

The combo of excessive antibiotics, chemicals from pesticides and preservatives in our food, eating a bland, unhealthy diet (alcohol, processed, refined sugar), <u>stress</u> and lack of sleep, can all contribute to an imbalanced or barren microbiome, unable to do its job properly.

Studies have proven how the state of our microbiome can directly affect our mood, energy levels and immune system.

I witnessed this firsthand.

Once I understood all this, I completely changed the way I thought about food and drink.

Instead of ingesting whatever I fancied, abusing my insides, I thought about my gut like the delicate, wonderful organism it is.

I embraced trying to nourish it with whatever was going to build back that rich diversity and support a healthy microbiome – so it could support me, my energy, my immune system and eventually be less sensitive and more robust. It can all get a little complicated as everyone is different of course, but to build back a healthy gut my rule of thumb was:

I avoided:

- Processed food.
- Refined sugar.
- Alcohol.
- Starchy carbs (bread and pasta).
- All gluten.
- All lactose.

I prioritised:

- Vegetables and salad.
- Slower energy release carbs (rice and potatoes).

- Quality protein (fish, meat, eggs).
- Fruit (but not too much).
- Lactose-free yogurts and cheese.
- Gluten-free bread and oats.
- Healthy fats (nuts, seeds, avocados, olive oil).

I aimed to have lots of colour on my plate as a general rule.

Eat the rainbow.

Fall in love with kiwis!

Were common mantras I tried to follow.

It took a lot of self-discipline and organisation, but eventually after three to four months my symptoms did begin to reduce, some altogether.

Yes, but, Charley, why should we care about your gut?

Because everything starts with a fit and healthy physical body.

Let me explain.

STEP 2 – THE BODY BASELINE

Physical first; mental second.

Before you can really start trying to explore the inner workings of your mind, start meditating, get a coach, try to get clear on what you really want or start building new habits, you've got to get on top of your physical health first. You don't need to wait until you get ill to discuss certain things with your doctor.

It's easy to forget the basics but remember, your mood, your energy levels, your ability to concentrate, be calm and even content are all linked to your physical health.

- Are you hydrated?
- Are you hungover?
- Do you have good gut health?
- Are you getting enough sleep?
- Are you eating the right food?
- Do you get regular sugar lows?
- Are you intolerant to some foods?
- Is your nervous system stuck in overdrive?
- Do you have too many toxins in your body?
- Are you lacking any basic vitamins and minerals?
- Do you have enough oxygen pumping around your blood?

Your physical health is the precursor to everything else.

If you hit the accelerator with a dodgy engine then you're likely not going to get very far.

Think about if you are getting the basics right (exercise, hydration, nutrition, sleep).

Think about if you have any bad lifestyle habits that might be holding you back.

Think about if you have any underlying health concerns that need attention.

Do what you can to establish a solid foundation of energy and vitality – a solid *Body Baseline*.

Remember what I said... making change requires energy and commitment, it also requires intuition – sensing the tracks. So we need our physical body firing on as many cylinders as possible. STONG BODY, STRONG MIND.

Yes, Charley, but don't you need a strong mind to be able to make these commitments to healthy habits?

Good point, and to an extent yes. But right here, *Step 2*, I'm just talking about getting the basics right to give your mind enough energy and your body enough vitality to give you the right foundations. Later you'll come to see how vital factors like clarity, consistency and discipline are to drive sustainable healthy habits and reach more serious physical and health-related goals.

The single most important tool I'm constantly falling back on for a hard reset is my *3-Day Body Baseline Toolkit.*

Whenever I'm feeling suboptimal (anxious, lethargic, paranoid, jittery, overwhelmed, miserable or de-motivated), maybe after an indulgent weekend, holiday, or just too many days of eating crap, not exercising enough and generally not looking after myself – I know exactly what I have to do to get back on track and it's only ever three days away. There is something very comforting and reassuring about that. To know what to do, and to know the pain is usually temporary. That I'm just three days away from being clearer, calmer and more content.

To help you get started – here is your very own Body Baseline 3-Day Challenge:

BODY BASELINE RESET

A simple, actionable 3-day reset to reboot your energy, focus and mood.

WHO'S THIS FOR?

- You've let things go over the last few days, weeks, or months.
- You want a no-nonsense approach to get your health routine back on track.
- You feel sluggish, demotivated, or low in energy.
- You're feeling overwhelmed, anxious, and on the edge of burnout.
- Your mind is scattered; it's hard to focus or concentrate.

WHAT TO EXPECT?

- Quick and achievable: get back on track in just 3 days.
- Rediscover how vital the basics are for peak performance.
- Gain a toolkit you can reuse anytime to stay aligned.
- Build your own personalised reset for the future.

THE 3 DAY CHALLENGE

STEP 1: TAKE INVENTORY   Rate your state on a scale of 1 to 10

START: DAY 1

- /10 Current Mood
- /10 Energy Level
- /10 Concentration

TOTAL /30

END: DAY 3

- /10 Current Mood
- /10 Energy Level
- /10 Concentration

TOTAL /30

STEP 2: HABIT TRACKER

BASICS	GOALS	Day 1	Day 2	Day 3
Water	Minimum 3 litres per day			
Diet	Zero processed food, refined sugar and alcohol			
Exercise	Minimum 30 minutes per day			
Sleep	Minimum 8 hours			
Social Media	Zero – remove all apps			

STEP 3 – DAY 3: RETAKE INVENTORY

STEP 3

THE ESSENTIALS

'Before crossing the threshold of uncertainty, gather the pearls of knowledge and wisdom as your guiding lanterns.'

RUMI

THE BOHO BUDDHA

'This is going to be your first taste of mindfulness.'

Alex Montalenti had welcomed me into his Downtown condo with open arms and a big smile, like a Floridian Buddha. A bit tubby, goatee beard and the signature white linen collarless shirt reaching down to his knees – the universal guru style.

'How are you doing today?' He said it like he really meant it.

We stood opposite each other in the living room. He stayed still and grounded – the opposite to those awkward hurried intros when they can't seem to stop talking. It was calming – but my antennas were still up.

He pointed over to the off-white faux leather corner sofa, but my eyes were drawn to the balcony.

'Wow, Alex – this view is insane!'

We were on the thirty-ninth floor, it was like peering out of a plane window coming in to land. You could see all the way from Miami Beach across Biscayne Bay to Brickell. Glorious Miami twinkled like a panoramic postcard.

We'd settled in and were sitting next to each other on the sofa. Alex had given me my Chopra Center meditation course booklet and was walking me through our plan for the three sessions.

How did I end up here?

Why was I talking about 'meditation' with a stranger? Meditation was something that had never really occurred to me.

Why the hell would anyone want to meditate?

The closest I'd got was the *Our Father who art in heaven* at boarding school before a custard cream and juice.

Wasn't meditation for mumbo jumbo yogis?

If it wasn't for Jelena, I'd have been more sceptical – but I was willing to give it a go.

Alex walked me through Session One.

'Meditation is a technology that benefits body, mind, and soul.'

He paused and looked up at me from the booklet to gauge my reaction. Maybe even searching for approval.

I didn't want to give him too much enthusiasm, just a semi-approving look. Part of me was still a bit sceptical, maybe a bit stubborn, and didn't want to admit he was making an impact until I was truly convinced.

But I did like where he was going.

All right, man – keep going.

He walked me through the first few paragraphs, his soothing voice almost sending me into a daydream. I was drawn more to observing him than the words he was reading, so I had to concentrate – but the real gems popped out at me anyway...

'Meditation is not about forcing your mind to be quiet; rather it's a process to rediscover the quietness that's already there.'

I had a flashback to the chaotic, adrenaline-fuelled days in South America.

'During meditation the body shifts into a state of restful awareness, which counterbalances the fight or flight response, and this has physical and psychological benefits.'

'Here, take one of these,' he said, holding out a little tub of raisins.

A raisin?

'This is going to be your first taste of mindfulness.'

I had to focus on holding the raisin, seeing it properly, touching it, smelling it and really tasting it before I got to actually swallow it. It felt ridiculous, but to be fair the process hit home. Usually eating a raisin would be a totally automatic, unconscious exercise, but this made me deliberately move all my attention and senses onto the raisin – I was immersed in the present moment. I didn't really know why that mattered yet – but I just went with it.

OK, we're already an hour and a half in – when are we actually going to do some meditation?

Alex wasn't quite finished priming me – it made sense though. For something as intangible as meditation, I think he wanted to make sure I really knew what the whole point of it was.

For me also, I was never going to buy in unless it made sense. I needed to trust that sitting with my eyes closed in silence for fifteen minutes wasn't a complete waste of time.

'Right, Charley – let's go next door, shall we.'

At last.

Tie-dye drapes, Balinese wood art, incense burning. We'd transitioned from the classroom to the sanctuary.

'I'm going to give you your personal mantra – it's important you write it down and keep it to yourself.'

'om   am [aam]   namaha'

He was about to teach me a technique called Primordial Sound Meditation (PSM). Using sound in the form of mantras to take us on an inward journey. The word *mantra* means instrument or vehicle of the mind, and in this case, the mantras were used for their sound or vibrational purpose – to help interrupt the flow of meaningful thoughts and eventually help us slip beyond thought into silence.

I liked the idea of my own mantra – it felt unique to me, special. He created it by triangulating my time, date and year of birth.

Alex came and sat down next to me on the floor cross-legged. 'Right, Charley, now I want you to close your eyes and let me guide you.'

I could feel the heat of his body next to me. It felt weirdly intimate sitting there alone with another grown man.

'I want you to relax, let go of the tension in your shoulders, Charley, your face, your eyes. Let go in your stomach and your hips.'

And one by one, I did. Releasing little fibres of clenched muscle.

'Now I want you to bring your attention to your breath. Follow the air moving deep into your lungs and tummy, and then follow it back out again. Follow it in, nice and slow, and follow it out, nice and slow... ahhhh.' He sighed as he released his own ball of air.

'Keep going like this, Charley, breathe in, and breathe out.' He spoke slowly, and softly – practically whispering. 'If thoughts pop into your head then just gently let them go and come back to your breath.'

Just a few minutes in and my body started to sink into a rhythm, the popcorn of thoughts in my head had started to settle down. I noticed some more tension hiding in my cheeks so I let my jaw hang with my mouth wide open.

'Now, when you're ready, Charley, I want you to practise your mantra, just like we spoke about. We'll do the first few together – here goes...'

'om   am [aam]   namaha'

We said it in unison out loud. I could feel my throat vibrate – that was the idea, the words were designed to create a certain frequency.

'om   am [aam]   namaha'

We said the words gently and gradually, like monks in a monastery. I followed the sounds closely with my mind.

'And one more time out loud, Charley. You're doing great, this time a little softer. The next three are just whispers and then just carry on in your head.'

'om   am [aam]   namaha'

It was like I was casting my own spell. Now only a whisper.

'om   am [aam]   namaha'

The vibrations danced ever so delicately around my vocal cords.

'om   am [aam]   namaha'

'om   am [aam]   namaha'

Then, they switched off altogether. I silently pictured the words in my mind.

'om   am [aam]   namaha'

The transition melted me down into the next level.

'Remember, Charley, any thoughts that creep into your mind, just detach yourself from them. Observe them like cars on the highway – just let them pass by and then bring your attention back to *om am namaha*.' Somehow, he was still in sync.

I kept going, repeating my mantra – keeping my attention on those words. Dancing shapes began to fill in the darkness behind my eyelids – like a kaleidoscope. I was sinking into a deeper labyrinth. Then something happened – something I'll never forget. My mind gave way. It was like my brain muscle decided to let go just like the other parts of my body, all the little synapses eventually deciding to cut themselves some slack.

I'd been switched on 24-7 for years. I hadn't even known how to switch myself off. It's hard to describe how it feels when you finally find the switch.

I allowed myself a flutter of excitement – feeling I'd stumbled across an antidote to my burnout and something to add to my arsenal forever.

I got back to it...

'om   am [aam]   namaha'

The patterns and light contrasts became more mysterious. I kept going for some minutes, teetering between consciousness and sleep.

'OK, Charley, whenever you're ready, slowly bring your mind back to full consciousness.

'Take your time.

'Now slowly open your eyes.

'Namaste.'

Stillness.

The air in the room was suspended. The Balinese Buddha ornaments seemed to command more stature and I noticed more the spaces between them. I stared forward at the wall, trying to absorb how different I felt. I was grounded and calm, unaffected by a bombardment of thoughts. There seemed to be a lot more space in my mind; it was still, sober and uncluttered. Everything seemed to stop, I was looking at the room through a new lens, a new reality where I was completely present. I felt calm, calmer than I can ever remember having felt in my life.

I turned to Alex and we smiled at each other.

He knew.

I wanted to hug him, but my Britishness held me back.

In Tim Ferris's book, *Tools of Titans*, he reveals the tactics, routines and habits of billionaires, icons and world-class performers. Arnold Schwarzenegger to Reid Hoffman to Jamie Foxx. Out of the 112 profiles in the book, the single most common thread was some form of meditation or mindfulness exercise built into their morning ritual. I had no idea how popular and effective it was.

Where had I been?

THE SPACES BETWEEN THE SPACES

'Have you read his book?' whispered the Michelle Obama lookalike sitting next to me.

'Yes,' I whispered back, smiling, pausing for the next cue.

She leant in a touch closer this time – like we were kids at school.

'What's it all about, dear?'

I liked her – there was a cheeky wickedness about her. The auditorium was starting to get louder as the seats began to fill – mutterings of excitement as we all waited for Eckhart Tolle to begin his talk. I leant in even closer so she could hear.

'It's all about the importance of being in the present. Detaching ourselves from negative thoughts. He talks a lot about how living in the present moment can free us from suffering and help us discover a deeper sense of peace and fulfilment.'

I could hear the audience mutter 'Eckhart Tolle'.

I was in Downtown LA for Summit Series. Think Burning Man meets TED Talks. Early investors in Uber, tech entrepreneurs, academics, thought leaders and change makers from around the world descended onto a makeshift campus for three days of workshops, talks and culinary delights. Big names like Larry Page, Richard Branson and Jeff Bezos were regular fixtures. Everyone seemed excited to explore, learn and make new friendships.

The crowd went quiet as a small, unassuming man with grey hair, a slight hunch and a tweed professor's jacket shuffled onto the stage towards a small wooden chair and table on which sat a pot plant and glass of water. No music, no fanfare, just silence.

He spoke softly, his s's whistled like a crisp hiss of a snake as his lips came together. Nobody moved – if they did, we couldn't hear what he was saying.

'Half of you will be utterly bored by me and half of you will not.'

I'd already read his international best seller – *The Power of Now*. And was hungry for more.

'The spaces between the spaces,' he began again.

I was hooked.

We sat there for an hour listening to Eckhart stooped in his chair – he didn't disappoint.

'One day you may catch yourself smiling at the voice in your head, as you would smile at the antics of a child.' Another of his lines I loved.

At the end Tolle led a short meditation, by the end of which some had nodded off and some had already left shaking their heads. But when it was time to leave, those of us who had stayed sat there, unable to move, mesmerised, like an audience at the end of *Star Wars* as the credits roll.

Tolle was right – the room had split between the converts and the disaffected.

Two months before, I'd have probably buggered off too. But now, post meditation, post reading his book, I got what he was saying and it all came down to this:

'Unease, anxiety, tension, stress, worry – all forms of fear – are caused by too much future and not enough presence. Guilt, regret, resentment, grievances, sadness, bitterness and all forms of non-forgiveness are caused by too much past and not enough presence.'

Tolle distils the mindset behind both into a single line: 'A perfect recipe for permanent dissatisfaction and non-fulfilment.'

I was starting to get it.

Anxious and stressed, worrying about the future? *Yes*

Resentful and bitter thinking about the past? *Yes*

Permanent dissatisfaction and non-fulfilment? *Abso-fucking-lutely*

He basically summed up every frustration that had been quietly building in my mind and then gave me the answer.

BE MORE PRESENT.

Reading messages on my phone while people were talking to me, pretending to listen with the intuitive 'yup', 'really', 'sure', 'wow', while actually thinking about where I had to get to next. My mind was constantly bouncing between the past and the future.

Why did she say that?

Did I come off too strong?

I need to reply to that email.

I'll sort it all out next week.

Tomorrow I'll go to the gym.

Once this deal closes, then I'll relax.

And on and on. An endless stream of thoughts that pulled me away from being *here*.

Tolle's outlook on life had begun to change how I looked at everything. I realised I was pissing in the present and I needed to do something about it.

I'll never forget fast forwarding to near the end of my life, imagining myself looking back, and feeling a cold wave of regret, thinking *was I ever really there?* Did I live my whole life through the lens of what's next?

This is something I still have to work hard at every day. Staying in the present is hard.

It was no secret either; it seemed like half the people I spoke to knew about *The Power of Now*... Uber drivers, waiters, gym instructors. It wasn't some mystic, academic, exclusive thing; it was all over main street.

Where had I been?

These days I feel like the book tries to stretch a few good ideas a bit too far, and I now know how much more I had to go and fish for myself. But at the time I read it, it all made so much sense to me and it's a book I would highly recommend if you're just getting started. But as you'll come to see, being present is by no means the only answer.

Let's lean into arguably the most mumbo jumbo word out there – *spirituality* (the non-religious sense).

AWAKENING, ENLIGHTENMENT, CONSCIOUSNESS.

This stuff wasn't really my cup of tea. I was more interested in models and Maseratis.

Where was it going to get me? *What does it all really mean?*

Well, imagine you're living in *Peppa Pig* world, everything is flat, two-dimensional as you see it. Now imagine you step through a door into the world of *Avatar*, a three-dimensional kaleidoscope of wonder and imagination. That's the best way I can describe it.

And for me, walking through that door didn't happen because of some fancy ritual or intervention, it happened slowly as I glided through some of the most elegant books I'd ever read. Books like *The Untethered Soul* by Michael A. Singer, and *Awareness* by Anthony De Mello. They quietly shifted my entire perspective on reality.

Here are some key takeaways to help you understand what I'm talking about:

1. The voice in our head is not us. We are the one who hears it. We are the witness of our thoughts.

2. By separating ourselves from these thoughts, we can see that most of them have no relevance.

3. Who we really are, our soul and spirit, is beneath all that.

4. Spirituality means waking up and realising this.

5. We all suffer because we automatically focus on what we don't have.

6. Self-consciousness, insecurity, anxiety and embarrassment are all forms of fear. Every day we are either feeling it or trying to protect ourselves from feeling it. When the Buddha said that all of life is suffering, this is what he meant.

7. This 'suffering' dominates our mind. We can never be free of it, until we are free from the part within us that is creating it.

8. Joy, beauty, love and peace tend to lie on the other side of this incessant neurotic thought.

9. Who we identify as gives us a lot of comfort and security. We resist questioning things and letting go. We fear losing what we know.

10. To detach our 'selves', we need to observe our beliefs, emotions and physical sensations, and try not to personalise what is

happening. Instead of saying, 'I'm depressed', we should say, 'I'm experiencing a depression right now.'

11. Celibacy, regular meditation, ice bath – all these forms of self-discipline are designed to help harden the mindset and maintain a level of detachment and resist the natural gravitational pull of unwanted thoughts.

12. Our spirit or soul, the witness of our thoughts, is somehow connected to something greater than ourselves, something magical and mystical.

With these new insights, it felt like I'd stepped into a whole new dimension. Reality itself had shifted. Things weren't binary or rigid anymore. For the first time, I could see how everything – ourselves, life, all of it – is subjective, malleable, controllable.

As corny as it might sound, I honestly felt like I'd woken up.

More conscious.

More alive.

You might be thinking: *OK, Charley, but what does that actually mean?*

I'll tell you (and here's why it's not just 'mumbo jumbo').

Instead of trying to describe what this state or shift is, let me explain what it's not. It's not being stuck in that default mode – reactive, impulsive, distracted. Living on autopilot. Like when I was heading to Mexico, chasing the next mission. My mind was hopping around like popcorn in the pan, constantly reacting to subconscious needs, childhood conditioning, ego, fear. Doing what I was 'meant' to do.

Doing what I'd always done. Not questioning, just following the programme.

We're all shaped by society, upbringing, movies, school, expectations. That programming shapes what we give meaning to, what we chase, how we feel, how we act. Most of us are just backseat drivers in our own lives. But waking up, becoming 'conscious', is seeing that programming for what it is. It's realising:

I am not my thoughts.

I am not my emotions.

I am not my reactions.

I can step out of this.

It's the moment you go from reaction to choice. From autopilot to awareness. Grabbing the wheel of your own mind.

That's what people are talking about when they say 'enlightenment'.

For me it was life-changing stuff.

And once I saw it, I couldn't unsee it.

It was like I'd stumbled upon the solution to the human condition. And thank God I did, otherwise I'd still be chasing my tail, stuck in permanent dissatisfaction. I began to think of everyone else, all my friends and family back home in England. It felt like I'd found a secret they all needed to know about.

Like me, they were the product of polite British culture, a nation covertly trying to disguise their self-consciousness, anxiety and insecurities with good manners and sarcasm, while at the same time operating under expectations to be a certain way and feel the need to prove their worth. I saw myself in them. Trying to prove I was enough. Quietly insecure. Always performing.

I realised the extent of the problem but could see how transformational this shift in perspective could be to so many people's life experiences.

This was the moment I went all in.

It's when I knew I had to start documenting everything.

'Enlightenment is the space between your thoughts.'

ECKHART TOLLE

'If you are depressed you are living in the past.
If you are anxious you are living in the future.
If you are at peace you are living in the present.'

LAO TZU

THE EYES DON'T LIE

At some stage I knew I would have to return home, but right now I was having too much fun learning who I was.

'You've got to check out *The Magic of Human Connection* – it's amazing!'

The workshop hadn't been the top of my list, even with my newfound appreciation for mindfulness, it sounded pretty out there. But everyone at my hotel (where mealtimes seemed designed to be collective experiences, so we all discussed what we were seeing, hearing, doing) had been singing its praises, so what the hell, I gave it a go.

Jessica Encell-Coleman. Early thirties, sporty, sophisticated, had a real get-up-and-go vibe – no frumpy, slow-talking Mystic Meg here.

There must have been about 150 of us in the marquee that had been set up on campus and we were instructed to split into two groups.

'Right, guys, I want this group over here to head over to the back of the room. Spread out, please, stand to attention and close your eyes.'

We were all a little bemused. She turned back to face my group.

'You guys, when I give you the green light, I want you to walk over there and give them all hugs.'

What? Is she serious? Hugs?

I was standing right at the front, and it felt like she was addressing me now, reassuring my puzzled look.

Really? I mean, come on. Consciousness yes but hugs now? Eeek.

'Yes, guys! HUGS!' The positive energy bounded out of her, the sort you had no option but to embrace, it was infectious.

She gave us a few more instructions and then released the huggers.

It was surreal – I felt super-awkward. I moved extra slow to see first what everyone else was doing. The first lady I walked up to was in her fifties. I could see she was waiting eagerly for someone to embrace her. I gave her a quick tentative squeeze with my arms and moved on, like a shy teenage kiss.

It was clever because the person being hugged would never know who was doing the hugging. So it removed any self-consciousness. The recipient could simply savour the hug from a stranger – free from judgement or anxiety. I noticed around the room people getting quite emotional. Afterwards I heard one lady say that she couldn't remember the last time she was able to hug a guy and not feel threatened by him.

I lined up my next customer, a middle-aged guy in a pastel red T. I was about to lean in but just then caught the eye of another dude with the same idea – I politely gestured him to go ahead. Tricky business this hugging – one had to move swiftly and decisively. Next up I spotted a big burly guy – someone else had literally just finished with him. He was wide open, I went in for the kill, hugged him tight. He was sweaty but I didn't care – I could feel he was relaxed, his body language was like *it's OK, don't rush off, stay for a few more seconds – I need this*. So I held his body tight to mine and relaxed into the hug the best I could – I took a deep breath and so did he. Then just like that we parted ways and I disappeared anonymously into the seas of huggers.

I probably hugged another three or four men and women of all shapes, sizes and ages. When they opened their eyes we were all standing back on the other side of the room. They will never know who they received hugs from. Weirdly I found it easier to hug the guys – I was worried that if the girls did see me, they might think I fancied them. Maybe it was a boys' boarding school thing.

Next up we switched around and I was there standing to attention with my eyes closed in anticipation. One hug after another, I could feel the love and the warmth – these people genuinely wanted to deliver me platonic love and good vibes – I felt myself starting to open up and trust more. I was getting into it, and it was weirdly satisfying.

I realised that I never really hugged anyone – I never really let anyone in. I was so guarded and anti other human beings unless they were a swimsuit model or someone else I was trying to impress. Had I chosen to become a lone wolf, disconnected from those around me, or had I just ended up that way? Naturally if you start off thinking you know better than everyone else, eventually you'll probably end up believing you simply *are* better.

'OK, guys, you're all doing amazingly – this is the BEST group we've had so far,' she fibbed.

'To finish up we're going to do something called the eye gazing experiment. On my signal I'd like you all to walk slowly around the room and when I say, turn to the person closest to you, take one another's hands and you're going to look each other in the eyes for two whole minutes.'

You could tell she was excited for us. It didn't sound that bad.

'It's harder than it sounds! Relax into it, guys!'

She kicked us off, it felt like musical chairs cruising around the room in anticipation. Before I knew it, I was facing a good-looking Swedish guy similar age to me, holding hands.

'OK now, get ready, everyone, we're about to start the first two minutes.'

I tried to fill the awkwardness with a typical British, 'I hate this kind of thing.'

He just stood taller, puffed out his chest and said confidently, 'Ah man, I love this shit!'

I felt inferior, annoyed with myself that I hadn't embraced it too – *maybe I loved this shit too? Why did I say that?* Was I ashamed, worried what he might have thought of me? He was like me but being more himself and owning it. It was a messy, awkward two minutes – I felt insecure and kept looking away. I just felt him judging me. It was like I'd started a race badly and couldn't recover. I couldn't wait to start afresh.

Next up I found myself holding a pair of soft clammy hands that belonged to an awkward-looking lady – probably thinking *what the hell am I doing here*. We began to stare into each other's eyes, I didn't know whether to smile or frown, I instinctively wanted to glance away but my eyes jittered as I tried to stay put. She was uncomfortable too – I tried to coax her with my body language as if to say *it's OK – we can do this*. I felt like she was gazing into my soul – I had nowhere to hide. But we both began to ease into it, two strangers willing each other to just be. I could feel all my instinctive habits kicking and screaming, wanting to break the moment, but they didn't – we stood there still and connected – it was quite something.

'OK, that's a wrap! Keep walking,' Jessica shouted.

I was still in a bit of a trance and not quite ready to move on – I instinctively wanted to put my arms around her – she reciprocated, and we hugged.

'Thank you – that was awesome. I'm Charley by the way.'

'I'm Sharon, you were so good at that – thank you.'

We moved on.

I felt closer to her than most of my friends I'd known for decades. I could be vulnerable with her in a way I just couldn't with someone I already knew. I remember crossing paths with her on campus a few times the rest of the week – we always smiled at each other knowingly – we had shared a special moment.

That workshop was mega – I left the tent feeling totally different to when I walked in. I was grounded, I felt open and more connected – it put me in a completely different state. To be honest it was a wake-up call – there I was thinking I was the jovial, outgoing people person. I was Carlos Ley: exciting, interesting, entertaining, a pro at chatting up women. But I wasn't really Carlos Ley, as I had started to accept now. And behind that mask was someone who actually felt very lonely, because no matter how many people he swept up into his orbit, he never let any of them get that close. It really hit home that I needed to unravel what was holding me back.

Little did I know though, more answers were just around the corner.

―

That afternoon I headed to a talk by Dave Asprey, founder of Bulletproof Coffee, successful serial entrepreneur and biohacking junkie. The kind of guy who'll do anything to optimise his body and mind: from cryotherapy and intermittent fasting to red light therapy, nootropics, and injecting himself with stem cells if it gives him a 1 per cent edge. He was obsessed with longevity and optimal performance.

I walked into this office space, finding myself in a small group of around thirty, so it felt quite intimate. But it was also a bit like the first day at school; a load of strange faces, some twos and threes sticking together but then a fair few reassuring singles too, flying solo like me, cruising around. I headed over to the trestle table where everyone had gravitated. There was this tall middle-aged guy, with slicked-back grey hair and wearing yellow-lensed Oakleys, holding court, dishing out Bulletproof Coffee (black with a lug of special 'grass-fed' butter to boost fat as a substitute for a carb-heavy breakfast). I grabbed one too.

Turned out the guy in the yellow lenses was Dave Asprey and after a few minutes he wrapped up the huddle, made his way to the front of the room, told us all to take a seat and instructed his sidekick to switch on the Instagram live stream so that his half a million followers could enjoy the experience alongside us.

He spent forty-five minutes or so explaining everything from how his goal was to live until he was 120 years old, to how he wore special skins on planes to protect himself from radiation, to how the yellow lenses were to screen the light pollution from his eyes. I was starting to go off him a bit.

But it wasn't until the end, after he'd invited us all to his biohacking lab in Santa Monica, that he said something that really piqued my attention.

There was a short Q&A, and someone asked Dave what the most important book he ever read was.

He paused for a second. It was odd, his confident bravado melted away and he looked quite raw and vulnerable.

'You know what,' he said, touching his face almost awkwardly and giving us a glimpse of someone who wasn't necessarily as confident as he had appeared so far, 'probably it was a book by John Bradshaw called *Healing the Shame That Binds You*. I read it when I was a young man, and it was the most important book I ever read.'

Turns out it would be the most important book I would ever read too – although it would take some time until I fully understood why.

BITCOIN & BILLIONAIRES

Next stop Silicon Valley.

I was on a roll – a self-searching sabbatical, a deep dive into an open-minded and mind-opening America.

Diego, the Chilean facilitator of VCX pitched me:

- Small group... twelve people.
- Entrepreneurs and investors, $10 million+ net worth and a few billionaires. Behind the scenes deep dive into the Silicon Valley start-up game.
- Chaperoned by the famous venture capitalist – Tim Draper.

'You think it's something you'd be interested in?'

Was I interested? Hell yes. All I had to do now was blag it.

'My *family* are landowners, we're in real estate and farming.'

I chose my words carefully – the wealthy South Americans talked about their 'family' like it was the firm, the powerhouse. I wasn't going to let on we had a modest farm near Brighton with a handful of rickety old cottages, struggling to break even.

I was punching above my weight, leaning on whatever I could to make me seem that bit more legit.

Silicon Valley to me was a faraway land – like fiction. A valley of silicon even, magically spinning out one billion-dollar start-up after another, like elves in the north pole.

Sunday evening, sitting in the busy lobby of the Sofitel San Francisco Bay in Redwood City. Possible VCX alumni awkwardly checking each other out, awaiting the welcome reception.

'Hey! Welcome to Silicon Valley, guys!'

Diego parachuted in, lit with energy and delight.

Just in time to lubricate the group and bring us together.

First, he embraced his Chilean comrades like old school pals, and then all at the same time he's greeting everyone, introducing us and dishing out our goody bags. There was a buzz now.

'Charley! So glad you're here, my friend. Here I want you to meet Carlos, he's Colombian.'

'Che... Carlos, me presento Charley de Inglaterra. Es un trader y vives en Miami.'

I felt right at home.

But hang on, could Carlos be one of the billionaires?

Turns out he was. Not only did his family own a Colombian bank, but he also had a chain of dentist practices across Mexico.

I was mixing with some serious movers and shakers. Fund managers, mining executives, real estate moguls, telecoms tycoons and even a salmon farm owner. Diego had drafted in businessmen from all over – a couple of Mexicans, a handful of Chilenos, a Colombian, a Hungarian, a Ukrainian and then me... the Brit from Sussex. We were all from traditional industries and here to learn about the sexy tech start-up game.

Of course, none of them knew I was close to broke. I'm not sure I'd really come to terms with it yet either. I was in denial. But I hoped that if I could just find some people who could give me guidance, help me find opportunities, everything would be OK. And in a way, it was. But not because of what they gave me. Maybe this mind-opening open-minded America would have more of an impact on the next steps in my journey than I expected, and in ways I couldn't at that point anticipate.

WILLY WONKA

Stepping into the Draper University building was like walking into Willy Wonka's chocolate factory. The Tesla car reception desk (literally a Tesla sliced through the middle and adapted to a desk), the oversize comic superheroes painted across the vast wall, the busy students scattered around different workstations – all at the behest of the prominent, Harry Potter-esque University emblem, a giant blue shield with the letter 'D' and a yellow lightning strike across an edge. It felt like fiction – but that was the whole point... the magic of turning fiction into a reality.

We had arrived at '*Hero City*'.

The group shuffled around the doorway, gazing up to the high ceilings trying to take it all in.

But when are we going to meet Willy Wonka?

We were in downtown San Mateo – a short bus ride from the hotel in Redwood City. It turns out that Silicon Valley is just the name of an area, essentially the southern San Francisco Bay region of California. It got its name because of the large number of silicon chip manufacturers and other technology companies that have their headquarters here. Spread across cities like Palo Alto, San Jose, Redwood City, San Matteo and Menlo Park it had become a thriving ecosystem for technology start-ups, venture capitalists and entrepreneurs. Stanford – the leading American technology and science university – was also right at the epicentre.

We were ushered into one of the classrooms and spread into the horseshoe configuration of chairs. I watched the irony of the fully grown business titans shuffling themselves into the plastic seat-desk-armrest combos.

'VCX Alumni... Welcome to *Hero City*!'

Tim Draper bundled in with gusto and colour. Dark and handsome, six foot four, he had that charm and presence about him. He was wearing a suit with his trademark Bitcoin tie... It wasn't the sort of polished look you'd expect a billionaire VC to command, his slightly scruffy sky-blue button-down Oxford shirt with a couple of pens clipped into his chest pocket made him look more like the friendly headmaster popping in to cover for the geography teacher.

'We're so excited to have you all here – this is the very first VCX programme. And thank you to Diego for organising everything. We've got a fantastic week lined up.'

He made us feel welcome right away – grateful even that we had taken a leap of faith. That's what Tim was about, having courage, taking risks, stepping into the unknown, being the *Hero*.

'I don't usually do this, but I want to tell you about my Facebook story – it'll give you a flavour for this place...'

He went on to tell us how he came very close to investing in Facebook when it was only getting started, but pulled out when they kept asking for more, suspecting he stood to lose money. He had been inches away from backing what turned out to be one of the biggest companies in the world. He shrugged it off with good humour, but I sensed there were still remnants of irritation deep down. The one that got away.

That was the thrill though. The game. We were all captivated. Tim, the scion of a Silicon Valley dynasty was the real deal. His firm Draper Fisher Jurvetson had backed companies like Hotmail, Skype, Tesla, Baidu and SpaceX, to name a few. His father, William H. Draper, after serving in public office under President Ronald Reagan, was one of America's very first venture capitalists. And now Tim's children were getting into the game – third generation venture capitalists. The Drapers were Silicon Valley blue blood, on a par with the likes of Sequoia, and Andreessen Horowitz.

Tim famously bought 30,000 Bitcoins in a US Marshal's auction that were seized from Silk Road, a black market on the dark web. At the time they were worth about $18 million – everyone thought he was crazy. Today at the time of writing they're worth around $1.2 billion.

He was always pushing boundaries – challenging the status quo.

Freedom to fail, was a well-known tag line etched into the fabric of his entrepreneurship university. They even taught science fiction instead of history to help entrepreneurs get more creative about the future, consider new possibilities and anticipate new technologies.

His students had to memorise a pledge and they'd recite it together each morning...

I will promote freedom at all costs, and I'll do everything in my power to drive, build, and pursue pride, progress, and change... I will fail and fail again until I succeed and explore the world with gusto and enthusiasm.

We'd walked into another world. A new mindset. A relentless culture to achieve and make positive change. There was a part of me that was really attracted to this kind of business philosophy, even if I didn't appreciate at that point how similar it was to many self-help philosophies. But I knew I liked the focus on principles, strategies and mindset – understanding yourself, your motivations, what success (and happiness) looks and feels like.

Back home this sort of rhetoric would get me thrown out of the pub.

Ay, look 'ere... that Charley's a bit full of 'imself, ain't he?

A hint of ambition and people tended to get suspicious. Not the done thing. Even though most of the people I knew from school were ambitious too, nobody would talk about it. I wasn't the only lone wolf. It really felt like every man for himself a lot of the time.

VCX week was one of the most memorable weeks of my life. Rich with new friendships, new ways of thinking about business, life, the future, and understanding the ins and outs of venture investing. We visited the Tesla factory, learnt about Bitcoin, and saw bespoke fabrics being made by 3D printer prototypes. But it wasn't until the very last day that I met a man who had the biggest lasting impact on me.

We were all scattered across the lecture hall waiting for the next tech titan to share their wisdom from the valley. An Indian American entrepreneur walked in rather unassumingly and casual, despite his evident intelligence and incredible success. Slider shoes, baggy sweater, late forties and thinning dark hair. He was the founder of Angel List, a platform where anyone could invest small amounts of money via syndicates into Silicon Valley start-ups.

He glided to the front of the room and greeted us. He had a kind smile and a glint in his eye – it was like he was a free spirit, on his own path, unaffected, radiating inner calm. There was something about him I was drawn to. His name was Naval Ravikant.

It's hard to explain but I think what I saw in him was everything I was searching for, even if I didn't have the words or realise it at the time.

It wasn't the start-up stuff that really stuck with me – it was his wisdom around life. He was like a modern-day philosopher, but his language was anything but 'mumbo jumbo', it was business-like, and I loved his bite-sized principles that were big in scope but clear and clever enough to stick in your mind and apply when it mattered.

One of my favourites was: 'It's not conditions that change your life, it's decisions.'

It had been my daily decisions, impulses and habits that had driven me to where I was today, so I could see that in order to change my life I needed to make better ones. Not how being spiritually enlightened could change my life – how making better choices could. That made sense, and it would make sense to my mother when I'd no doubt have to explain why I wasn't being brainwashed by all this 'mumbo jumbo'.

Naval helped me appreciate why any of the spiritual stuff actually mattered in the real world. He wheeled in the practical application that gave this theory some teeth.

- How my choices in life are clouded by my ego and identity.
- How meditation allows me to dive below them and unlock truth, clarity and direction.

- How important it is to guard your time to create space and stillness to think.

I'd spent years reacting. Starting businesses with mates, jumping at whatever sounded like a good idea at the time. Saying yes to things that presented themselves rather than carving out the space to truly think about who I was, what I wanted and why.

He helped me see too how the concept of gratitude wasn't just some airy-fairy idea. We're wired to think about what we don't have, what we lack – nothing is ever enough and so we're seldom satisfied, in fact we're permanently dissatisfied. Even the Buddha said, *desire is suffering.*

The utility of gratitude now made perfect sense. It was the ideal antidote to the dissatisfaction. I totally got now why I needed to write down three things I was grateful for in my *Five-Minute Journal.*

Practical application – the juice was worth the squeeze.

A few more of Naval's one liners I particularly liked were:

Be present above all else.

Reading is the ultimate meta-skill.

Compound interest creates real wealth.

Earn with your mind, not your time.

Watch every thought and ask, 'Why am I having this thought?'

Love is given, not just received.

He was giving us practical insights on how to think – not what to think. And I was soaking it all up like a sponge.

Shit, if I thought more like him, maybe I'd end up more like him.

The fact he was a successful businessman and not a monk made a big difference to me. It just made everything feel less mysterious and more matter of fact. And when he quoted people like Eckhart Tolle it gave me more confidence that I was on the right track, that this newfound conscious awareness was real, useful and tangible.

'That was my favourite talk of the week, Naval – thank you so much.'

'Here's my card – fire me an email anytime.'

I began following Naval on Twitter and listening to all his podcast interviews.

I began to heed his advice, read many of his book recommendations (panning for gold as he put it) and began adopting a lot of his life and business philosophies.

Another of my 'digital mentors' was Gary Vaynerchuk, AKA Gary V, who I was introduced to at Summit Series in LA. He was a fast-talking New Yorker whose schtick was all about the hustle and self-awareness. Light years ahead of the curve when it comes to digital trends – he owns a $250 million media agency called VaynerMedia and he's convinced he's going to buy the New York Jets one day.

A lot of Gary's sayings resonated with me too.

'Perfection is the disguise of insecurity.'

I'd built a whole identity around getting things 'just right', but I was beginning to see the cracks in that story.

Ed Mylett was another. He was a successful businessman turned self-development guru. He coined the phrase, *blissful dissatisfaction*.

This was super neat. The idea that as humans we're never going to be fully satisfied, and we're always going to have goals and desires that we want to work towards, but we have to try and find enough bliss in the process.

Not, we should live in bliss.

Or we should never feel dissatisfied.

But...

Blissful dissatisfaction

I loved it. Logical, practical, it made total sense to me. The simplicity coupled with the scope of it made it easy to remember. Now I refer to it a lot to check myself. It sums up the human condition in two words. That's the target, the sweet spot, the goal:

Blissful dissatisfaction

I'd been sceptical at first, but what really moved the needle was seeing a lot of highly successful American businesspeople embracing the 'mumbo jumbo'.

It was a slight case of, *shit, if they're into it then maybe I should be too.*

I looked up to them; they felt credible, like digital mentors. They gave weight to everything I was starting to explore, and gave me the appetite to keep going. I'd been lucky: top schools, great university, loving parents, but I was still craving real guidance. I'd thought I knew best, and ended up in a mess. What I needed was practical wisdom on business and life.

People always ask when the key moments were when I had a certain epiphany or major perspective shift – *what was it?*

And the reality is that bar a few special moments (which we'll come to), the way it all happened was just as Naval put it: 'At some deep level, you absorb them, the words, the concepts, and they become threads in the tapestry of your psyche. They kind of weave in there.'

And that's exactly what was happening to me – you don't realise it at the time, but these guides, books, talks and conversations were slowly weaving their way into what was to become Charley 2.0.

But right now, despite the groundwork, the experiences, the new healthy habits, the old wiring still ran the show more often than I liked to admit. A lot of information, not a whole lot of integration.

My six-month hiatus was over – I was back to full health, and I was excited to take the new me back home – the bronzed spiritual gangster eager to show it all off. But for now, I was still very much Charley 1.0.

We were packing up my apartment, I remember Carmen in her silk Hermès trousers and white tank top looking like she was in a *Vogue* campaign. I'd been seeing her for a few weeks – she was a ravishing Puerto Rican model.

It was time to say goodbye.

I was, in the words of New York columnist Candace Bushnell – the creator of *Sex and the City* – a 'modelizer'.

There were more modelling agencies per square foot in Miami than anywhere else in the world – I was obsessed. Models were my trifecta. They quenched my ego. They determined my mood, self-worth and confidence. With a model by my side, I was complete; without, I was insecure and worthless. It was that black and white.

Money, body, Instagram, job, apartment, friends; it was all designed to qualify me to date a model. And to me a stunning model meant more admiration and respect from everyone back home. The same 'everyone' I was still trying to outdo.

I headed back to the UK thinking I'd done the work and I could finally get back on track. Little did I know, though, the little pit I'd fallen into was about to turn into a rather large crater.

WHAT IS MEDITATION?

At its core, meditation is a practice that trains the mind and body where to deliberately place attention.

Meditation strengthens your ability to stay present, be intentional and gain control over your thoughts and emotions.

THE 3 LEVELS OF MEDITATION

LEVEL 1

MINDFUL MEDITATION

Practice
Place your attention on your breath or a mantra.
When thoughts arise, observe them without judgement and return to your focus.

Benefits
Be more present, strengthens concentration, helps to detach, reduces stress and anxiety.

LEVEL 2

DYNAMIC MEDITATION

Practice
Focus on emotions like gratitude, forgiveness, or compassion.

Benefits
Intentionally reshaping unhelpful mental and emotional habits.

LEVEL 3

INTUITIVE MEDITATION

Practice
Sink deeper into your body and reflect on key decisions or challenges.

Benefits
Enhances alignment with your values, clarifies long-term goals and builds confidence in your decisions.

A GUIDED MEDITATION PRACTICE
(10 mins max)

STEP 1:
Create the Environment:
Find a quiet space free from distractions.

STEP 2:
Relax and ground yourself:
Take a few deep breaths, release tension from your body and close your eyes.

STEP 3:
MINDFUL MEDITATION

Focus only on your breath. When your mind wanders, gently bring back your focus to your breath. (2–3 mins)

STEP 4:
DYNAMIC MEDITATION

Reflect on three positive moments or accomplishments from the past day to foster gratitude. (1–2 mins)

Identify one negative emotion or thought that is holding you back and pick the antidote. Once chosen, cultivate that feeling in your body, in your heart. Really feel. (2–3 mins)

'It's never enough' ➡ **Gratitude**
Racing thoughts, stress, 'what-ifs' ➡ **Presence**
Grudges, bitterness, past hurts ➡ **Forgiveness**
'I'm not good enough' / need approval ➡ **Self-Love**
Ego, comparison, proving yourself ➡ **Humility**
Inner critic, negative spirals ➡ **Reframe Positive**

STEP 5:
INTUITIVE MEDITATION

Focus on a pressing decision or goal then visualise different scenarios, immersing yourself in each one. Which one feels aligned with your ambitions and values?

Ask yourself:
'Am I choosing what's easy, or what will help me grow?'
'Which path energises me and aligns with my purpose?'

STEP 6:
CLOSING REFLECTION

Take a few deep breaths and reconnect to the present moment.

Quietly end the ritual by saying to yourself 'Namaste'. The literal meaning is 'I bow to you'. It's a way of acknowledging something greater than ourselves.

Finally reflect on any insights or ideas that arose and write them down.

BACK TO REALITY

My mother picked me up at Heathrow. It was grey and wet, and she looked tired. She had been up most of the night ferrying guests home after hosting a wedding function. My younger sister Nina had been shouting at her all morning, and the crops were waterlogged.

'How has everything been?' I'd asked her enthusiastically.

'Oh, you know, we've just been terribly busy as usual, Charley – it never seems to stop. Don't let me forget to stop off and feed the cattle when we get back. Johnny is away on holiday this week.' (Johnny had been working on our family farm since he was seventeen. He was now in his seventies.)

I very quickly came back down to earth and suddenly felt guilty about galivanting around the US, spending the little money I had left (or more truthfully, my credit cards) on self-improvement, while she was at home driving tractors, shovelling grain, mowing the lawn, running the small weddings business, and looking after my autistic sister 24-7.

'So tell me, how are you doing? Tell me about Miami – do you think you're *better* now?'

It always felt like it was wrapped up in concern as opposed to dripping in excitement, wanting to hear all my news and new experiences. We chatted. I didn't tell her half the things I'd been up to and definitely not with the appropriate enthusiasm – I dialled it all down to fit the invisible demure. It's hard to explain, but deep down I think I was afraid of not being how she expected me to be, too far away from her ways and her thinking. Perhaps I felt I couldn't handle her judgement, so I sat there with my designer shoes trying to resist being pulled back too far into the conformity I'd started to break away from.

We made it home. I'm walking along the wooden-beamed corridor – the whippets are jumping around, over-excited to see me, my sister Nina is following me into the kitchen. I could feel my head brushing against the ceiling – that was different I thought.

'You've grown, Charley,' observed my mother.

Mrs Liggett, our housekeeper since before I was born, was standing there waiting to give me a big hug.

'Don't you think he's grown, Mrs Ligget?'

Then it hit me. I'd grown taller from all the yoga – I was a tanned yogi, into meditation, green juices and clean living.

It was real. No wonder they were staring at me as though I was a stranger.

ROYAL POLO

A few months passed. It's summer and I'm sitting in the tent zipping up my boots, next to Prince William. I feel like a kid in a candy shop – it doesn't get much more high profile than this. I'd committed to playing the royal charity polo match months ago and there was no way I was going to miss it.

'Hey, Charley, it's good to see you – it's been ages...'

Prince Harry walks in and cracks his trademark smile, the one that the paparazzi and army vets love him for; the smile that will win the heart of a Hollywood actress.

'Life treating you OK?'

'Awesome, thanks, Harry – can't complain.'

As it happens, I'm broke, living back home with my mother at thirty-one and ashamed of telling anyone the truth, least of all Prince Harry and the man sitting beside me, a future king.

I'm clinging on to being the well-heeled commodity trader with a decent grasp of Spanish, but the truth is I'm a boarding-school boy, in over my head, afraid, and trying my best to make it all go away. Trying to pretend it's all good.

But hey.

I can't wait to get the photos of today up on Instagram – that will show them. Look at Charley. He's the bomb. Still here.

Growing up all I could ever think about was playing polo. Just like any other kid going to the footy at the weekend I'd watch my father play, mess around on the horses and romanticise about being like one of the majestically talented and good-looking Argentinian professionals. Maybe even get an iconic photograph of the Queen handing me a prize someday at Windsor, just like the ones of my father in the downstairs loo. He served in the Household Cavalry and ceremonial duties were very much par for the course. He enjoyed the pomp and prestige of commanding the mounted escorts alongside Her Majesty the Queen in his red uniform, white plume and silver breastplate sparkling in the glitz of the occasions. The army was his way into the world of polo and became a central part of his life.

It's a misunderstood sport for many reasons – but really there's only one way to describe it.

INTOXICATING.

Think Formula 1 back in the day. Ayrton Senna, James Hunt, the danger, the glamour, celebrities, royalty, models, paparazzi. Just instead of petrol, rubber and engines, it's the smell of fresh cut grass, pedigree horses, muscles and sweat, like 100m Olympians, and the sound of hooves thundering down onto the ground.

Imagine standing close to the finish line next to the rail of a famous horserace. The crowds, the tension, the thrill, the pack of horses thundering past – polo can be just as captivating.

Growing up, I could see that polo attracts some of the wealthiest people in the world, from aristocrats to oligarchs, and then come the beautiful women, the chancers, the lotharios, the fast money and the egos. *Carlos Ley?*

We had just finished the prize giving after the exhibition match. 'Let me introduce you to my son Charley – he's just back from Miami,' said my father.

'Gordon Troughton.' He put out his hand, standing to attention.

'Charley, how nice to meet you – your father and I are great mates, we used to be in the Army together.' I waited for the inevitable, 'Tell me, Charley, what do you do?' The dreaded question, I hadn't perfected the party line yet.

'I'm a commodity trader.'

Thank God he left it at that.

Maybe Gordon didn't notice my anxiety – it was painful. We finished our small talk and cracked on to the bar. My father walked proudly next to me, eyes scouting the crowds for some more of his buddies. He's immaculately dressed, a tie pin through his pastel pink Hermès tie, pocket handkerchief and crisp white shirt. That stint in the Army, the cad around town, the pomp and prestige of the circles he moved in were all delicately woven into his appearance.

'You look well, you're a good-looking son of a bitch.'

'Thanks, Daddy.' I grimaced.

He meant it as a compliment, but I'd started to see just how much weight he placed on surface appearances. Looking good. Being seen with the right people. The optics always seemed more important than what was actually going on underneath.

I didn't want to be as vain as he was, but I still secretly sought his approval.

'Is that a spot on your face? You must leave your face alone.'

I tightened and went into my shell momentarily.

I felt that obsession with how things *looked*, rather than how things *were* had held him back sometimes from going deeper in business, in relationships, in life. And deep down, I knew I didn't want the same fate.

He had a knack for spotting certain well-to-do faces the moment they appeared, steering me over for a quick handshake. In banking, it was a gift – building a network, working the room, collecting names. And he was brilliant at it. But it always felt a little one-way, charm flowing upwards for approval or agenda, rather than sideways for connection. Often I found myself rebelling, preferring to chat to the waiter instead.

'Charley, I still can't understand why you sold those lovely horses of yours.'

Huh, wait until you find out about the house.

He had no idea – I couldn't tell him how bad things were financially.

We were in the middle of the summer social calendar. Keeping up appearances was more important to me than ever. Chip off the old block, I guess.

I later came to learn that one of the strongest forces in the human personality is the drive to preserve the integrity of our own identity, and I was holding on hard.

But something else was happening – something I couldn't yet articulate. That hollow feeling I'd been covering up with work and women and the next deal, it was starting to surface. I felt anxious a lot of the time now, especially at events like this. My six-month sabbatical had been like hiding in a bubble – no one really knew me there. There were no expectations. No awkward questions about what I was up to. I could reinvent myself, be whoever I wanted to be.

Back home, reality hit differently.

Something was trying to reveal itself, something I'd been hiding from for years. A crack had appeared and I couldn't seal it. The veneer of Carlos Ley was crumbling, and for the first time, I couldn't numb the pain.

But it was more than that. It was like a crack had appeared and I couldn't seal it anymore.

I walked around the rest of the day like a self-conscious lamb hiding behind the uniform and facade of who I used to be. Paranoia had set in.

Charley, how's work going?

Charley, what are you up to at the moment?

I still didn't tell most of them what was going on.

Being a hotshot commodity trader had defined me. Without realising it at the time, I feared what would happen if I couldn't be that person anymore, the person everyone expected me to be, the person that gave me my self-worth.

If I couldn't be that person then who the hell was I?

'Many of us have worn masks for so long that we're not even sure what's actually underneath anymore. We've lost track of where we end and the mask begins, of who we really are. That's why removing the masks is not only terrifying, it's painful.'

LEWIS HOWES, *THE MASK OF MASCULINITY*

CELINE

'You've matched with Celine'

'You have a message from Celine'

'Hey, Charley... How's it going? Nice photos :)'

Each prompt induced another flutter of dopamine. Wasn't she one of my favourites? I tried to recall among the hundreds of girls that I'd swiped right as I instinctively pulled up her profile.

Celine

French Lebanese

Notting Hill

Fashion

Bingo

I scrolled through her photos on Hinge (my preferred dating app). She was a European version of Kendall Jenner. Brunette, olive skin, wafer thin, I could tell from her bikini shot at the beach cabana in Mykonos. Another next to her father outside their whitewashed town house in West London, the spring sun radiating down onto the brilliant pink cherry blossom and her trendy oversized rainbow fabrics. Both of them were striking, effortlessly cool and clearly wealthy. Maybe my new carefully choreographed photos had done the trick.

The topless beach pic with my friend's younger sister. *Look, I have a great body and I'm friends with girls I'm not trying to sleep with.*

Hiking with two mates with their arms around me. *Look, I have some guy friends too.*

Sitting on the back of my car with three kids and my polo sticks. *Look, I'm a family guy, great with kids but also play polo and have a Range Rover.*

Walking off a small propeller plane in Los Roques. *Look, I travel to exotic places, and (used to) have money.*

All designed for girls to look at me in a certain way.

In my mind Celine was girlfriend material, and I quickly became fixated. I almost saw her as a prize asset.

Shit, if I could just start dating her that would fast track my problems away, I'd be someone again.

'Let's switch to WhatsApp, I'm not on here much.' I lied

'Here's my number – message me x'

Experience taught me you had to get them off the dating app, there were too many other guys, too many distractions. Especially for someone like Celine.

A whole day went by. Was she going to message? What had happened? Had I been too forward and blown it?

At last, my WhatsApp alert chimed.

'Hey :)'

Gotcha. Relief.

I touched her name and maximised her profile photo like a detective, checking for more clues. Boho chic festival vibes with friends; her lean, tanned legs were accentuated by black jean hot pants and Dr Martens ankle boots. I wanted her even more. *Don't screw this one up, Charley.*

Messages pinged back and forth for a few weeks. I tried to be flirty, cheeky, kind, intelligent and even aloof at times, trying to match her laissez-faire demeanour. If she waited a whole day to reply, I'd do a day and a half. I was rolling out the playbook.

Incoming messages made me feel excited, energised and in control. My whole world was lit up with hope in the minutes, hours or days it took to craft a reply. But the moment I pressed send it was like dropping a bomb of black ink into a glass of clear water – my whole body filled with worry, paranoia and anxiety. Had I gone too far? Why wasn't she replying despite being online? Who else was she talking to? Was I being too keen? It could go on for days.

Ball in my court – in control and excited.

Ball in her court – paranoid and anxious.

This girl I'd never met was literally determining my mood, minute to minute, hour to hour, day to day.

Finally, though, it was time to meet.

Sloane Square, Colbert, the well-known French brasserie. It was a safe bet, relaxed, chic and the 'Euros' loved it.

'Don't be late!' I teased her.

It was a Thursday after work, just before 6 p.m. I'd arrived early to get settled in and find a good spot, but the place was rammed. We'd have to make do at the bar and I found myself in a familiar pose, alone, squeezed between two groups propped up against my elbow, trying to look cool and unflustered.

'At the bar... you're late! ;)'

I pulled my shoulders back and stood a fraction taller to compensate for the insecurity starting to creep in. It was ten minutes past, can't be long now.

Then I spotted her.

She floated into the foyer wearing a long quilted duvet coat and was greeted by a waiter. I pretended not to see and planted my face back down into my phone.

'Hello, you!'

I looked up animated and surprised to see her just a few feet away.

'Celine, hey!'

I took the lead and gave her a warm hug – as if we'd done it before. Some of it had rubbed off on me, glimmers of new Charley peeking through.

'So nice to see you.' Carefully trying to avoid any online dating judgement from bystanders.

'Excuse me, do you mind if we... Cheers, mate.' We wedged ourselves into a gap at the bar, the place was even more crowded and getting rowdy. It really wasn't ideal but there was no going back now. I felt a sweaty back forcefully reverse into mine, vying for territory. I braced myself and nudged him back to protect our space and Celine slipped closer into the pocket between me and the bar. I was on edge and getting agitated, but we were nice and close now. She wore hardly any makeup – her deep green eyes and square jawline didn't need it. Boyish features, independent demeanor, clearly her father's daughter.

'Let me take your jacket, there are hooks under here.'

'Ah thanks, Charley, I think I'll just keep it on for a bit, I'm a little chilly.'

'Are you sure?'

'No. I'm fine.'

It was short and sharp. We'd created this chemistry online and got comfortable chatting but now it was like starting all over again.

I tried catching the bartender's attention. Nothing. Tried again. Still nothing. I felt invisible. Was he ignoring me on purpose? Paranoia crept in – I needed to prove I could order a damn drink. I leaned over the bar: 'EXCUSE ME!'

Ten minutes later we were finally clutching our gin and tonics – thankful for the props. 'Cheers, Celine, it's nice to finally meet you properly.' She smiled back. We settled in and began the familiar dance, like two animals inspecting one another in the wild, only dressed up in the influences of modern society.

The awkwardness began to ease, and we got into a rhythm. The words didn't really matter, they were the excuse for us to observe how we were together. I went into autopilot... favourite restaurants, London hangouts, dating history, destination bucket list, keeping fit and growing up. I concentrated far more on how I came across while her senses absorbed me.

'What are you up to this weekend?'

'I'm actually going to Milan with my dad, we have a place there.'

'Sounds amazing, is that for work? What does he do?'

'Finance, he runs a private equity fund.'

She didn't allude to much else, I sensed she was used to playing things down and it made me even more intrigued. Maybe I'd meet him one day, maybe we'd go to Milan together, maybe he'd give me a job.

It was nearly time to wrap up; I took a moment to take it all in. Celine, seemingly unattainable, internationally chic, was leaning against my shoulder. Maybe this could actually work.

'Let's get the bill, shall we.' I jumped in before she could. 'Have a great time in Milan, take care.' I didn't mention any expectation of seeing her again. I knew that I needed to let her come to me now. If she didn't, I knew it was over.

—

Three days later.

Nothing.

Hadn't she thought about me at all?

Didn't she enjoy our drink?

Had she found out that I was broke?

'Hey, Charley! How was your weekend? I'm so sorry for being useless... walked into a shit storm at work on Monday. How are you? I really enjoyed our drink last week ☺'

In one chime, my whole world turned back around. Green light.

Things developed quickly. Daily messages, voice notes, memes. I'd hop on the train to London for dinners, cinema, walks. Running commentary on everything.

Out of nowhere Celine had become a major feature in my life – I thought about her 24-7 and quickly forgot about everything else. It was four weeks of pure excitement, she was filling up my cup, and my mind would run away with thoughts about how to move things along faster... to taking her away for a weekend, to making her my girlfriend officially, to getting a place in London again so I could be closer to her.

'Morning, Charley, chat a bit later?'

It was 8 a.m. and felt a little odd; she hadn't messaged me for a few days since we last saw each other. I tried not to overthink it.

Later that day I was up in town, standing in Berkley Square Park, West London, after a morning of interviews. It was midday, the sun was boiling hot, and I was pacing back and forth under the tree's shade trying to avoid breaking a sweat into my suit. The phone rang.

'Hi, Charley, I just stepped out from work as I saw you called. Listen, I'm really sorry but do you mind if we stop seeing each other, I'm just not feeling it.'

What?!

There was only one way to describe it: excruciating.

I felt sick. Dumped again. What was wrong with me? The pain of rejection throbbed around my body. I felt empty and anxious. How I felt was entirely disproportionate to what had actually happened; I'd been given the cold shoulder from a girl I met on a dating app after just over a month.

But for some reason it meant something so much more.

I'd been clutching at straws, I thought that Celine was going to solve all my problems, a shortcut. I'd have something to feel good about again, to give me confidence, even admiration – look at me, I'm back.

Instead, I got the train home to Sussex that afternoon from London Victoria back to my mother's house. Staring out the window at Battersea Power Station with that sinking, spiralling, panicky feeling.

'Hello, Charley, how did it go?' I hopped into my mother's car outside our local station, she was there like she'd always been growing up – and I could even feel this time the hopefulness in her voice that my date had gone well, maybe some good news finally for her broke, burnt out, 31-year-old son who had to move home? I was pretty good at putting on a brave face – 'Oh, it was OK' – but it was something about the melancholic moment, sitting in the car, wipers running, spitting with rain and dark – I looked down into my lap and admitted 'not very well' and with that I erupted into a flood of tears.

'I don't know what's wrong with me – why does this keep happening?' (There had been a string of rejections recently.) 'I can't take it anymore. It's not just that, it's everything, everything's going wrong. I love being here with you but I've lost my independence, I hate having to borrow money off you, I don't feel myself – whenever I go out I feel like I'm faking it. I feel empty and lost – I don't think I'm very happy.'

It was the first time I'd really admitted how I was actually feeling – I'd been putting on a brave face and I was clutching at straws. I went to bed that night staring at the ceiling, thinking to myself *how the hell did I end up here?*

―

I'd done the work in Miami – the meditation, the gratitude practice, the yoga, the digital mentors. I'd come back feeling like I'd figured it out. But it was becoming clear now that I'd only been scratching the surface. It took an emotional setback like this to show me that I still had a long way to go.

But to be fair, these tools *did* help. More than I realised at the time. They didn't fix everything, but they grounded me. They became my mental baseline; the foundation I needed to weather the storm and make sense of the chaos.

They helped me stay above water, slow the downward spirals and start seeing things a little more clearly. They gave me just enough space to observe my thoughts instead of being completely ruled by them. Enough breathing room to remember that *this too shall pass*. To remind myself how lucky I was to have my health, my family and time.

The digital mentors I was following kept me going too. They gave me a sense of direction, opened doors to new ideas and created a flywheel of growth.

And while I hadn't fully grabbed the wheel of my life yet, I'd realised for the first time that there *was* a wheel to grab.

That's the real turning point. I was awake but still mostly operating on old habits and old conditioning. I hadn't changed much yet. I was still stuck in a lot of the same patterns.

That's why it's hard to change. Even though I was learning so much you can see how it's hard to change habits of a lifetime – to stop being how you've always been. It takes energy and desire.

The Essentials didn't transform me overnight, but they did give me the tools and footing I needed to keep going. And that made all the difference.

STEP 3 – THE ESSENTIALS

You can't do calculations without knowing some basic maths.
You can't learn a language without knowing some basic grammar.
You can't transform your life without some basic ideas.

Think of these *Essentials* like that.

Just like the Body Baseline, these *Essentials* are the same but for the mind; another vital precursor to making change happen.

1. The Now

Living now, experiencing the present moment. Not up in your head daydreaming about what happened or what you have to do.

This is important because if you are seldom present, you are asleep, wrapped up in your own thoughts and not able to experience the wonders of life.

2. Meditation and Mindfulness

Mindfulness is becoming aware of what is. Mindful eating, listening, walking. Not doing something while not being aware of doing it – drifting in your mind.

Meditation is the practice of consciously moving your attention from one thing to another. Deliberately moving your attention from your to-do list to your breath or mantra.

The practice of being intentional with your thoughts and emotions is critical to controlling your mind and changing your state.

3. Consciousness Awareness (Waking Up)

The ability to switch off your mind's autopilot. It's the shift from reacting to choosing, from being controlled by thoughts and emotions to observing them with clarity and space. It's realising: *I am not my thoughts. I am not my emotions.* It's not living reactively, impulsively, or chasing validation. It's not being stuck in the programming of your upbringing, society or ego. It's not just doing what you've always done without questioning.

This is important because it enables peace, presence and the power to choose how you live. It calms your nervous system, helps you understand others and frees you from the cycle of constant dissatisfaction. It's the beginning of real transformation.

4. Gratitude

The practice of feeling grateful is the remedy to the human condition to always operate from lack, never enough and never satisfied. It is a method used to re-train your mind to feel satisfied, content and happy. It is the antidote to permanent dissatisfaction.

5. Guides

Individuals whose insight resonates with you and whose guidance you trust to elevate your life. You might relate to some of the teachers and mentors that I've experienced, but equally there are many other resources, thought leaders, philosophies and techniques out there.

My advice would be to follow your gut. It doesn't need to be complicated. Ask yourself simple questions and allow yourself to give honest answers – instinctive ones.

What makes sense to you?

Who can you relate to?

Which people are you drawn to and respect?

You'll find that some stick and others won't. But then one thing will lead to another, good people know good people.

Follow your genuine curiosity. I've shared some of my favourites.

It's a minefield out there, that's why I wrote this book for you.

STEP 4

KNOW THYSELF

'True transformation begins when we unravel the mysteries within ourselves, understanding the depths of our thoughts and emotions.'

UNKNOWN

SWITCHING GEARS

The Essentials had helped me navigate my burnout but I just couldn't get back to feeling my old self. Instead of being confident, upbeat and with direction, I was tired, empty, heavy and uninspired with life. I'd lost my mojo. I didn't really feel like doing anything or seeing anyone. If I did, I'd have to put on an act. What I'd learnt in Miami had been impactful, but I just knew there was something still missing.

Now I needed something else, something more.

In my *Five-Minute Journal* one of the prompts is to write down how you want to feel, what state you are searching for or want more of. Nearly every day for a whole year I'd write a combination of the following:

I am...

Happy relaxed and free

Strong and confident

Light and natural

Calm and in the moment

These were the feelings I was lacking.

I was searching for a better **state**, a more liberated, happy, passionate, selfless, carefree Charley. I wanted to feel like I used to when I was growing up.

I came across a quote by the French writer Anais Nin that struck a chord. 'And the day came when the risk to remain tight in a bud was more painful than the risk it took to blossom.'

And that pretty much summed it up. I felt suboptimal, and I was fed up with it. I needed to push myself and get to the source of my unhappiness. Green juices and yoga were all very well, and everything else I was still doing (my rituals, meditation, journaling, etc.) helped to relieve some of the anxiety and uncertainty, but for the most part it was all surface level. What I hadn't realised is that I was flawed, driven by obsessions and insecurities and the situation I'd got myself into was inevitable.

I'd done nothing to really change as a person. I'd fooled myself into thinking that I had it all sorted. I needed to go below the surface, dig deeper, get to the root of things and explore the workings of my mind. I needed to figure out how my psychology was screwing me up.

I'd been trimming the grass when I should have been pulling out the weeds.

I needed more answers.

Change: Inspired by intuition, fuelled by courage.

AN UNBRIDLED STALLION

It was a sizzling hot British August bank holiday – a few university mates and I were frolicking around like the children in *Swallows and Amazons* enjoying the sunshine and North Norfolk beaches. My buddy Jamie had invited a bunch of us up for the weekend.

'Charley, you're not really leaving tomorrow morning, are you – it's a bank holiday Monday. You should stay.'

We were sitting in the wooden sailing boat as we chugged back to Burnham Overy. They thought I was mad.

'You're going where?'

'It's a seminar,' I said. 'Consciousness and Human Evolution.'

'Sounds pretty "mumbo jumbo" to me, mate.'

'Yeah, something like that,' I laughed.

The next morning – 8 a.m. I'm at the Millennium Hotel in Gloucester

Road where fans, giddy with excitement, are streaming through the door. I could sense marathons of struggle, optimism in there somewhere, buried beneath years of false hope and disappointment. Tickets had sold like hot cakes – I only got mine from a lucky last-minute resale on Facebook. We were all here to see Dr Joe Dispenza, the American bestselling author, scientist and all-round transformation guru. His work operates at the intersection of neuroscience, quantum physics and spirituality – but most fundamentally he believes that our mind has the power to heal our body.

According to Dispenza, he had a serious cycling accident that left him with six broken vertebrae, and he was told by four of the best surgeons in California that he would need a complicated operation to insert metal rods into his spine – but he was determined to find another way.

After extensive studying into the relationship between the mind and body, he started to practise visualisation and meditation techniques that he believed could help him heal. After just nine and a half weeks, he was back on his feet, and shortly after that, back training again. He regained full mobility without the need for surgery.

It was this first-hand experience that encouraged him to dedicate his life to helping others use their thoughts and emotions to heal their body.

So, what the hell was I doing here?

I didn't have a chronic physical ailment. But when he explained that his work didn't just apply to physical problems but also helped people change the way they feel, it really piqued my interest. He spoke about how we can use our mind to create new and positive emotions.

It resonated with me in my search for answers.

Why not give it a go?

—

The conference room was dark. Production, lighting and camera teams were making their final checks. Seats were filling up. There was a buzz of anticipation. I could see rows of middle-aged women with their notepads at the ready, eager to meet their icon. I sat down next to a grey-haired woman who turned and gave me a friendly smile – we were about eight rows back from the stage and close enough to a side door where Joe was getting mic'd up.

'Hello, I'm Charley.'

She reminded me of one of my old schoolteachers, draped in colourful loose-fitting clothes, bangles galore, clutching a brace of freshly sharpened black and yellow HB pencils.

'Miriam.' She smiled warmly.

'Been to see him before?' I asked.

'No, just YouTube. Oh, but I've read his book too – *Becoming Super Supernatural*, it was life-changing for me. Joe's my rock star.'

She couldn't help but blush.

'Well, let's hope it's all worth it!'

I thought about the crew back in Norfolk. Was I crazy sitting here in this hotel basement, about to listen to some 'mumbo jumbo' about consciousness when I could be drinking Pimm's with my best mates?

I took a photo of the big screen and WhatsApped it to the group: Welcome to Consciousness & Human Evolution

The stars and galaxy vibe made it look even more out there.

'Made it!' I wrote.

I wanted them to know that I hadn't been bullshitting. It felt good to be doing something constructive, to have chosen to be here, in the moment, out of my comfort zone, on my own journey and uninfluenced by the people around me. I'd been brought up to be, think and behave a certain way – here I was taking back a sense of agency, opening my mind rather than simply reaching for anyone offering me a ready solution. And this was the first time I'd felt like that.

It was time for Dispenza's keynote. The energy dialled up as he confidently strutted onto the stage. Fifties, grey with boyish good looks – a performer with a gift for being able to communicate science, philosophy and spirituality. He'd been finessing his craft for decades and now the world had caught up. He looked the part too: a well-fitted black tee, pressed jeans and polished black shoes. He couldn't help his charming smile. It wasn't his style to play up to the celebrity status, but he had the X factor; it oozed out of him.

He opened with a simple line: *'Consciousness put simply is awareness, and awareness is paying attention and noticing.'* I loved the clarity of his language.

Dispenza was getting into his rhythm... serenading us with his note-perfect delivery. He asked us to turn to the person next to us, look each other in the eye and introduce ourselves as 'supernatural geniuses'.

He got the chuckles he was hoping for, and it wasn't long before we were all dancing to his tune, even finishing his sentences...

'Nerve cells that fire together...'

'WIRE TOGETHER!'

He reminded us that we are not hardwired to be a certain way for the rest of our lives – *'You are marvels of adaptability and change... would you agree?'* he said.

'Science is the contemporary language of mysticism.'

'It is science that demystifies the mystical.'

Miriam and I were sold.

He went on to explain how 90 per cent of our thoughts are the same thoughts as the day before – that our brain is a record of the past, that it's a memory bank. He explained how people wake up in the morning and they're an artefact of everything they've learnt and experienced to this moment. And every single one of those memories has an emotion associated with it.

He described how thoughts are the language of the brain, and feelings are the language of the body.

He went on to say something like the moment you feel unhappy – the moment you feel unworthy, the moment you feel discouraged – now your body is in the past.

And then he explained that if you believe that your thoughts have something to do with your destiny, then your tomorrow is just going to be more of your yesterday.

'Yes, or no? Turn to the person next to you and explain that...'

Another wave of approving laughs echoed across the room. It was like a gymnast effortlessly pulling off the Yurchenko Double Pike, and then saying... *now you try!*

He went on – elegantly describing how then once the emotion is stored in the body, then the body becomes the mind of that emotion. He explained how we become predictable, our bodies on autopilot, dragging us into a future based entirely on our past. We lose our free will to the program.

'Bloody hell, Miriam, this guy is good, isn't he?'

She was scribbling ferociously – bangles galore clinking together, and without stopping she peered up at me momentarily, smiled and gestured towards Dispenza on the stage as if to say – keep listening, there's more...

He went on to speak about how our personalities can just be a manifestation of our habits. If we keep thinking the same way, making the same choices, following the same patterns, eventually we'll end up doing the same things on automatic. It all starts being part of an unconscious process. But is that who we really are?

That's when it really began to sink in.

The power of our subconscious.

I'd been on autopilot ever since I could remember.

There was I assuming that I'd been thinking for myself, but in fact, I'd just been reacting to all those same impulses and emotions lingering in my subconscious.

The urge to post another vain picture on Instagram. Needing to hook up with another model. In a hurry to be the big shot – cutting corners. Desperately trying to impress people. Ego, insecurity, admiration, perfectionism, fear. I had never really been in control. I was on autopilot, trying to please my teachers, my father, my vanity.

Miriam tilted her head again towards me – I could feel her breath.

'Isn't it incredible... we're so unaware of it, the subconscious... while it's the source of our sadness, joy, anger, love, desire, fear, jealousy and so much more...

'Just think about all those fancy wellness fanatics trying to "make change"' – rolling her eyes sarcastically with the trademark air quotes gesture – 'most of them don't have a scoobie about this stuff, honey, they're just narcissists with Green Goddess juices and a yoga mat.'

I laughed out loud – Miriam cracking me up, where did that come from?

But she was right, and it didn't take long for me to clock it was the perfect description of *moi*.

I jotted down on the page:
Subconscious Awareness → *Self-Awareness* → *Choice to Change.*

Little did I know, the biggest revelation was just moments away.

He explained that if how we think, feel and act forms our personality – then surely our personality creates our reality. So then if we want to create a new reality – a new life, we'd have to change our personality! It made sense.

He went on to say something like – then you would have to start thinking about what you have been thinking about unconsciously and change it – you'd have to become conscious of your unconscious habits and behaviours and modify those. *'Yes or no?'*

YES! This is exactly what I'd been hunting for. How to *actually* change, go below decks. Not just being the narcissists with a Green Goddess juice and a yoga mat, as Miriam would put it. Dispenza kept going. He was poetic, logical and captivating. We were at the end of the rainbow, the sharp end, at the cusp of more answers.

He explained how you have to look at those emotions that we hold so dear and how we have to decide if these emotions belong to our future.

I thought about some of my urges, impulses and emotional habits that I'd become so used to. Old and new.

Needing to be the centre of attention.

Needing to prove.

Needing to be perfect.

Worrying what everyone thinks.

Being envious of other people.

I thought about how hard it would be to step away from these emotional habits etched in my psyche. I realised that I was getting close to the precise intersection of where real change happens, consciously thinking about the subconscious and pondering how one might intervene.

'This is the game – now you're on the field...'

'The body bucks and kicks like an unbridled stallion...'

His writing was barely legible as he excitedly jotted illustrations for us on the old-school paper flip chart... it felt like he was building up to his crescendo.

He told us how people who have an uncompromising will, who sit there returning the body back to the present moment, are taming that resistance. That's the real battle. And sooner or later, when our will is greater than the program, the body realises it's no longer the mind and it surrenders into the present moment. There's a liberation of energy – you free yourself from the chains of those emotions that keep you in the familiar past and the predictable future. And everybody who does that says the same thing: it was worth it.

He drove the point home: the breakthrough doesn't come from outside. It comes from mastering yourself. And when the body finally lets go and relaxes into the present, joy follows and torment ends.

'How many people understand me?' he grinned.

'Bloody hell.'

I turned to Miriam and blew out my cheeks in awe.

Light bulbs were switching on in my head left, right and centre.

It all started to make proper sense. I could see for the first time how powerful my subconscious was; my conscious mind was the smaller, weaker part.

Dispenza's barely legible illustrations (something like these) summed it up nicely:

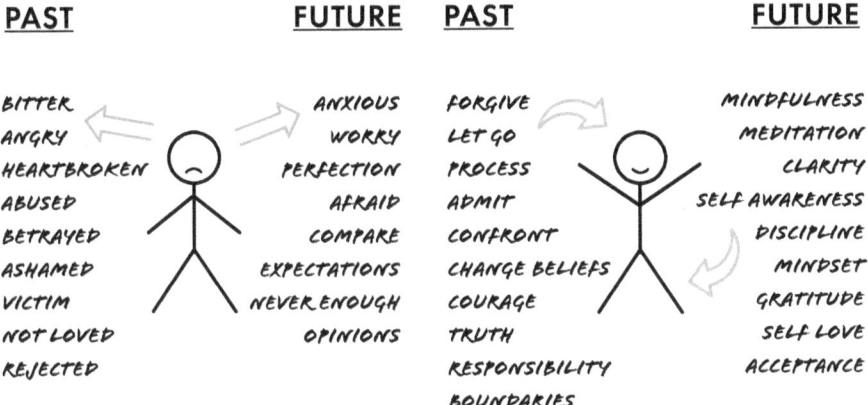

I began to see how much work I had ahead of me; to understand who I was and find my mojo again. I needed to ask some hard questions and take an honest look at myself. But instead of feeling overwhelmed, I felt uplifted. I wasn't scraping around in the dark anymore – I could now see the path forward.

Break time

I perched on the end of a concrete buttress outside Gloucester Road Tube Station, ready to sink into my ham and cheese baguette. My shoulders dropped as I bathed in the heat of the summer sun – I took a moment to observe the passers-by and felt this reassuring sense of relief. It was like I'd just finished the end of term exams. My quest to get back to how I was before – confident, happy and with direction, was slowly beginning to take shape. Podcasts, books, speakers, workshops. The brash American world of self-help was beginning to get through to me – a stiff Brit who thought he had all the answers; that there was only one way to live.

'Hey, man, do you mind if I...'

A young Indian guy about my age gestured at the spot next to me.

'Sure.' I shimmied my things across.

'How you finding it?' He'd seen my wristband.

'Mate, it's pretty damn powerful, right?!'

We compared notes. It was cool to see how someone else similar to me was also so energised by Dispenza. It made me realise that I wasn't alone on this solo journey; there were thousands of people out there looking for answers too.

'Fancy some of these blueberries?'

He held out a fresh punnet of ripe, deep purple berries.

I couldn't resist.

The blueberries triggered the flashback. All of a sudden I'm 14 years old, sitting down for Sunday lunch in the oak-panelled dining room at home.

Sitting next to me was Dr Jan de Winter, after thirty years as a radiologist at the Royal Sussex Hospital, he was now the leading cancer prevention specialist and had set up a charity which my mother was chairman of.

'Dr de Winter?'

'Yes, Charley?' he replied in his gentle tone.

'If you could just choose one thing to eat to keep you healthy what would it be?'

He smiled.

'That's a very easy question to answer, Charley.'

He took a moment to wipe a spot of gravy from the side of his mouth with the white linen napkin. He was a gentle, good-looking man with olive Austrian skin.

'Blueberries, dear boy... They're packed with antioxidants and other essential elements. This is one of the healthiest things you can eat.'

I took note. *Hmm, blueberries.*

Flicking back into the present moment outside Gloucester Road tube in the sun with my Indian friend, I could taste the sweet ripe berries pop in my mouth.

That was random, I thought.

'So where are you from?' he asked.

I gave him a glazed look as my mind was still drifting in the past. There was something else, something connected to this moment. It was like there was a word on the tip of my tongue and it was about to come to me. Something relevant.

BANG. Then it hit me.

'Man, this is so random... So, you know you offered me these blueberries, right? Well, I had this memory.' (I explained about the lunch) 'But, man, it's the book, Jan de Winter's book, which he gave me when I was 14 years old standing on the porch of our house saying goodbye. I never used to read any books, but this one was different. It was pocket size, packed with these memorable sketched illustrations... Easy to flick through... You know, lots of big text, lists and bullet points. *How to Die Young at Ninety – A Blueprint for High Quality Living*, it was called.

'It was all about diet and exercise. Smoking, drinking etc... you know. But get this. There was one chapter heading – one illustration – that was different to the others, one page that I remember like it was yesterday: *Emotional Stress*, it was titled. All about how negative emotions like fear, anxiety, anger and jealousy can be just as harmful to our health as all the obvious stuff.'

> *Stress has a debilitating effect on the body's immune system; though it is not the actual cause of the illness, it may be the determinant factor which swings the balance in a borderline condition. This is why certain illnesses cannot be explained in purely physical terms and why other factors such as anxiety, insecurity, emotional tension and stress play such an important part in their causation. Anxious people take much more out of themselves and thus become vulnerable to ill health.*

'It's crazy how similar it is to what Dispenza was saying this morning. It's like the two doctors' narratives are intertwined like spiralling DNA. Both of them hitting home just how much our emotions can impact our health.'

'That's very cool. What did you say the name of the book was again?'

He plugged the letters into his Samsung.

'It's true though, right, Charley? It is Charley, right?'

I nodded hurriedly and urged him to keep going. The enthusiasm was compounding between us.

'Emotional stress is a silent killer... We become workaholics, or even someone can do something to us years ago, they've disappeared but we hold on to that feeling, whatever happened, we repeat the feeling over and over in our body – it haunts us and plays havoc.'

I was nodding agreeingly, trying to hide my drifting attention as I realised he was describing me: the workaholic, getting burnt out, still stewing over how my success compared to peers of mine.

I remember getting home that night, digging out the book, reading this page of questions and despite all the work I'd already done, feeling that the bottom section still resonated the most.

HOW TO DIE YOUNG AT NINETY

Questions on Emotional Stress
(Any answer in the affirmative is favourable)
Are you calm and confident
Do you sleep well
Do you find time to contemplate
Do you meditate
Have you a desire to help others
Do you have someone to love
Do you have someone you can lean on
Are you glad to be alive
Are you able to express your emotions
Does your work satisfy you

(Any answer in the affirmative is unfavourable)
Are you nervous and insecure
Do you worry about things
Are you particularly afraid of cancer
Are you easily angry
Are you inclined to bottle up your feelings
Do you tend to be jealous
Do you feel lonely
Do you feel fed up
Do you easily harbour a grudge
Are you often depressed

The big question quickly became, *how was I going to get rid of it? How was I going to change my emotional state?*

I kept searching.

BASIC INSTINCTS

'Charley, when are you actually going to stop reading all these books? Haven't you read enough? You must be spending a fortune on all this mumbo jumbo.'

Sitting at the kitchen table, I tore open my latest Amazon delivery. *The Chimp Paradox*, by Professor Steve Peters, spilled out of the package, and I saw my mother roll her eyes – she was more into Jilly Cooper and Jeffrey Archer. I flicked through the book with curiosity as my mother and sister began one of their familiar mealtime routines.

'NINA! NO, COME ON, I'M SORRY THIS IS RIDICULOUS. HOW MANY TIMES HAVE I TOLD YOU?'

My mother's face was wrought with disbelief as Nina piled a fourth scoop of vanilla ice cream into her bowl while simultaneously drenching it in chocolate sauce. Her fair, innocent complexion had been preserved throughout her thirty years. Her skin, delicate, unaffected by make-up, alcohol, or smoking. Her cheeks were flushed from her signature hot night-time bath and she was wrapped in her favourite pink Minnie Mouse dressing gown. She was like a child in an adult's body.

'Nina, you can't possibly eat all that! What did the doctor say? No wonder you get these tummy aches. How are you ever going to get fit and healthy!?' (The polite way of putting it.)

My mother stretched over to take the bowl away from her.

'NO!' she screamed, slammed the table and snatched it back in a fit. 'YOU CAN'T TAKE IT AWAY, MIMI. YOU CAN'T TAKE IT AWAY. I WANT IT. YOU CAN'T MAKE ME. IT'S MY DECISION.'

'Nina, don't you dare speak to me like that. You can leave the room if you're going to yell at me like that.'

So began another forty-five-minute showdown at the dinner table. Nina digging her heels in, shouting and screaming at my mother. My mother patiently and rationally trying to explain the logic behind manners and self-control to her 30-year-old autistic daughter.

'I'm sorry, I won't do it again. I didn't mean it. Please forgive me.'

It would end with an apologetic hug, craving my mother's unconditional love once again. We all knew it would just be a matter of time until the next episode.

Nina struggles with logic and rationalising situations. She finds it hard to grasp why consequences matter.

I had been reading Freud and learning about the *id* (the primitive, selfish, instinctive part of our brain) and the *superego* (our moral conscience), and I couldn't help thinking about how Nina's *id* was clearly more dominant than her *superego*. It really highlighted for me how real this constant battle is between our primitive survival instincts and our more developed rational mind.

I went up to bed early that evening with my new book, *The Chimp Paradox*.

By now I'd read hundreds of self-development books, but this one slotted straight into my top ten, and here's why.

My three key takeaways are:

1. There are effectively two beings in our head. The primitive, emotional Chimp, and the rational Human.
2. We're separate from our Chimp. It's me the Human vs the Chimp. I want one thing and my Chimp wants another.
3. The Chimp is five times more powerful than the Human. We shouldn't try and control it; willpower only goes so far. We need to learn to work with it – *Chimp Management*.

And here's my favourite quote from the book:

It's your Chimp, an emotional machine, that is overpowering your Human mind. It is not you doing these things, it is your Chimp that is hijacking you. Having a Chimp is like owning a dog. You are not responsible for the nature of the dog but you are responsible for managing it and keeping it well behaved. This is a very important point, and you should stop and think about this because it is crucial to your happiness and success in life.

It made perfect sense to me – *Chimp Management*.

The Chimp loves all the quick fixes and instant gratification: fast food, sugar, booze, porn, caffeine, sleeping in, playing it safe and spending cash. It loves to judge, compare, complain, and collect likes on Insta. It's a pleasure seeker, a dopamine addict.

But I on the other hand want the opposite. I want to be healthy, exercise, have no regrets, feel content, at peace, take risks and be successful... short-term pain for long-term gain.

Now I could see why the age-old principles of *self-discipline, self-control, willpower, routine, and one's environment* were so vital to dial down the Chimp and dial up the Human.

No discipline → No Chimp management → No long-term gain

But what about *actually* managing those emotional chimp-like tendencies that are making me feel permanently dissatisfied?

My neurotic Chimp, forever stressed, worrying about what might be around the corner, nothing ever being enough, needing to matter, needing to be loved, afraid of what people might think.

I'd heard all the proper mumbo jumbo jargon before... gratitude, sure... but self-love, acceptance, compassion etc. – it wasn't really my cup of tea.

As I lay there though, in the same bedroom I slept in growing up with the pony club rosettes scattered along the school photograph frames, toy soldiers in formation along the mantlepiece, Lion, Owley and Doggie huddled on the armchair, I read on. And quickly the penny dropped. It clicked. I could see for the first time why the juice was worth the squeeze, why anyone would actually want to practise these mumbo jumbo methods.

- *Gratitude*. That's the antidote to the never enough, always wanting more.
- *Being present*. That's the antidote to worry, stress and anxiety.
- *Forgiveness*. That's the antidote to anger, resentment and bitterness.

- *Self-love.* That's the antidote to insecurity and needing to matter.
- *Humility.* That's the antidote to grandiosity and ego.
- *Positive thought.* That's the antidote to magnified negativity.

I was sold. I could see the practical utility.

Professor Steve Peters likens this *Chimp Management* to sweeping leaves.

Ignore the leaves too long and they pile up, fester, decompose and they're hard to shift. A little bit of sweeping each day keeps things tidy and manageable. I realised that it's a practice one has to develop.

A little sweeping each day. I thought that analogy was pretty neat.

It gave me a renewed conviction to keep going with my morning routine and meditation practice. I needed to maintain my *Chimp Management* to avoid the creep of permanent dissatisfaction.

Instead of chasing the end of the rainbow, I was training my mind to be happy with what I had. As coach John Candy said in the movie *Cool Runnings*, 'A gold medal is a wonderful thing, but if you're not happy without it, you'll never be happy with it.'

I certainly wasn't home and dry yet, but I had begun to notice changes.

I could see now how I'd been using Instagram for nothing more than an admiration accessory. Every slick, carefully choreographed picture was really just designed to momentarily catch a bunch more likes, like a tonic to soothe my insecurities. There was I thinking Carlos Ley in his D&G trunks on the beach in Mykonos would notch up a few more brownie points but really it was me saying... *Hey everyone, I feel shit about myself deep down so can you sling me some likes so I can feel better?*

The thought of posting another selfie made me cringe.

I noticed how sticking to my morning ritual, going to the gym and eating the right things helped me feel calmer, more grounded and able to make better decisions.

And when my Chimp popped up, I knew that's where those thoughts were coming from.

Another packet of crisps.

Bugger the gym, I'll go tomorrow.

Damn, he looks impressive.

Urgh. I wish I wasn't broke living at home.

That bastard – I'm going to show him.

Why isn't she replying to my text?

When the 'leaves' were scattering on the floor I was armed with the tools to dial down the Chimp and dial up the Human. I was developing this awareness, perspective, understanding of how my mind was working and that gave me a real sense that I had better control over myself – my own mind.

As I closed my eyes, I thought about Nina again and how she would never get to experience a lot of the things I probably took for granted – romantic relationships, having a family, going on holiday with mates, getting a driving licence. I could be impatient and tough with her at times, but right now I melted into a deep sadness and guilt. Life wasn't fair for Nina. My mother once said she wished Nina was born with one leg rather than her mental disability, so at least she could have her fully functioning mind and lead a more normal life, and I agreed.

I took a moment to acknowledge how lucky I was.

EGO

Freya Ridings' beautifully soothing voice gently roused me from a deep sleep the next morning.

I lay and listened to another verse before swivelling out of bed and intentionally placing the souls of my feet on the blood-red carpet. I used the contact between my bare skin and the warm fabric to reset my mind into the present moment. It was a ritual, a primer – step one that I'd picked up from *How to Live a Good Life* by Jonathan Fields.

The song, 'Lost Without You', was still gliding out of my iPhone strategically positioned on the windowsill away from my bed. I shuffled over to stop the alarm; it was still pitch-black outside.

04:59 a.m.

Discipline = Freedom. The alarm was labelled.

The little personal touches helped me embrace the early mornings as something I wanted to do, something that I was curating, rather than some godforsaken punishment. It was about changing my relationship to parts of my life, reframing whether they are painful or pleasurable, and contemplating the meaning I gave things.

I began my morning routine:

- Warm shower
- Stretch and podcast/audiobook
- Meditate...

Since my Chopra Center course with Alex in Miami, almost nine months ago now, I'd been pretty good at sticking to the practice – I'd average about five days a week, sitting for five to fifteen minutes just to maintain the habit. Some days my mind would be jumping around all over the place, and it would be virtually impossible not to wander off on a daydream or constantly think about how much time was left on the clock. But other times I'd be calmer and found it easier to sink into a deeper state, holding my attention on my mantra, bathing in the vibration... 'om am namaha'.

But I was getting results too. I was getting better at observing my thoughts and intentionally placing my attention where *I* chose to, and there would be these little moments during the day when I could put this new skill to use.

Catching myself about to put someone down. Then choosing not to.

Wanting to interrupt and talk about myself. Then keeping quiet.

A negative thought. Then observing it and trying to change my perspective.

Learning about meditation in the *Essentials* step gave me the concept and that was great. But it wasn't until I actually *practised* it regularly that I realised how powerful it really is.

Because when you boil it down, meditation is the act of moving your attention from here to there, from this thought to that one.

That's it.

It's training your mind to be *deliberate* about where you place your focus. And that's everything. Because your focus drives your emotions, your behaviours and ultimately your results.

Meditation, I realised, is **personal mind control**.

If you can practise choosing one thought, one feeling, or one response *over another* – that's the crux of change.

And I was definitely starting to feel like I had more control over my impulses.

Why the hell had no one ever told me this before?!

I sat in the armchair in the corner of my bedroom with my eyes closed, hands resting on my thighs, thumbs and forefingers touching, and used my breath to relax into my body. Not even the birds had begun chirping yet – it was deathly dark and silent.

Midway through my meditation I moved my attention to gratitude.

I reminded myself how healthy and fit I was, how lucky I was to be so loved by my family and close friends, how lucky I was to have what was really a very privileged life. But I didn't just think it, I felt the gratitude in my body, in my gut, I got emotional. I did this day after day after day and slowly but surely my angst around not being where I wanted to be began to melt away into a new perspective of patience and appreciation. It wasn't so bad after all.

I was retraining my mind to be happy with what I had.

I moved on to deal with the resentment and anger I carried towards things that had gone wrong for me in the past. It was weighing me down, sapping my subconscious energy, as Dispenza would put it. I didn't want to carry it around with me anymore. Placing my left hand on my heart I tried to sink even deeper into my body with each breath and then attempted to separate myself from those negative emotions. I tried to witness them, be the watcher, detach myself from the feelings, and then I started to conjure new deliberate sensations of compassion and forgiveness. It wasn't easy, but I knew it was the only way to rid myself of the negative angst.

My mind started to wander.

Flash back to a few years before. I'm sitting next to my friend Anna on our EasyJet flight back from a holiday with friends in Croatia. I'm smelling the sweet lashings of Nivea aftersun she just caked on in the departures lounge. My Hublot watch and gold chain are contrasting nicely against my sun-kissed skin too.

'Charley, why can't you just be *yourself* and stop trying to be so cool.'

We're reminiscing about the trip.

It struck a nerve.

I'm defensive.

Dismissive.

Pissed off.

'You don't understand, Anna, I've worked hard for all this success.' I snapped back. Attempting to justify my self-importance.

She winced, sipped on the dregs in her plastic cup and peered out the window, as if to say... *get me away from this arrogant guy.*

But why did that comment make me so angry?

Because in hindsight, she was right of course. I was trying so hard to be my alter ego Carlos Ley, the big time Latin American commodities trader with a lust for fast living and fast women.

Anna missed the Charley she used to know. But at the time I had no idea, and there was no way I was going to agree with her.

This was classic Chimp behaviour. My ego was doing everything possible to cling on to the identity I'd created. The money maker, the womaniser, the very things that defined me – the things I thought made me matter.

So, when anyone like Anna came along and criticised or challenged my personality; what I stood for, what gave me confidence and swagger, she was attacking and threatening the very thing my Chimp needed to stay alive – my ego. And so, my Chimp literally went APE and fought back. It snapped, belittled and disregarded any criticism, desperately trying to defend what I stood for.

Anna had rattled my cage.

The popular American author Ryan Holiday talks about how desperately our ego loves to cling on to our identity in his book, *The Ego Is the Enemy*. He says, how psychologists often say, that threatened egotism is one of the most dangerous forces on earth. 'The gang member whose "honour" is impugned. The narcissist who is rejected. The bully who is made to feel shame. The imposter who is exposed. The plagiarist or the embellisher whose story stops adding up.'

It was so true.

And then it hit me. There I was thinking I was being clever and confident, but actually all my behaviour was just based on me being afraid deep inside. The whole thing is counterintuitive; we think ego gives us confidence and self-esteem but actually it's founded on fear. Being afraid of not mattering, and not being loved.

Bloody hell.

That's why it is so damn hard to take a real look at ourselves.

That's why it is so damn hard to make big changes in our lives.

The ego fights, kicks and screams to protect the status quo.

My ego had been controlling my life and holding me back big time.

It all seemed so obvious and simple now.

The bigger the ego, the bigger the dreams, the bigger the expectations, the bigger the lengths we go to, the bigger the stress and the bigger the fall.

And how true was that.

I'd gone from buying expensive watches to impress the Miami swimsuit models, to borrowing a tenner from my mother to fill up the car.

What a mug.

I began to notice egotistical behaviour play out around me. Friends, colleagues, family, acquaintances, all oblivious to how such a dominant force inside of them is controlling their lives. Not being able to admit mistakes, not asking for help, not accepting criticism and not wanting to have honest conversations.

Only the more reason to keep going.

Keep documenting my journey.

Keep writing.

I heard someone once say, 'The more you know the less you say.' I had begun to understand why.

DING

The *Insight Timer* app chimed the end of my fifteen-minute meditation and brought my wandering mind back to full consciousness. I brought my hands together into the prayer symbol and raised them to my forehead.

'Namaste.'

EGO: 'Like a monkey with epilepsy on a hot tin roof being stung by bees.'

SPIRITUALITY,
BY ROGER S. GOTTLIEB

PRIDE

'Morning!' (Sunday.)

My mother was scrubbing the radishes by the sink listening to Radio 4 as I came down the back stairs into the kitchen.

'There's an article about James in the *Telegraph* today, I left it out on the table for you.'

I sat down, pulled the *Telegraph* magazine towards me, and immediately clocked the familiar photograph of the handsome 21-year-old, arm wrapped around his glamorous mother, Clare Milford Haven, and his whole life ahead of him.

James Wentworth-Stanley was one of the coolest, best-looking and genuinely kind people I knew when I was in my twenties. When he was at Newcastle Uni, he had a minor operation to correct a varicocele on one of his testicles, but soon after became paranoid that the surgery had left him impotent.

It got to him, he started to feel deeply depressed, and even ended up in A and E telling the staff he felt anxious and suicidal. He had spoken to his mother and his family a few times on the phone, but never admitted to them exactly how bad he felt.

Only ten days after the operation, James tragically took his own life.

Although James wasn't a close friend, it's by far the biggest tragedy that I have known in my lifetime. His mother Clare is sure that pride played a big part in holding James back from asking her for help or admitting how bad he really felt. Clare has since founded James's Place – a charity set up in James's memory offering men in suicidal crisis free one-to-one therapy with centres in Liverpool, London and Newcastle. The article was celebrating the charity's first centre in Liverpool.

Sipping on my cup of PG Tips, it struck me how similar pride can be to ego and how destructive the seemingly positive word can be. It's often threatened ego dressed up as pride. I definitely didn't tell my family a whole load of stuff I was feeling – I was afraid of what they might think, I was too proud also.

- I was too proud to ask my mother or brother for advice.
- I was too proud to admit how I was really feeling.
- I was too proud to contemplate speaking to a psychologist.

I'd finished my charred croissant caked in butter and lime marmalade – about to head back upstairs.

'Would you like to come with me to Hassocks as my plus-one this evening? Sheila's having a watercolour exhibition at her house – it's a fundraiser for Help for Heroes.'

The thought made me wince inside – a struggle at the best of times, and another reminder of my circumstances.

What's the point? my mind would mutter.

'Er, I think I'm just going to stay here if that's OK.'

I was slumped over the table with my head in my hands. Maybe I did want her to ask if I was OK.

'Not to worry. Forecast isn't looking too good, the poor crops, we desperately need some dry weather...

'Nina's got a dentist appointment at twelve – would you mind taking her? Johnny needs me down the farm.'

I shovelled the crumbs around my plate like a grumpy teenager and didn't respond. It was like I was in a hefty dark cloud, infected with a black ink, numbing any spark of positivity.

Surely she must see that something's not right?

Was it because she really couldn't tell? Or was she too busy? Or maybe because she was too afraid to ask... afraid to hear what I might say...

That I feel depressed.

'Come on, Roxy, come on, Blue... outside.' She beckoned the whippets and grabbed her car keys.

'Is everything OK, Charley? You're very quiet.'

And all of a sudden there it was. But instead of soothing me, the words stunned me. Panic ripped through me.

'Huh? What?'

Like I'd been caught doing something I shouldn't.

'Er... Yes, I'm fine... just a bit tired.'

'What about Nina?' she asked.

'Oh, yes... er twelve o'clock, sure.'

And just like that she was gone, along with my opportunity to tell her how I was *really* feeling.

I sat there pondering what had just happened.

I remembered reading about this exercise called 'The Why Ladder' in Dean Graziosi's bestselling book *Millionaire Success Habits* (it's way less cheesy than it sounds). In trying to really get to the bottom of something you keep asking yourself *why* until you get to the crux of it. Just like this...

Why was I so afraid to tell her?

I guess I was afraid of what she might think. Worried about not being how she expected me to be and seeing that strained look of concern on her face.

Yes, but why was I so afraid and worried of what she might think?

I suppose because it's important to me what my mother thinks, and I don't want to let her down?

Yes, but why don't I want to let her down?

Uhm... I guess because her reaction, her judgement, would make me feel exposed and might confirm to me what I fear the most... that I'm not good enough.

Crikey.

I found it easier to speak to strangers about how I felt. There was less pressure, less judgement and less expectation to be a certain way, a certain type of boy, man, son. It was easier to avoid judgement from family and friends, prickling my insecurities. No wonder I resisted telling them how I really felt: lost, rudderless, wondering what to do.

So much of life had been about living up to the high standards of my parents and their world. To be admired. To make them proud. To fit within their framework of what a 'good life' looked like.

My mother, principled, noble, thoughtful and selfless, instilled into me the importance of being a good boy, representing the family, doing things properly and so on. (And I'm glad she did.)

My father's angle was different, but the result was similar. For him, I think it was important I looked good, so he looked good.

Either way, the combo meant one thing: looking good mattered. A lot. Appearances were a priority.

Gosh, wasn't Charley on good form.

Gosh, isn't Charley looking well.

It's what I lived for.

—

'The youth of today can be a bunch of self-centred, over-sensitive snowflakes.'

A classic line from my mother as she served up the pork chops and green beans.

Dinner time. We're back at the kitchen table.

We're getting into another of our lengthy debates about my favourite topic and my mother's least favourite – *feelings*.

'Oh come on, just admit it, maybe if you opened up a bit and spoke about stuff you'd feel more alive and connected,' I try.

She doesn't budge.

'Charley, you know me, I don't do problems, I don't see why I need to speak about my problems and feelings.'

Another favourite line of hers. I went quiet – how could I try to make her see that it's not so black and white?

'Do you think it would have been self-centred and selfish of James to speak up and talk about how he was feeling?'

The words sit between us. She goes very quiet.

It's no one's fault, it's just how things have been for generations. And for a lot of us Brits it's just not 'the done thing' to talk about our emotions and problems.

The old vs the new.

King Charles vs Prince Harry.

The stiff-upper-lip vs the progressive oversharers.

Where should we draw the line?

I believe there's merit to stoicism, resolve, the stiff-upper-lip – who wants everyone flouncing around needing to feel self-expressed 24-7? But when there is something important that needs to be spoken about, to the right person, in the right situation, too much pride can be a killer, just like it was for James.

Pride can be toxic, it can be dressed up as arrogance and entitlement, even pomp and prestige. Most of us don't even know we're doing it – it's subconscious.

SHAME MAN

Later that evening.

'Did you read that book I gave you a few weeks ago?'

'Which one?'

'*Daring Greatly*, by Brené Brown... You know, that lady who did the TEDx talk that went viral.'

She looked bemused; it can't have made much of an impression.

'You know, the one all about shame and vulnerability.'

'Oh yes.' She winced. 'I gave it a go, Charley, but I just couldn't get into it; it didn't really make much sense to me. I did try – I know it's one of your favourites.'

I thought about Brené Brown's famous quote... 'Vulnerability is the last thing I want you to see in me, but the first thing I look for in you.'

I was guilty.

There I was trying to get my mother to open up, when I was too afraid to tell her how I really felt.

She looked tired, I could see that she just wanted to get on and didn't need any more of my self-righteousness pontificating. I'd already pushed her enough today.

'Thank you for supper, Mimi.'

I headed upstairs to my room with a heavy heart and pensive mood.

Was all this stuff really worth it? Was it really helping?

I was having my doubts.

Spiritual gurus, pseudo celebrity scientists and American self-help mentors.

Versus my mother. The most formidable, patient, loving, stoic, gracious and hard-working person I know.

Who should I listen to?

Maybe she does know best.

Maybe I was being brainwashed.

I was thrashing around in the dark... invisible hands pulling me in different directions.

My desire for more answers, to feel different, and the lure of the self-development world against the comfort of the status quo, not wanting to hurt or upset my family and worrying about what people might think.

I was on a solo journey.

At times I had no idea where to go next.

But it was the accumulation of warning whispers inside my head that were showing me the way...

They will judge...

They will criticise...

They're afraid of change...

Just keep going...

Trust yourself...

Be brave...

The book that shifted that Bulletproof Coffee, biohacking junkie Dave Asprey from cocky to quiet was resting patiently on my bedroom desk. The book I'd ordered months ago when I was in Los Angeles.

The book that he said changed his life.

The book I'd never opened.

The book with the black-and-white front cover that looked as appealing as a school textbook.

Healing the Shame That Binds You, by John Bradshaw.

But why had it changed his life?

The man who seemed to know virtually everything there is to know about change, development, body and mind.

What the hell was it?

I began to scan through the pages.

Bradshaw kicks off by explaining how this thing called 'shame' can take over our identity – to believe deep down that we're a flawed human being.

That's intense, I thought. *A flawed human being?*

Can't possibly relate to me. Yes, I had issues, but I didn't think things were that bad.

He talks about how it stops us embracing and expressing our 'true self', and instead one creates a cover up, a mask, or 'false self' to guard against revealing who we really are.

Our emotions become 'shame bound', he says; we're afraid to express them and we stay in hiding.

I immediately thought about a mate of mine from uni. I always suspected he was hiding something behind his flamboyant A-type bravado. (Classic deflection – spotting it in others before I could see it in myself.)

'We become the nice guy, the people pleaser, the joker, the perfectionist, arrogant, whatever we need to do to guard against exposing our true self. It's exhausting and we can get burnt out.' (*Healing the Shame That Binds You*, John Bradshaw, published by Health Communications, Inc.)

Hang on a second. I got burnt out...

I'm a nice guy, a people pleaser and a perfectionist...

'If our parents don't know how to be intimate with one another, or how to express emotions, or how to communicate properly, or how to love themselves, then it's unlikely the kids are going to be able to do any of these things either.'

I reminisced about the past thirty-odd years...

Were my parents ever really intimate together?

Did they ever really express emotion?

Hardly.

Bradshaw goes on to explain that when children are prevented or discouraged from expressing themselves and developing their own autonomy and purpose, they're left with unmet needs, 'a hole in their heart', and grow up to be adult children, never really happy deep down, needing to forever *prove* themselves.

Jesus.

I blew out my cheeks.

It felt like he was describing me... always trying to prove, achieve and be admired. But unmet needs, 'a hole in their heart' – could those apply to me too?

Bradshaw definitely had my attention. I kept going.

'Neurotic shame is the root and fuel of all compulsive/addictive behaviours.'

'I'll be OK if I drink, eat, have sex, get more money, work harder, etc.'

'Worth is measured on the outside, never on the inside.'

It was the first time I'd ever contemplated that I might be some sort of addict.

Until now I'd thought that any of that sort of stuff was reserved for alcoholics and drug addicts.

But maybe I was addicted to admiration.

And according to Bradshaw, it was because deep down I didn't feel I was good enough and felt I needed to prove myself. A human doing rather than a human being, as he put it.

There was more, he got onto relationships...

'With a false self, intimacy is impossible.'

'Love addictions.'

Shit. Busted again. I always experienced fireworks when meeting a woman I liked, feeling a churning mix of excitement and anxiety as soon as we started to text and date. I definitely felt passion, but I quickly became convinced each time that it was actually love. And that's what I was addicted to.

The resemblances got even more disturbing.

'... in my beginning relationships I always went too far and wanted too much. If I met a girl and we hit it off, I immediately began talking about her in terms of marriage – *even after one date!* Once she was in love with me, I expected her to take care of me like a mother.'

Uncanny. I'd never even realised I was doing it – but it was true. Bradshaw was describing himself, but he may as well have been describing me.

There was no hiding from it. Page after page, it was like looking in the mirror.

ANOREXIA NERVOSA ... was the next chapter heading. I'd have skipped past if it wasn't for the girl I'd just been dating. Or to put it more accurately, been dumped by after another two-week love addiction. She'd been telling me about her own anorexia, so I was intrigued with what Bradshaw had to say... 'Anorexics most often come from families that are dominated by perfectionism. Affluent families are often focused on self-image actualising. Respectability and the upper class have a very special look and image to keep up.'

It was so true, I thought to myself... some families put so much importance on appearance and looking good.

'The following patterns predominate: perfectionism, non-expression of feeling (no talk rule); a controlling, often tyrannical and rigid father; an obsessive mother, completely out of touch with her sadness and anger; a pseudointimate marriage with great pretence at looking good.'

Jesus. More similarities.

Children should be seen and not heard, my father always used to say at the dinner table.

Bradshaw connected the dots:

'The anorexic person takes control of the family with her starving and weight loss. She is a metaphor for what's wrong with the family. She is rigidly controlled, denies all feelings, and is super achieving and encrusted in a wall of pretence.'

I'd never thought about any of this before, but it made sense to me.

But what did this all really mean for me?

I wasn't an alcoholic, or anorexic or suffering from a severe addiction.

Did this stuff *really* apply to me and my family?

Surely not. Surely we weren't that bad?

I thought about it. What were the facts? What was real?

I thought about how both my brother and I were in our mid-thirties and both single.

I thought about how obsessed I'd been about needing to prove, needing to be admired.

I thought about how excruciating it was when I got dumped after just a few weeks of knowing someone. Maybe it was because deep down I didn't feel good enough... ashamed... and the rejection was just rubbing salt on the wounds. I wasn't in love with them, I just needed them to love me.

My father was all about the pomp and prestige. The right friends, the right schools, the right clubs, the right godparents, the right haircut.

My mother – immaculate always, skinny, a workaholic, always doing everything for everyone else, never ever kicking back and letting go.

Had my parents screwed me up?

Did I need to *heal the shame that was binding me?*

Or were we just another old school British family?

I suppose the big question I had to ask myself was... *Did I feel that I needed to achieve, prove and be admired to ultimately feel that I was good enough and worthy of people's love and respect?*

And if I'm honest... the answer was *Yes.*

Maybe Bradshaw was right. I'd been trying to fill a bottomless void with external gratification.

I was ashamed of what people might think of me.

I was ashamed of being with a girl that didn't meet a certain standard.

I was ashamed if I didn't look good when I saw my father.

I was ashamed about what people thought of my autistic sister.

I was ashamed of living at home with my mother.

I was ashamed of looking weak, and ashamed of failing.

I was ashamed to tell people I was feeling shit.

I was ashamed of all this and more. Because of how I felt about myself deep down. Shame was keeping the real me in hiding. Now I knew why this book had changed Dave Asprey's life. This 'shame' was screwing up his life too. Bradshaw helped him to see it... that 'aha' moment.

Now I could see it too.

Now I had to heal the shame that was binding me and go on to change the course of my life... just like the Bulletproof Coffee man, Dave Asprey, had done all those years ago.

It all made sense now. The game was on.

But how?

- *How to feel secure?*
- *How to learn to really love?*
- *How to build inner confidence?*
- *How to build back my self-worth?*
- *How to really get back to feeling good again?*

I now knew what everyone meant by 'doing the work'. I had to keep looking inward. Nothing on the outside was going to change how I felt on the inside.

The slightly less cynical Brit kept going – determined to get to the promised land.

Thank God I did.

'A lot of parents will do anything for their kids, except let them be themselves.'

BANKSY

SABINE

And there we were – sitting opposite each other in the beige consulting room just off Sloane Square. Dr Alexiou, *call me Sabine, please*, probably wasn't much older than me. She was wearing a creamy, almond-coloured silk blouse, a green tartan skirt and dark blue suede knee-high boots; they were flats, business-like, but her legs still looked long and elegant. She had a touch of Jemima Khan about her, the same soft but curious eyes looking at me through a dusty blonde fringe.

I was trying to think myself into the role of the patient but that made me feel uncomfortable. I was wondering if I would come to regret taking my friend Nicole's advice to see a therapist only a few weeks ago.

'You know the thing is, Nicole, I just don't feel like being out and about at the moment. I just feel like I'm faking it, I prefer to stay home – I suppose I feel like I've kind of lost my mojo.'

She was sipping tea opposite me on the sofa as we looked out onto Kensington Gardens. Tall, blonde and sporty, she oozed goodness, heart and confidence.

'Listen, have you thought about going to see a psychologist – my boyfriend's been seeing one for ages and he absolutely swears by it.'

I chuckled. 'No, no, it's OK – I don't need that – it's not that bad.'

Seeing a psychologist still seemed a little extreme, despite everything I had already done. I knew there was a stigma attached. Other people thought it was a sign of failure, a sign of weakness. And I convinced myself that the kind of self-help I had been exploring would cover enough of the ground, without having to see a shrink!

'Come on, trust me – something's telling me you'll really like it and get a lot out of it – you may as well give it a try.'

We had been good friends for a few years now, she could see something through my eyes that I couldn't.

'Look, you know he plays for England and loads of sportsmen have them now.'

My ears pricked up.

'Hang on. The England players are into it?'

'Yes!'

'Shit, well, in that case maybe I might give it a go,' I said with a cheeky enthusiastic smile, acknowledging my fickle U-turn.

A bit of FOMO and pro sportsmen making it OK was all it took. In that moment I felt like it was OK to ask for help.

So here I was with the French-Greek lady I'd been referred to by my GP.

The room smelt faintly of Chanel and was pleasantly spacious, bathed in sunlight flooding through the dormer windows. I'd immediately known which chair to take because it had a fresh glass of water and a box of tissues beside it.

As if I'll need those.

'How have you been?'

Her tone fell somewhere between kindness and business-like detachment. Her accent was international, European, intelligent.

I looked at her, shrugged, exhaled and smiled all at once. Why did I feel as though I'd known this stranger all my life? She had managed to make me feel comfortable immediately. I suddenly remembered the Charley who had been more open to things like this back in the US, the Charley who had listened to Jessica Encell-Coleman and Alex Montalenti.

She picked up her notepad and pen, and I began.

Commodities... trader... talented, success, money, high risk... 24-7... burnout, confidence, ashamed, insecure, failure, identity...

She interrupted with questions and pushed for clarifications. She was listening intently and that encouraged me to go into even more detail. I told her everything...

Girls, obsessions, Miami, denial.

I wanted her to know that I wasn't a novice either...

Spirituality, self-development, books, talks, meditation, wellness, routine.

And then the real reason I was here...

I'd lost my mojo.

I didn't feel like going out anymore.

I wasn't myself.

I caught her glancing at her watch. 'We've run a little over.'

It was already five minutes past the hour – it felt like I'd only just started.

'Charley, thank you for telling me all this. It sounds like you've been through a lot.'

Her sympathy was like a tonic. All of a sudden it mattered more to me than trying to avoid the stigma of needing it.

'I'm confident that I can help you; it'll take some work, but we'll do it together.'

'Thank you.'

We did some housekeeping, I confirmed that I wanted to continue with the sessions (even though I had no idea what to expect), and before I knew it, I was back on the street hailing a cab to go home.

Was Nicole right? Could this be the answer?

—

We were about halfway through the next session; we'd moved past the 'what happened' and into the present.

In a soft voice, Sabine asked, 'And have you really been happy, Charley, are you happy now?'

She said it like she really wanted to know, like she was talking to the little boy I'd once been. I wanted to say the right thing. To be a good boy. My automatic thought was to say *yes, yes I'm fine* but in the pause, as the last few years flashed before me, the struggles, the striving, the trying to prove myself, I realised – welling up, perhaps definitively for the first time – that, no, I wasn't happy.

'Not really,' I said, 'I've just been trying so hard,' before erupting into full-blown tears and reaching for a tissue.

And right there and then, it all started to dawn on me.

- *Was I alone most of the time?* Yes
- *Did I ever really care about other people?* Not a lot
- *Did I think I was better than my friends and family?* Most of the time
- *Was anything ever enough?* No
- *Was I trying to please everyone, so they'd like me?* Yes
- *If I stopped and thought about it, was I really happy?* No

What had struck me was that instead of just 'losing my mojo', in actual fact I wasn't really fine – I was fundamentally unhappy. Even when I was chasing the dream and seeming to catch it, that high was actually pretty shallow.

I'd been fooling myself.

She sat there opposite me in silence as I sniffled and composed myself.

'It's OK,' she said.

'I guess that's good, right... you're going to tell me it's good to cry?'

I managed a smile. It felt like a relief, like I was allowed to stop the pretending, to hang up my boots for a bit.

To let go.

We switched tracks and began to explore the past thirty-odd years, piecing together how and why I'd become the person I was today... like detectives.

Tell me about your mother... her parents... her childhood...

Your father... what's important to him... how long was he in the army... their relationship... the divorce...

Boarding school...? How old were you....?

We dug into my upbringing and every now and again she'd reach for her pencil to jot down a note. It was like taking an exam. I wondered what prompted her – what the eventual outcome was going to be.

'I want you to close your eyes and think back to when you were a little boy. Take yourself back to a time when you were unhappy or afraid.'

I uncrossed my legs.

'Right, now close your eyes and look for the feeling.'

And there it was, Coral Reef Water Park; the fear set in as we drove past. It signalled T-minus ten minutes until we arrived at my boarding school. Sitting in the passenger seat I turned to my mother with tears pouring down my cheeks,

'Mimi, I really don't want to go back.'

I was seven years old and about to be dropped off for another three and a half weeks. It felt like a lifetime. My father was all for it though; it was where all his mates sent their boys.

Not long after, we're walking down a school passage, lined with activity boards, the dining room seating plan, the games board – smart mothers' perfume lingered in the air, their heels echoing against the freshly polished wooden herringbone floor, fresh haircuts, loud voices and overenthusiastic teacher smiles welcoming us back.

'Charley, let's go and drop off this new blanket in your dormitory.'

We head to Dorm 49 – it was small with just four other boys and my dormitory monitor, Tiggy. I'd been getting cold at night, so we'd bought a new extra-thick blanket to go over my duvet. Mimi draped it over my bed and lovingly tucked it in around the edges, as if to do it for each night she wouldn't be there. Already I missed home; the whippets, Tan the Labrador who used to sit by my bed, my sister. It made me sad. But each night it would get a little easier, the boarding school machine of regimental routine slowly began to blur the warm memories of home life.

'Right, let's go and see Mrs Briars, then I really must go, Charley.'

Panic.

We headed back downstairs.

'Hello, Charley,' Mrs Briars said, smiling as she acknowledged my mother.

She was kind, warm and motherly. I looked up to see all the other boys scurrying around the classroom, like a holding pen of weaned lambs without their mothers. A few said hello but I wasn't ready yet. I held Mimi's hand tightly, still holding on to home. They chatted for a few minutes and then it was time. I wanted to press pause; I wanted it to all slow down.

'Can we go outside for a second, Mimi?' I wanted to be alone with her – there were too many people around.

'You'll be OK, Charley; you'll go and see all your friends and I'll see you in a few weeks at your football match.'

I squeezed her tight, smelt her familiar perfume. 'You be a good boy for me,' she said.

That nearly set me off, I felt afraid of letting her go, scared of facing everything that lay ahead of me, I didn't want her to abandon me.

'Very good. Now open your eyes.'

Sabine's voice brought me back into the room. I was surprised how vividly I could remember it all.

But what did all this have to do with me getting back on track?

She paused, leaving a mildly awkward silence, which it was my job to fill with more of my own words but this time I refrained.

It worked.

'Have you ever heard of "Boarding School Syndrome"?' she said into the silence.

I shook my head like a moody teenager – still not understanding the relevance.

'You should read Joy Schaverien's book. You'd be amazed how many men, in particular, who went to boarding school suffer from depression, intimacy issues and suppressed emotions.'

'Interesting,' I said, wanting to show I was listening and being open-minded, even if I wasn't accepting this related to me. This still sounded like something relevant to other people more than it did to me.

'Young men's early attachments to their parents are broken and it causes trauma that is often hidden. The schoolboys conform to survive in the masculine, macho environment and often develop a veneer of confidence to disguise their vulnerability. It can have all sorts of effects on them later on in life.'

Did I detect sympathy in her voice? She'd clearly met some of these men and seen first-hand how their lives were being affected.

'A bit like John Bradshaw's *Healing the Shame That Binds You?*' I said. 'Hiding your true self, ashamed of expressing real emotion, covering it all up and ending up compensating with obsessions and addictions? Freud and Maslow too… they talk about unmet needs in childhood.'

Once again flexing my knowledge, I was doing my best to shimmy away from being the subject of the discussion.

'Exactly, Charley! I see so many men with a history of failed relationships, or workaholics, alcoholics, or even those just desperate to be loved and admired because deep down they don't feel good enough.'

Once again, I wasn't ready to admit she was describing me.

I know how homesick I used to get, but I never considered how the experience might have affected me.

Trauma was a big word.

'I mean, I was so lucky, though, Sabine, my parents gave me the best upbringing anyone could have asked for. I went to some of the best schools... we had everything we wanted. You know, how could I complain really?'

She scribbled something else into her notebook. I wondered what she was writing in there.

But our time was nearly up.

'So do you live nearby?' I broached the subject of her personal life.

'Actually no, Madrid.'

'Ah wow, so you commute every day?'

'No, just a few days a week, I have a little place in Belgravia.'

She said it just like any of her smart international neighbours would have – casually, with that air of European sophistication.

I didn't want to overstep the mark though, so left it at that.

'Same time next week?'

'Sounds good!'

I gathered my things and headed out the door.

'Oh, Charley?'

I turned back to find her sitting in her chair, iPhone in hand, observing me through her chopped fringe.

'Trust the process.'

I felt a knowing smile steal across my lips and I nodded. 'I will. Thank you, Sabine.'

She smiled back, showing a little more of herself than maybe she wanted.

A LATE LUNCH

It was just after 1 p.m., I was running a little late, I wanted my father to know I'd got things going on. My shoes were all polished up and I was a tad smarter than usual but subtle enough that he wouldn't realise the extra effort. Striding along Jermyn Street in London (anxious not to be too late either), I was feeling optimistic, maybe a touch apprehensive too. Today it was going to be on my terms. I had booked the table. No more long stuffy lunches at one of his clubs. I hadn't seen him for a few months and I felt like the slate was clean again.

'Hi there, I have a reservation under Charley Law... a quieter table in the corner if possible,' I said to the Italian hostess. She doesn't even look down. 'Yes, hello, Mr Law, your father, Captain Law, is already waiting for you.' Of course he was... and I knew that affectionate endearing smile she gave me... He'd already had his wicked way, she'd already been charmed by him.

'Hi, Daddy!'

He stood up and gave me a massive hug. 'Happy birthday, my son.' He was looking at me full of admiration. 'Great spot, well done – I moved us to this table, the other was bloody noisy – next to those old battle axes over there,' he said indiscreetly.

'Now, Brush [one of my nicknames], have a look and see what you feel like, you can have the salmon, the carpaccio, the croquettes look good, the—'

'It's OK, Daddy, I can read it myself, thank you. You just focus on what you want.' I tightened up.

'Oh excuse me, could you come and take our order?' The waiter did a pivot and came over flipping his notepad open, clicking his pen.

'Yes of course, gents, what can I get you?' he said.

'Daddy, I haven't had time to read the menu,' I muttered loud enough so the waiter felt my annoyance.

'Oh, hello, it's my son's birthday – he's thirty-two.'

The guy smiled awkwardly – trying to give a shit.

'Could you tell me if the lamb is cooked fresh? I'd like it pink please.'

'I'll have to ask the kitchen, sir.'

'But surely you must know if it's cooked already?'

'I'll ask the kitchen, sir.'

'Oh, just make sure it's pink,' he snapped as I cringed – I knew how the waiter felt.

The regular circus had begun. I was starting to think *what am I doing here?* I gave the young waiter that apologetic smile as he took our orders but the damage was done and he was dismissed.

'Now I hear your mother is off to see Matthew in Singapore.'

It was a secret; my mother didn't want him to know she would be away from the family home. I felt the same angst and annoyance she would have felt by his smug intrusion. That control he always tried to exert; at dinner, on holiday, by the sports field. Who had he charmed? He smiled, knowing that he wasn't meant to know.

'Now tell me, how's that book of yours going? What's it *actually* about?'

'It's going well actually. I've finished the research and planning, and I've just started putting pen to paper. It's about what I've learned from...'

'Sounds very vague.'

I let him speak.

'I'm putting together my memoirs... Now, how's that Devon girl you were seeing, she was rather nice, you've got my eye, Brush.'

'Oh, we stopped seeing each other, it didn't really work out,' I muttered, not wanting to tell him that I got dumped.

'What a shame, did you get found out?!'

His face lit up and his thin lips tightened around a grin.

For him it was just banter with his 'playboy son', but for me the words cut deep.

'Did you get found out?'

Wasn't I good enough for her?

'Plenty more out there. I had more crumpet than you've had hot dinners!'

'Could someone top up my wine?' He leaned out from his chair as another waiter passed by.

'Of course, one second, sir,' he said, just attending to a family peacefully tucking into their main course.

I can see my father getting agitated. The service was a little slow and he's feeling the effects of two glasses of Chablis.

The waiter returns and limply picks up the bottle of white wine from the ice bucket. He wasn't to know that the Captain was waiting to pounce.

As he slowly poured the wine into his glass, my father snatched it out of the poor boy's hand.

'Oh, give it to me, you blithering idiot,' he shouted, as the young waiter looked on, shocked and embarrassed.

As I watched my father, I felt myself retreating, turning back into the little boy sitting at our dinner table at home, listening obediently to lectures about what to do and how to be while he slurped his way through another bottle of claret, interrupting my mother to the point where in the end she gave up and didn't speak. I could feel it in my nervous system, the strain in my stomach, my racing heart. I could feel exactly what the waiter was feeling – how the Captain's bellow had dealt him a body blow. I thought to myself, *stand up and walk out*, but

I didn't. I couldn't do it to him, he would be distraught. I was afraid of how he might react. A betrayal too, after everything he had given me…

A first-class education, horses, holidays, cash for school trips and university, chauffeuring me around, at my beck and call – doing whatever it took to give me supposedly the best childhood anyone could ever ask for.

So, I stayed at the table; I stayed there for him.

'Daddy, I have a meeting at two thirty,' I lied. 'Do you want coffee?'

We get the coffee and the bill, I gave him a reluctant hug, hurried out of the restaurant and took a long walk to my afternoon therapy session.

I'm sitting in the waiting room, early for my next session with Sabine, remembering how, when my parents were getting divorced, I'd inserted this passage from Kahlil Gibran's *The Prophet*, into a letter to my father.

> Your children are not your children.
> They are the sons and daughters of Life's longing for itself.
> They come through you but not from you.
> And though they are with you yet they belong not to you.
> You may give them your love but not your thoughts,
> For they have their own thoughts.
> You may house their bodies but not their souls,
> For their souls dwell in the house of tomorrow,
> Which you cannot visit, not even in your dreams.

I wonder now if he even read it.

NOT ENOUGH, NEVER ENOUGH

'So, Charley, how have you been?'

That now familiar question signalled the start of the session.

I took a breath before launching into what I'd been holding onto for the past forty-eight hours.

'Not great, Sabine, to be honest. I don't know why this keeps happening to me. You know that girl I was seeing, not Celine, someone I met afterwards. We broke up. I thought it was going really well, I thought she could be the sort of girl I could start dating properly, but after we went out the other night – and you know – it went well, I thought she had a good time, but the next day she called me up and ended it.'

'Did she give a reason?'

'I mean, kind of; she said that something didn't quite feel right to her. Honestly, Sabine, I'm not sure how much more I can take of this... It keeps happening to me, I don't know what's wrong with me, I don't know what I'm doing wrong.'

I leant forward in my chair, elbows rested on my thighs, hands clutched, and head bowed.

She could tell I was flustered. 'It's hard for me to know what you might be doing without being there. Did anything happen? Could you have put her off somehow?'

'I really don't think so.' I paused to go over it in my mind one more time. 'No, honestly, I don't think so – it's just odd, everything felt fine.'

'You're good-looking, well educated, got a lot going for you; I can imagine there must be many women in London that would like to date you, Charley.'

That would normally have helped ease my paranoia but yet another rejection was really making me doubt myself.

'Maybe I'm just trying too hard? You know, it's like I'm always anxious and afraid of it not working out.'

She sat up a little in her chair, as if we'd stumbled onto something important.

'Yes – you're operating from a place of fear, aren't you? If the relationship doesn't work out, what does that say about you?'

I looked down. I knew where this was going.

'Deep down, Charley, I think you believe you're not good enough. And every rejection confirms that fear. So you're performing, trying to be what you think they want, terrified they'll see the real you and leave.'

She paused, letting it sink in.

'But the irony is, by never showing them who you really are, you're guaranteeing they can't actually connect with you. You're rejecting yourself before they get the chance.'

Ouch.

'You know...' she continued delicately. 'Sometimes if girls can smell desperation, then that's not a good thing.'

I took a moment to absorb what she had just said. It hurt, but she was right of course, and I knew it. I just hadn't wanted to admit it to myself. I was needy and desperate.

'I'm just bored of feeling like this, Sabine – I never used to be like this.'

'You're going around looking for someone to fill up your empty cup, Charley... and that's not a good place to be.'

It made sense.

'So how do I fill up my own cup then?'

She smiled gently. 'As we are,' she replied confidently.

I waited for more. I was eager to hear the elixir to my pain.

'Just as we have been... gently, carefully, moving you away from the beliefs you're holding on to... letting go... getting perspective, delicately rebuilding your self-confidence, your self-worth... helping you to feel more secure.'

It took time, but over the weeks and months, slowly but surely the anxiety began to dissolve and behind that I could feel myself getting stronger again emotionally. I guess I was healing on the inside, becoming more secure again. I had had a crisis of confidence, but that didn't need to be permanent. The key was getting to understand myself, because you can't fix the car if you don't know how an engine works.

And that is what I was starting to do.

> 'The human is the only animal on earth that pays a thousand times for the same mistake. The rest of the animals pay once for every mistake they make. We have a powerful memory. We make a mistake, we judge ourselves, we find ourselves guilty, and we punish ourselves.'
>
> *THE FOUR AGREEMENTS*, DON RUIZ MIGUEL

'What was it like growing up at home? Did you date many girls? Close your eyes again and think back if you like.'

We danced around my formative years – I coloured in for her what it was like growing up in the Law household.

'Thank you for sharing that, Charley, it's really interesting. Your mother sounds like a remarkable lady. I'm guessing your parents weren't that intimate with each other before they got divorced?'

'No, I suppose not. I never really remember seeing them being close and loving with each other. Actually, I kind of think for my brother and I, the whole girl thing growing up was a sort of no-go area. Talking about them, inviting them home, discussing a relationship – it always felt like we were doing something wrong, or they weren't ever good enough.'

Sabine made some more notes.

It was approaching the top of the hour, and once again I didn't feel like I was getting the answers I craved. How long was this all going to take?

'OK,' she said ominously. Exhaling. As if we'd reached a milestone... 'I'm going to give you some homework to take with you this week.'

Sabine pulled out a textbook called *Reinventing Your Life* and passed me two batches of photocopies. It was like being back at school, two textbook pages copied landscape onto A4 with those untidy, skewed black and white edges from the photocopier.

'I'd like you to read both these chapters please and then complete the exercises – we'll discuss next time.'

—

I found a bench in Duke of York Square. I popped open my plastic folder and slid out the first set of photocopies:

I'M WORTHLESS: THE DEFECTIVENESS LIFETRAP

Yikes, that sounds pretty hardcore, Sabine.

THE DEFECTIVENESS QUESTIONNAIRE

For each description you had to score one to six to find out the strength of your '*Defectiveness Lifetrap*'.

I grabbed my biro.

No man or woman could love me if he/she really knew me.

Not completely fair but definitely some truth there [2]

I am inherently flawed and defective. I am unworthy of love.

Hmm, I'm not sure, maybe a bit harsh [2]

I have secrets that I do not want to share, even with the people closest to me.

Probably yes [5]

I hide the real me. The real me is unacceptable. The self I show is a false self.

Probably yes [4]

One of my greatest fears is that my faults will be exposed.

Maybe that is right – it's what I told Sabine [5]

I devalue my positive qualities.

Yup [5]

I live with a great deal of shame about myself.

Seems that way yes [4]

It had my attention. I kept reading.

THE ORIGINS OF THE DEFECTIVENESS LIFETRAP

'Someone in your family was extremely critical, demeaning, or punitive toward you. You were repeatedly criticised or punished for how you looked, how you behaved, or what you said.'

Really? Sounds pretty serious – that wasn't me, I don't think. I mean, my father was quite critical and mildly domineering, but surely this is going too far.

I made a little squiggle on the page and kept going through the list.

'You were rejected, unloved, emotionally abused, blamed for everything that went wrong in your family, always told you were worthless... and so on.'

This was way off-piste, not me at all. I had a happy childhood – safe, secure, wanting for nothing, with lots of opportunities. Where was Sabine going with all this? Still, in my eagerness to search for answers I kept going.

'Many people who have grown up being criticised and made to feel defective *compensate* by trying to be superior in some area. They set high standards and strive for success and status.'

Well, that is pretty much how I am – always striving for more success and status. Maybe there is something here?

I'd never thought about how parts of my personality could be linked to compensating for things that might have happened growing up.

I wanted to know more.

List Signs That You Might Be Coping with Defectiveness Through Escape or Counterattack (i.e. by avoiding or over-compensating).

'Are you hypercritical of other people?' *YES*

'Are you defensive about criticism?' *YES*

'Do you devalue the people you love?' *SOMETIMES*

'Do you overemphasise status and success?' *YES*

'Do you try to impress people?' *YES*

'Do you ask for reassurance incessantly?' *YES*

Shit.

And there was more...

'A narcissist is someone who lacks empathy, blames others for problems, and has a strong sense of *entitlement*. People like Elliot [Case Study Character] have developed this narcissism to fight back against their underlying feelings that no one will ever love or respect them. It is as if they are saying to the world: "I will be so demanding, act so superior, and become so special that you will never be able to ignore or criticise me again…"'

'The end result, though, is that he has status and success, but he still does not have love. <u>He is looking for love but settling for admiration</u>.'

It was a sucker punch – I was left stunned and pensive. I was like… *oh shit that really is me.* There was no denying it. I couldn't hide from the words on the page. I couldn't fire back an insult or laugh it off. I just stayed sitting there, coming to terms, and getting more and more agitated by the obese pigeons pecking crumbs at my feet. They didn't even flinch when I tried to shoo them away, they just kept turning in circles as if they were doing it on purpose.

I didn't like what I was reading. *A narcissist? Really?*

It's strange, you'd think these shocking realisations about myself would send me to a dark place – but in fact it was the other way around. I was like *oh shit, that makes sense*, now I know the symptom I can find the antidote. Getting to the source of things, not thrashing around in the dark anymore, not knowing why the same things kept happening to me. Now I could finally do something about it and turn my life around.

I wanted more. I suddenly remembered the next chapter – *what the hell was that about?*

IT'S NEVER QUITE GOOD ENOUGH, THE UNRELENTING STANDARDS LIFETRAP

I hurried through the next questionnaire:

I cannot accept second best. I have to be the best at most of what I do.

Some of the time [3]

Nothing I do is quite good enough.

Hmm some of the time [3]

I strive to keep everything in perfect order.

Yes! [5]

I must look my best at all times.

Yes! [5]

I have so much to accomplish that I have no time to relax.

Mainly yes [4]

My personal relationships suffer because I push myself so hard.

I think so [3]

My health suffers because I put myself under too much pressure.

Yes definitely [5]

I deserve strong criticism when I make a mistake.

Yup [4]

I am very competitive.

Yes [5]

Wealth and status are very important to me.

Yes [5]

Got me again.

I kept reading.

'The primary feeling is pressure. You can never relax and enjoy your life. You are always pushing, pushing, pushing, to get ahead. You fight to be the best at whatever you do, whether it is school, work, sports, hobbies dating, or sex. You have to have the best house, the best car, the best job, make the most money, and look the most handsome or beautiful. You have to be perfectly creative and perfectly organised.'

Once again it was like I was looking in the mirror. I thought back to the days travelling to South America, nothing was ever enough. As soon as I got what I wanted, my default was, *what's next?*

I'd never really contemplated that this feeling of nothing ever being enough and my perfectionism could be holding me back. I'd thought it was always what set me apart from everyone else.

I was given a card on my tenth birthday and there was a badge attached to the front with a smiley face saying, '*It's not easy being perfect*'.

I was chuffed, I thought, *this is me – I am perfect.* I wore it with pride that day, and then it stayed on my bedroom dresser and throughout my teens, twenties and early thirties. Thinking about it now, clearly it was just a frivolous birthday compliment – but I'd taken it seriously, and for the most part, one way or another, I'd felt that I had to do it justice.

From time to time, I used to look at it and genuinely think to myself *it's really not easy but I am perfect. I must keep up the work.*

The 'not good enough' and the 'never enough'.

It was a relief. Finally, I knew what I was dealing with.

I shuffled the papers back into my black plastic folder, clicked the poppers together and threw my crusts at the pigeons.

The Indian philosopher Jiddu Krishnamurti said, 'The ambitious man is the most frightened man because he is afraid to be what he is, because he says, "If I am what I am, I shall be nobody. Therefore, I must be somebody."'

I thought to myself – *how true.*

FAREWELL

My weekly sessions with Sabine had helped me understand my own mind and start to feel more emotionally sound and more like myself. I felt strong again. It was time to move on.

Session twenty-two. Five minutes to go. I knew what I had to do.

Sabine reached across for her dark green leather Smythson's diary – ready to schedule in next week. Now was my chance.

'Sabine, you know as December is around the corner, I was thinking maybe this would be a good time to pause things for a bit. I'm feeling good, in a much better place and...'

'Of course! I think it's a great idea, Charley. You've done so well; I'm really pleased with your progress. I'm not sure you need me anymore.'

And that was that. We stood in the doorway.

'Take care, Charley.'

It felt like the end of term. 'Can I give you a hug?'

She looked less surprised than I expected. I felt we'd grown close.

'Of course!'

I embraced her long enough for it to be meaningful but short enough not to weird her out. I can't tell you how good it felt. It marked a major milestone – one of those moments you look back on and consider what life would have still looked like if all this hadn't happened.

If you asked me, *yes but, Charley, how did all this therapy actually help you?*

I'd say the three big ones were:

1. Primary Pain – Feeling Shit

Painfully coming to terms with what I'd been avoiding. That I did in fact need therapy. That I was depressed. I was able to finally let go and face the collapse of the identity I'd built up. Pretending I was fine. Faking confidence.

I needed the safety net and the mirror.

2. Connecting the Dots – Clarity

Something that I'd never even begun to consider. How my upbringing and schooling impacted the young man I'd become. Probably the area where I had the most resistance and denial too. *'But I had the best childhood anyone could have ever wanted.'* Yes, but what about emotionally? Realising that as a sensitive young boy, going to boarding school at seven meant switching into survival mode, falling into rigid conformity and expectations. Doing what I was told, being how I ought to be – all very well-meaning – but likely not quite what *I* needed to develop my self-worth, my own agency, become my own man.

Instead, I learnt how to bury my insecurity beneath the appearance of a well-mannered nice guy, desperate to please, desperate to be admired. I began to realise just how much this had shaped my personality, how my personality had shaped my decisions and how those decisions in business (overly agreeable and ego driven), in dating (mistaking admiration for love) and within myself (low self-esteem) were affecting my life.

Accepting the reality of this was something I battled with. I felt guilty even considering my parents had anything to do with all of this. I didn't want to blame them; I love them deeply, and I know they did their best. But their psychology shaped mine. Their values, their relationship, their way of dealing with emotion (or not dealing with it) had all trickled down.

3. Standing Up – Green Shoots

Sabine helped me turn invisible influence into something I could finally see and name. I started to notice how certain comments – from my father, from friends, from voices I'd internalized over the years – had quietly shaped how I thought about myself, about relationships, about what mattered.

Once I saw it, I couldn't unsee it.

And slowly, I started pushing back. Creating boundaries. Spending less time in situations or with people who reinforced the old ways of thinking I was fighting to move away from.

I had to pull out some weeds to let the new flowers grow.

But more than that, the work started to build something real inside me.

Self-worth. I stopped seeking validation from everyone around me. I started trusting my own judgment.

Confidence. Not the fake bravado I'd performed for years – real confidence.

Calm. The constant anxiety that used to hum in the background? Gone. I could finally breathe. I felt at ease.

Emotional control. I knew myself better – self-aware. I could catch the impulses, the tendencies, negative thought patterns, the old triggers and make more intentional choices.

Resilience. When setbacks came, I had the tools to deal with them.

Pain moved to peace.

Confusion gave way to clarity.

Agency started to grow from within.

We'd done the heavy lifting.

So, was that it, all sorted?

Had I come to the end of the road – finally done with what I'd once quite dismissively considered 'mumbo jumbo'?

I didn't see it that way anymore, but did that mean I didn't need any more of it?

I came to discover that this was the point in my journey where a lot of people stopped.

What else is there to do?

I don't feel unhappy anymore, I don't have constant anxiety. I think I get it all now.

But remember, I wasn't after average. I was in search of great, better, wonderful.

I'd gone from minus three to plus three.

But what about a fucking ten?

I was on a mission now. Documenting as I went – for me, yes, but also for everyone else who might be stuck where I'd been. If I could crack this, maybe I could help others do the same.

STEP 4 – KNOW THYSELF

Take a breath.

You can see it's a lot, right? To really understand yourself.

But can you see why it's so important to look inwards?

Can you see how it's easy to be the 'narcissist with the Green Goddess juice and a yoga mat'? Thinking you're working hard on yourself but not really – not actually being self-aware, not going underwater, as I like to say.

Hopefully you can see how vital this step is.

Introspection and reflection allow you to understand why you are how you are.

Why bother, you might ask?

Because introspection is the gateway to change.

If you have a problem with your car, it might not be obvious what the cause is. So before being able to solve the issue, it's important to first take a look under the bonnet, right? Here are a few examples of things in life that might not be going your way (reasons to start looking under the bonnet).

- You struggle with relationships.
- You never really feel satisfied.
- You work ALL the time.
- It's excessively painful when you get rejected or criticised.
- You've lost that light joy feeling you used to have.
- You need to be a perfectionist.
- You often people please.
- You insist on getting wasted every weekend.

- You have trouble expressing emotions.
- You keep losing.
- You constantly need approval from other people.
- You're on the edge of burnout.
- You don't feel how you want to feel.
- You feel like you should be happier than you are.

Sure, it can be uncomfortable, but I'm telling you the relief, the perspective, the *'oh shit, that all makes sense now'* clarity – it all massively outweighs the discomfort. All of a sudden you know what's going on, you're not thrashing around in the dark anymore. You've got to the source, the symptom, and it's a gamechanger because now you can do something about it.

You can't start untangling a piece of string until you've tinkered around a bit first and identified which bits go where.

Yes, but, Charley, how to actually do this?

It starts with introspection (self-reflection). Meditate, journal, write, ask close friends, family or colleagues for real honest feedback. Speak to a therapist, read self-development books, go to workshops, do personality tests, experiment with psychedelic drugs, but only in jurisdictions where it can be explored safely, legally and with qualified health professionals. They all lead to more self-awareness.

You'll have to see what works for you, my friend. But just remember, however uncomfortable these conversations or thoughts might be, you need to lean into that because all the things you are looking for lie on the other side of that discomfort. Discovering your real self is the difference between living a life of freedom instead of conformity. Feel the fear and do it anyway. These are all ways for you to face yourself and understand who you truly are.

After you've connected some dots, keep going, keep untangling.

To heal.
To let go.
To forgive.
To process.
To rebuild.
To overcome.
To create new beliefs.
To create new mindsets.

Go slow, be patient and be kind to yourself.

You might feel lonely, lost, confused, or isolated from others while you try to figure things out. This is quite normal.

Don't think of it as a bad thing.

Some things you won't see until you start looking for them. So being lost is a good thing. It's the gateway to finding yourself. To rebuilding your life.

You might not be able to see it yet, but I promise you it's true.

Just have faith.

Before we move on, I want to tell you something important – something that is seldom spoken about. At this point, you are going to be a little vulnerable and susceptible to influence. Remember, you are (quite rightly) opening up parts of yourself you would usually keep hidden away to find the answers you are looking for. So just please remember, no matter how desperate you might be, never lose your own sense of agency. Have your wits about you and be careful who you work with and whose advice you act on. I've seen too many good people take wrong advice or at least follow advice that wasn't quite right for them, and it can have serious consequences.

Trust your own judgement.

No one has all the answers. But sometimes the questions people ask you are more important than any answer they could give you. That way, people can help you find answers within yourself.

Go slow and try to understand yourself fully before making any major life decisions.

Self-Awareness = Choice to Change

STEP 5
RESPONSIBILITY IN ACTION

'Self-awareness without action is like knowing the way but never embarking on the journey.'

UNKNOWN

REBUILDING

After moving back in with my mother when things fell apart, I'd started to rebuild. I got a job, rented a flat in London, and life started to regain some rhythm. I landed a role at a boutique trading house, doing iron ore out of Africa. Small team. Entrepreneurial set-up, confidence coming back.

The transformation work was paying off. I was making better decisions, thinking longer-term, less impulsive. The job wasn't my dream, but it gave me stability while I figured things out.

I found a cheap basement flat in London. You could barely swing a cat – but it was mine and it became my base camp.

The kitchenette-living room had just enough space for my trusty desk and the solid oak bookshelf crammed with all my nonfiction. I'd filled the walls with inspiration quotes, goals and pictures of the leaders that inspire me. I'd gone from private jets in Panama to a Pimlico bedsit – but I was determined to build back up again.

I felt the wisdom from the likes of Buffett, Munger, Bezos, Ravikant and Draper was starting to rub off on me. I was less of an unguided missile and more of a Land Rover kitted out with GPS and some extra fuel tanks and tent on the roof – ready for the long road ahead. I started to understand what people meant when they said 'hard work is its own reward'.

Every morning before work, I'd sit at that desk and write. The book had become more than just documenting my journey – it was my purpose. I'd seen how much this stuff had changed my life already. The reading, the therapy, the frameworks, the breakthroughs.

I knew I was still on my own journey – there was more to come – but I saw how overwhelming, confusing and time consuming it could all be. Hundreds of books. Dozens of gurus. Conflicting advice. I was determined to distil what actually works. Document as I went. Help others avoid years of trial and error.

Two hours every morning, I was building the book as I continued to re-build myself.

NO MAN'S LAND

I'd decided to start getting back out there again socially. It was at one of the biggest events on the summer social calendar – the Goodwood Festival.

The July summer sun was beaming down onto the famous English racecourse carved into the South Downs, and I was captivated by the iconic grandstands along the final furlong, bursting with quintessential colours, singing familiar rhymes, dusting up an air of romantic nostalgia.

I spotted the head honcho, Charles Gordon-Lennox, custodian of Goodwood Estate and the 11th Duke of Richmond, cruising past the parade ring making a beeline for his private box. I clocked the signature cream suit fresh back from his favourite Savile Row tailor – my guess, a fine blend of linen and cotton, just enough for that structured, polished look without the creases. Three buttons on the jacket giving a nice high V so his lapels could neatly frame the timeless sky-blue shirt and navy woollen tie combo. Charles was brilliantly British, but his look, finished off with the oval eggshell glasses and grey curtains, just hollered European chic.

My posse was huddled around the Ladbrokes desk next to the Whispering Angel bar.

'Shit, mine practically came last!'

'Which one are you backing next?'

'Sam's dad owns No.6 – worth a punt apparently.'

The usual cabaret unfolding.

'There he is. Charley!'

I got a hard smack on the shoulder and turned around to see an old school pal smiling up at me.

But shit, I can't remember his name.

'Maaate! So good to see you, looking dapper as ever,' I blagged, reaching out to give him an overenthusiastic handshake.

Did he notice my second take? Could he see my brain whirring away behind my eyes?

'Charley, so good to see you. What are you up to these days?'

I flinched.

What the hell am I meant to say – oh, I've just finished therapy, moved back to London after a stint at home – starting over?

The old me would have just blagged it, spun a yarn: *mate, awesome thanks, work going really well, seeing this new bird...*

This time I felt naked, awkward, even paranoid, and not quite sure how to be. I'd taken off the old clothes but hadn't quite figured out what the new clothes were yet.

'Hang on, look, here they come – which one are you on?' I deflected.

By the time the horses had whizzed past the finishing post he'd got swept up in the crowd. I stood on the periphery alone, slightly detached. It's not like I hadn't been socialising – I'd been living in London again, working, seeing friends, dating. But most of my time had been spent in one-on-one catch-ups, deeper conversations, time with my family, or immersing myself in either personal development or my job. I wasn't exactly used to big social events anymore, lots of acquaintances, and the small talk that comes with it. So part of me felt a little gun-shy, like I was stepping into a different rhythm.

Everyone's attention all of a sudden shifted to two English roses approaching – willowy blondes. One in a popular royal blue Zara dress and the other in a tailored tweed suit – perhaps Holland Cooper. The gang greeted the girls – I recognised one of them, but not well enough to say hello.

Christ, I thought, *was anyone going to introduce me?*

They didn't.

I felt invisible.

Left out.

Like being back at school wanting to join in but not knowing how. More anxiety was creeping in; I crossed my arms awkwardly.

What the hell was going on? Wasn't I supposed to feel better after all this therapy?

I felt a sudden need to talk to someone.

A need for a drink. (I'd quit.)

A need for some admiration.

A need for some attention.

The relics of Carlos Ley were trying to lure me back to my old ways of being.

I nearly gave in...

Mate, did you hear what happened to me...

Mate, have you heard so-and-so was cheating on so-and-so...

Mate, let's go do some shots and find some girls...

But I resisted.

I caught the impulse.

I stood fast against the bravado.

Shit, it was uncomfortable. I felt like an addict needing my fix.

I guess that was self-awareness. I guess it was precisely what Joe Dispenza had spoken about:

'...*you'd have to become conscious of your unconscious habits and behaviours and modify those – yes or no?'*

'...you are freeing yourself from the chains of those emotions that keep you in the familiar past and the predictable future.'

'The body bucks and kicks like an unbridled stallion.'

Sure as hell felt like it.

The rest of the day was like walking a tightrope. Refraining from falling back into the old version of me, the person everyone perhaps wanted to see.

What must they be thinking? What's happened to Charley?

But my anxiety and discomfort slowly began to melt away throughout the day, although never disappeared altogether. Weirdly it was quite empowering – like being at a party sober, having control over myself.

If I didn't know any better, I'd have thought that I'd lost my confidence and flair that day. Enough to drive anyone to a double Jaeger Red Bull. But luckily, I knew that I was letting go of my ego. That part of me that I now knew was founded on fear. That part of me that Sabine, my therapist, had helped me to see was wrapped up in my borderline narcissism.

I was still recalibrating. Still filling up my cup.

I'd come so far, made so much progress, and it was important to acknowledge that.

BUT.

I wasn't there yet. I still wasn't entirely satisfied.

Sabine had helped me go from a minus three to a solid plus three. I didn't feel shit anymore. I felt OK most of the time.

But I didn't want OK. I didn't want to just be plus three for the rest of my life.

I wanted it all. Success AND happiness. A plus ten.

I wanted to feel how I'd felt at the best moments of my life: playing sports at school, running clubs at university, trips with friends, playing polo in Argentina, even family time on the farm. Bursting with energy, direction, clarity, confidence, joy.

My intuition was telling me that there was something more, something better on the other side of all this.

But where to next?

Was I ever going to have any fun again?

I wasn't going to settle. I wasn't going to have any regrets. I needed to find more answers.

SADHGURU

It's the midst of the British heatwave, and I should have been sipping lemonade in the garden, settling in to watch Prince Harry tie the knot with his American actress bride, Meghan Markle on TV. But no – my old uni mate Pete had dragged me off to the O2 to watch Sadhguru speak, an Indian yogi, mystic and 'visionary', as he called himself.

'Pete, mate, this better be worth it.' Whilst I no longer considered the things I was doing 'mumbo jumbo', Pete sometimes took things to another level – numerology, psychics, reincarnation, etc. I was wary that that's what I was about to get.

By now I was getting a reputation for missing things, Bank holiday weekends in Norfolk, and now the royal wedding. But I knew how far I'd come, so I was even more determined to keep going.

Ushered into the vast conference hall – it was so big you could see a sort of haze in the air, there was that familiar drone of the AC, the muttering of thousands of people and the clunk of metal chairs – it felt like we needed a pair of binoculars to see the stage. We sat there patiently; I started streaming the wedding on my iPhone.

Eventually Sadhguru made his appearance – he flashed up on the huge screens and I could easily make out his gentle eyes, his white Father Christmas beard and his beige turban. He spoke softly, he was cheeky and had a wry smile. He did this little quirk where he ended each question with a '*isn't it?*' It had a semblance of cockney; he'd pause and gaze into the crowd knowingly, '*isn't it?*' I liked him immediately, the guy was full of charisma, charm and wisdom. I switched off BBC iPlayer – sorry, Harry – and grabbed my note pad.

We were two hours in – another four to go. *How the hell am I going to make it through this?*

One minute I was frantically scribbling down gems, and the next I was fidgeting in my chair, manoeuvring to get comfortable. I took another swig of my water and placed it back onto the empty chair between Irena and me. She was a young Middle Eastern lady who had come to the event alone. She was tapping notes into her iPad – but we were completely out of sync. It was like Sadhguru's words were little personalised carrier pigeons – some for me and some for her. It made me realise how different messages can relate to different people at different times in our lives.

I also felt a sort of common bond between Irena and the other strangers in that vast room. People from all walks of life; they were all here to learn and listen. They were humble and curious – maybe in search of a better life or more clarity. I took comfort in being among thousands of other human beings who were also on a journey – I felt like it was more normal to be on a journey than not to be.

There were so many great insights and takeaways I jotted down:

'*If we come to terms with mortality, we gain an ease about our existence.*'

I loved that. Perspective is everything. He also gave us a tip to constantly be reminded when we look at our watch – time is ticking.

'The nature of our minds is to protect our identity – gender, race, status, religion, creed, nationality, etc. This is why we always fight for our beliefs.'

Hearing this from a spiritual leader just cemented in my mind how relevant it was. I had held on to being Carlos Ley – the smooth-talking Latino commodities trader – and convinced myself this character was my actual identity. This kind of defensiveness is such a fundamental part of our resistance to change.

'You have to understand these human nature aspects of mankind and psychology to try and untap true bliss.'

And this summed it all up for me. It reconfirmed everything that I'd been doing – trying to understand the inner workings of my mind, slowly untangling the angst and trying to feel great again.

It was working.

'What happens within us should happen our way, not someone else's way.'

This confirmed my new thinking even more: Stop looking to the outside to determine how you want to feel on the inside. I like to think of it as walking up to a stranger on my commute to work and saying, *hey, do you mind telling me what you think of me? I need to know how I'm going to feel today!*

It's crazy to think how much I was being influenced by everyone around me. *If I could just change enough things on the outside, I could change how I felt on the inside.*

My whole life I'd been dancing to the tune of the pied piper instead of having the confidence, belief and self-worth to figure out my own melody – my own groove – and dance to my own beat.

I'd been trying to be all things to all people. But all this 'mumbo jumbo' had helped me to claw back my sense of self.

Quietness.

Self-respect.

Self-compassion.

Thinking for myself.

Being more assertive.

Standing up for myself.

There were no major breakthroughs or stunning aha moments at the event, but it was days like this that convinced me to stay on the journey. Sadhguru helped reinforce things I'd heard already; he explained things in more relevant ways, and taught me new things.

It struck me that all this 'mumbo jumbo' stuff wasn't just an afterthought, it was central to our existence. Universal. Foundational to building a happy, whole and fulfilling life with meaning and purpose. And I was right to be giving it the attention I was.

All sorted then, right?

A PARADOX

Friday morning. The Lansdowne Club, Mayfair

I sat alone at a quiet corner table; one I'd carefully chosen. I was shuffling the newspapers, fixing my collar and sipping my tea, attempting to dissipate the nervous energy.

I was about to confront my father.

I'd asked him to meet, but now I felt like a schoolboy waiting for the headmaster. Still, I reminded myself, this was for the greater good of our relationship – to hopefully bring us closer.

'Morning, Brush!' he said as he approached, beaming like we were about to hatch some mischievous plan together.

Grey suit, cream Turnbull & Asser shirt, signature mint green froggy Hermès tie. The Captain in full uniform. He pulled out his chair, sat, and pointed his chin as he tucked his napkin into his collar.

'Bloody good sausages here. Have you ordered?'

I smiled weakly. He was radiant – full of charm and joie de vivre. And there I was, about to bang on about feelings.

He poured the tea and began buttering toast. Completely oblivious.

We breezed through small talk. Then I cut to the chase.

'Daddy, do you mind, I'd like to talk to you about something important.'

He looked up, a touch surprised. 'Of course, tell me.'

'Well, you may have noticed... I've been a bit distant lately.'

'You have – I just assumed you've been terribly busy.'

'I haven't actually been that busy. The truth is, I've found it increasingly frustrating when we speak, or spend time together.'

He stayed quiet – I kept going.

'I want to see you more; I want to spend more time together... but it's hard. I feel like you never really listen. I'm sorry but I just want us to be as close as possible – I love you.'

'I don't understand, what's so frustrating?'

'It's nothing new, Daddy – stuff we've spoken about so many times before – you know, speaking about women the way you do sometimes, despite asking you not to; when we're out, and you're short with waiters or dominate the conversation – I nearly walked out of the restaurant the other day I was so embarrassed. It's hard to even finish what I'm saying a lot of the time without you cutting me off – I just feel you don't really respect or listen to what I'm saying most of the time – it's usually a monologue, not a conversation, and I just switch off. I'm sorry to say all this but I just shut down, it's not enjoyable and it makes me not want to be there.'

I'd got it all out – it felt like he was listening. Maybe this could be a turning point.

He sat there for a few seconds. He was hard to read. Had I infuriated him? Was he sad? Was he going to let go and finally understand?

I started to feel a bit guilty as I momentarily saw the little boy in him – a vulnerability, getting told off. But then he delivered the line that I'll never forget.

'Charley, you're terribly sensitive, you know.'

I couldn't believe it. I went straight back at him. 'That's not the point! This isn't about being sensitive. It's about having some respect and listening to me for once.'

'Oh, all right, Charley,' he said, wincing – showing the first signs of irritation.

I think I had said enough.

'Look, it's good to have these conversations and I'll certainly take this on board, but you really mustn't be so sensitive.'

There it was again, but this time I let it go.

Oddly, despite feeling like I'd hit a brick wall, at least the conversation seemed to dissolve a lot of my pent-up frustration. I think he felt it was the first time we'd really 'spoken' in a while too. I remember giving him a hug and walking off thinking to myself if there was any hope – would he ever change or listen. A paradox – more love and connection but also more frustration and judgement. I didn't know how it was going to pan out.

A LANDMARK MOMENT

Two years passed in London.

The trading job gave me stability and breathing room. I'd built back some savings during that time, and more importantly, I'd worked hard to clear the mental noise. Success and wealth creation still mattered to me, but what was driving me had changed.

When our trading model started running out of steam and the market shifted against us, I saw it as a sign rather than a setback. I'd been feeling the pull to go out on my own again – but this time, on different terms.

I didn't think I was slipping into becoming Carlos Ley again. On the contrary, I felt I was applying many of the lessons I had learnt through self-help. While I won't pretend the old patterns had vanished completely (part of me still wanted to prove I could make it), this was now less about ego, short cuts, big risks and chasing an outcome. It wasn't for the watches, the cars or the girls. It was to build a life I wanted. It was to back myself, have a go, not have regrets. I wanted to play the long game now, build something meaningful, be intentional and create financial freedom for myself.

I had just enough capital saved from the past two years to fund the setup and give it a proper go.

I spent months researching materials of the future – what would power the energy transition, EVs, semiconductors. I was methodical this time. Commissioned research. Built financial models. Thought long-term.

But the more I dug in, the clearer it became: the capital requirements were too high, the geopolitical risks too complex, the technology too uncertain.

Then I had my aha moment, something I heard Bezos say - instead of chasing what's going to change, focus on what's going to stay the same.

Building materials. Infrastructure. Boring, but essential.

That led me to consolidating small aggregate and industrial minerals mines in Colombia – the government was investing billions into infrastructure and there would be demand for decades.

It felt like a good idea. Lower risk, asset-based, consistent cash flow. I could build slow and steady. So I started the business and got to work.

On the personal side, the self-development books kept arriving. The writing continued. The unsuccessful romances piled up.

I was in a better place – no doubt about that – but I wasn't thriving. Something was still missing. I didn't feel complete, whole. I was still searching for that 10 out of 10 – truly loving life.

Meanwhile, I kept hearing whispers of this supposed 'seven years of therapy in seven minutes'. Breakthroughs. Rapid lasting change. I was sceptical, but you know me – I had to get to the bottom of it.

A friend recommended the bestselling book *EST: Playing the Game the New Way*, by Carl Frederick. It was a cult classic.

One passage in particular jumped out at me: 'Yep, the shrinks of the world make $200 every thirty minutes by agreeing with you. They're just expensive friends, who help you find the right pictures on the videotape, take a long and hard look at them, and then make you write about them. In fact, they help you drive yourself even deeper into the mud next to the pictures, by having you analyse what was going on. And this process keeps you firmly anchored in the past.'

Was this me? Had my therapist made me wallow in my past?

It was enough to make me want to sign up to the globally renowned personal development programme – Landmark – which was based on the principles of the book.

Unknowingly, I was about to embark upon the very thing that would become the point of no return. The hopefully ultimate solution to my unresolved questions.

We'd convened on the top floor of an office block around the corner from Euston Station. Sitting in the third row from the front, waiting for Gerry, the seminar facilitator, to wrap up his monologue was like anticipating the starting gun at the 100m. That unnerving space between opportunity and embarrassment. He was like a retired actor from Hollywood, the accent, the flamboyance, the sincerity in his giving a shit about us Brits, all sitting there skipping between suspicion and belief in our minds. I reached my hand up in the air – directly and reluctantly. My heart was already palpitating, but I knew I had to push through the fear. My lone hand caught his eye just as he was ending his last sentence, the sea of hands that followed were irrelevant – I'd timed it perfectly.

'Right, who else would like to... Yes, you, sir.' He pointed to me. I didn't need to look around – I knew it was me. I stood up and walked to the front of the room, took hold of the microphone and looked up to the 300-strong audience. What the hell was I doing – I should be watching England play the All Blacks in the semi-finals of the Japan Rugby World Cup like every other normal person in the country that Saturday morning but instead I was at The Landmark Forum, a well-known self-development weekend workshop.

My leg quivered as I stood at the mic. I took a deep breath and began apprehensively: 'OK, so I've already done quite a bit of work – had therapy etc.' Blah blah.

'I know that I am how I am because my dad was like this and my mum was like that.' Blah blah blah. 'But for example I'm still petrified of what everyone thinks of me, even everyone in this room. I feel like a fraud standing up here with nothing that wrong with me.'

Gerry interrupted me. I waited for the sympathy, some soothing words of reassurance and praise for getting up there. I looked at him in his three-piece suit, teeth popping out of his big smiley mouth.

'Stop, stop,' he said, holding up his hand like he was shielding light from his eyes. 'Look at you, just look at you – it's pathetic.'

What the hell? He's ridiculing me in front of everyone. I looked to the girls in the front row for some support and reassurance. *What a prick*, I thought.

'I can't see your name badge, what's your—'

'Charley,' someone shouted out; either someone who I'd been speaking to earlier or someone who could see my name badge.

'Everyone just look at Charley. Charley, you fade into the background like a dull piece of wallpaper. Do you have a girlfriend?'

'No,' I replied.

'I'm not surprised,' he snapped back.

I looked again at the girls for some pity and sympathy, but they just looked at me as if to say, you're on your own now, son.

'Why would anyone want to hang around with that?' he jibed.

Then, in a marginally more sympathetic tone, he went on: 'Charley, you've been playing the victim for God knows how long, you're all wrapped up in your own pity, blaming everyone else.'

His words pierced my shell like a bullet. What he said was undeniable, it was black and white, he was so right and I had never seen it. I'd even come up here for some pity. I could feel the way I was standing, hunched over, earnest – lusting for pity.

'Charley, these stories and ideas you have created in your head from whatever happened in the past, they're your stories, your interpretation of life – you chose them so it's up to you to change them now, not anyone else.'

I'd been getting it completely the wrong way around.

I'd been trying to blame my parents. All that time I'd spent at home with my mother it had been her I'd been trying to change rather than myself. But it was all on me – it was my responsibility. Yes, I had been tinkering around the edges of me at the same time, but I had never really accepted accountability. I still liked being the victim too much – victims are blameless, and they are often also powerless. But I wasn't powerless. I was just making excuses.

'Now, Charley, how do you want to be – what are you?'

Silence.

My brain couldn't function – I was in shock up there and couldn't think. He helped me along.

'Charley, you're a strong and powerful young man, aren't you? I can see you're a leader.'

YES!

That was it – something clicked. Carlos Ley wasn't really a leader. The lone wolf had no pack following him. The only thing I had following me was my own sense of victimhood. But to become a true leader meant seizing my own sense of agency.

Deep down that's what I knew I was and wanted to be but no one had ever said this to me before. Yes, my father always expected – no, demanded – success from me, but I was still a weak sheep, pursuing someone else's definition of making it. I didn't really believe in that dream because it was somebody else's. But now I had my own. And it had been hiding just beneath the surface all along.

I looked out at the sea of faces, a few were muttering about something in the room – a few faint gasps; I didn't know what was happening.

'Look at you now,' Gerry said. 'You look different – two foot taller. Now turn to the room and tell us all how you are now, who you are.'

I turned my attention to my body. I did feel different, he was right, my shoulders had dropped, my chest was out, my head was up.

'Yeah he does,' someone shouted out.

And there, just like that, in a room full of strangers my life changed for the better.

I realised something so powerful, something I had no idea about, a total shift in my perception of myself. It was like learning to fly.

I walked over to shake Gerry's hand and then sat down, bowed my head to hide from the attention and then my eyes swelled with water and as I blinked – tears fell in unison into my lap. They were tears of relief, tears that had been waiting for years to be released, to express the weight of my emotions.

Shortly after, we were dismissed for the next tea break. I stood up and made my way to the door. Someone said, 'Hey, Charley, you were amazing; the stuff you said really helped me too. I could really resonate.'

It was reassuring to hear but my mind was firmly fixed on step two of the process. The breakthrough wouldn't be complete without Gerry's prescribed real-world action-taking.

I walked outside to call my mother.

'Hi, Mimi, are you OK?'

'Hello, Charley. Yes, all's well here, how's your event going?'

'It's actually pretty amazing, Mimi. You won't believe it but I just got up in front of everyone.' I cringed slightly imagining her picturing me on the microphone. I closed my eyes to say the next bit. 'Mimi, he made me realise that I've been playing the victim all these years, I've been so hard on you and blamed you for so much. I'm sorry for being so hard on you, Mimi.'

There was a brief pause. 'Ah, Charley, it's OK. You were a little, but I just want you to be happy.'

Her words only reconfirmed it all, and then for the first time ever at 35, I said it: 'I love you, Mimi, you're the best Mimi in the world and I'm sorry for everything.' I rushed the last bit as I choked up and I could feel the tears run down my face again.

'Ah, Charley, I love you too, thank you for saying that.'

I'd never felt so close to her. I felt her put her arm around me as I held her to my ear in the rain on the busy pavement. I felt relieved, liberated, like a child, but proud and grown up like a man. We said goodbye and I just stood there as the people surged past me – clear-headed and still, everything seemed to slow down.

Shit, I thought... *liberated, like a child...* those were some of the words, the STATES I'd been searching for... the STATES I'd been writing in my journal.

I took a deep breath and just thought – WOW, that's it. That's rapid change.

What I had been researching was true – you really can make internal shifts quickly. It didn't have to take weeks, months, or years. It was just a matter of challenging my mindset. Confrontational? Yes. But I was ready for it, and realising I wasn't a victim and that I'd been hoping someone else would come along and fix everything for me changed everything. It was a revelation. It was empowering as hell.

After the short break I went back inside for the next session, grabbed my notepad and began to piece it all together.

Sabine had helped me a lot, she gave me a more stable footing, but this direct approach, calling me out was exactly what I needed. This was real proactive change – taking responsibility. It *was* like doing years of therapy in minutes. It made me realise too that conversations that we don't want to have are usually the ones that we need to have the most.

But that's not all, and I don't say this lightly, but if there's one idea in this book that could genuinely change everything for you, it could be this. Central to the programme was the idea that we can develop negative or unhelpful beliefs in life and these are often created from our interpretation of what people have done and said to us.

Here are some examples of what I mean:

- You were teased for your appearance at school → *I'm not attractive.*
- You were constantly compared to others growing up → *I'm not good enough.*
- You only got attention when you excelled → *I have to achieve X to be valued.*
- Your parent withheld affection when you needed it most → *I don't deserve to be loved.*
- You failed early and no one encouraged you to try again →

- *I'll never be successful.*
- You were abused by someone → *I'm worthless.*
- You were rejected again → *There must be something wrong with me.*
- You got hurt when you trusted → *I can't let anyone in, I'll just get hurt again.*

Whatever we've interpreted from other people, experiences, life – has created certain beliefs within us. Or said in another way, we create opinions about ourselves.

Stuff Happens → Beliefs
Cause → Effect

And these beliefs or opinions form our personality.

What we think, feel and say. How we show up in the world. The choices we make.

It's a common view to think that our personality is precisely that – our personality, and that can't change, right?

Well, here's the mother of all insights.

From all the work I've done, one way or another, this is what seems to lie at the leading edge of work done by a lot of prominent philosophers, positive psychologists and religious leaders.

In a nutshell, if we created the belief by ourselves (albeit often subconsciously – without realising), we can now choose to change that belief consciously.

You *can* change your personality.

And it comes down to *interpretation*.

Growing up we're forming all these ideas, opinions and beliefs about ourselves unknowingly. Most serve us well, but some start becoming a problem when we realise that they're getting in the way of what we want in life.

And in that moment, if you can recognise which belief is holding you back, however personal, unfair or horrible the experience that made you have it might have been, and then you can acknowledge that despite what happened, it was still *you* that chose to *interpret* the *meaning* you gave to what happened – then that is a major breakthrough in itself.

And so if you interpreted the meaning and created that belief, then you can now consciously decide that you don't have to think about yourself in that way anymore, and you can choose to create a new belief to replace the old one.

If you did it back then, you can do it again.

And that's where yesterday ends and tomorrow begins.

Responsibility in Action.

We (mis)interpret the meaning of certain interactions and experiences.

We (mis)interpret how what was said or what happened relates to us.

We might take things literally when they weren't meant that way.

We might have a more sensitive disposition to others.

We might tend to take things to heart.

For example, I (mis)interpreted from my mother that intimacy was wrong and was ashamed to show affection. It's ridiculous to think that my mother believes that intimacy is wrong – but that's what I (mis)interpreted.

I objectified girls, judged them physically, saw them like trophies, a status game and set ridiculously high standards. Some of these traits I picked up from my father and mirrored them. But he never said, *Charley, this is what you should think*, it's what I decided to (mis)interpret from him. I can't blame him for being him. It's my job to be like *OK, I picked that up, it's not working for me so now I want to change.*

Another level deeper. I failed to recognise that whoever did or said things to me in the past that I held onto, were likely reacting to their own complex psychology, playing out their own insecurities, beliefs, needs and fears, their own blame, or their own pain, and I just happened to get in the way. But I decided to take their actions to heart, I personalised a lot of it, took it literally, (mis)interpreted that this is what they actually believe about me so I must think it too.

This is where I was going so wrong. I'd been *(mis)interpreting* things from the world around me and therefore believing a whole bunch of unhelpful things about myself. That I wasn't good enough, I didn't deserve to be loved, and more recently – *poor me*.

Landmark helped me realise that I'm not responsible for my past, but I am responsible for my future, and these were exactly the sorts of insights I was looking for.

Carl Frederick, the author of *EST*, was right – I had been wallowing in my past, firing and wiring pity into my mind, self-absorbed. The narrative running around in my head was: *look how everyone else made me like I am today.* I needed to stop pointing the finger at everyone else and turn it around to point at myself, take personal responsibility and just decide to change. It was less navel gazing and more hard action – this is where Landmark and other similar methods are so powerful.

My therapist laid some great foundations, but I don't think I'd ever have made this sort of progress without Landmark. But I wouldn't have been able to skip therapy either. For me this was the right sequence. I needed the gentler therapeutic approach to start, not just to feel stronger again, but that slower process was needed in coming to terms with things.

Depending on what you might be trying to overcome, where you are in your journey, how sensitive or impatient you might be, you can usually gauge if you're ready for a more direct and confrontational approach to change.

I think we're all different and can tolerate different things at different times.

I missed the mother of all rugby matches that day, but I found a part of me didn't actually mind. What I was doing instead was changing *my* life.

COLLATERAL DAMAGE, SACRED BOND

'Anyway – you must need to go.'

I'd usually snatch the opportunity to wrap things up so I could get on – rushing onto the next thing. But less so these days.

'Actually, I don't, Mimi – I'm not in any hurry.'

We sat next to each other in her smart Mitsubishi pickup – workman-like yet elegant just like her. It was 5 p.m. December dark, we'd parked up outside the front door, the wipers were frantically flicking away the heavy rain, and the AC was blowing to fend off the condensation.

'I'm afraid your godmother isn't doing so well – I don't suppose she's got very long left now. Tristan [her son] and I have been texting – he's worried about his father not coping so well. He said he wishes he'd just open up and talk about it rather than pretending it's not happening – he's keeping it all bottled up.'

She pulled out her phone to read one of her WhatsApp messages to him:

'Tristan I'm so sorry to hear that. I'm afraid it's a generational thing – we're not very good at talking about our feelings. Charley tells me all the time I need to open up more.'

Ouch.

I felt a sense of guilt wash over me. All those painful conversations in the kitchen by the Aga – she had been listening after all.

I got what I'd wished for but hearing her say it made me sad. The thought of her judging herself.

She paused. There was something else on her mind.

I'd learned from Sabine when to shut up – how to give those shy, tender expressions a chance to rise to the surface and transform into speech.

Another splatter of rain on the windscreen... then it came.

'We've had a pretty good time together, haven't we, Charley – over the years?'

I felt my heart melt with more guilt. It was unfamiliar vulnerability; she was searching for reassurance.

Shit.

How much had she been reminiscing?

How much had she been beating herself up?

I knew how selfish I'd been over the years. How hard it had been caring for Nina, the relentlessness of keeping the farm above water and the pain through her divorce. She had been robbed of so much joy and there I was making her feel bad for the way she raised me.

What a prick.

'But I sometimes think I could have been a better mother to you.'

I had to tilt my head slightly to hold back the tears. 'What are you talking about? Mimi, you HAVE to listen to me. It was impossible for you to love me more than you do – we've talked about me growing up, home life and school because it was important for me to connect the dots and piece things together so I could understand how I became the man I was and what I needed to work on to make some changes. But that's on me. There's no blame, there's no criticism – it's my interpretation of the world around me and it was my responsibility to choose and change whatever I want about myself. Your openness and willingness to talk gave me that awareness and understanding I needed. Mimi, you brought me up in the best way you knew how.'

She kept listening intently, I needed to keep going – I couldn't risk not hitting this home. I couldn't deal with the thought of her beating herself up and me being responsible for more hurt.

'There's no real right or wrong way, there's a spectrum; over here you have hippie parents – do what you want, smoke some weed, and over here you have controlling authoritarian parents who beat the discipline into you. You and Daddy were probably around here,' I said, pointing to the middle and a touch to the right. 'But in the end, it doesn't really matter where you are across that spectrum, because every little girl or boy is going to interpret things differently – some of us are more sensitive, you know?' She nodded. 'We're all conditioned one way or another. But what does matter, is that if someone isn't happy, they're looking for answers and need to understand and express themselves, then having a parent or parents that are open to talking things through, it's... it's, um, like a sort of remedy. The most dangerous thing is not talking – but we did and we unlocked stuff, didn't we? We unravelled the knots between our souls and look at us now, Mimi – the conversation we're having now, we're much closer, don't you think? Does that make sense?' I pleaded. My eyes welled again. I desperately needed her to understand to relieve my guilt.

'Sort of, Charley.'

I'd shifted from blame, to acceptance, appreciation and love, but I couldn't erase the words I'd spoken to her in the haste of wanting to point the finger while trying to figure myself out.

The damage was done. I could try to move on but that didn't mean she would.

It's easy to forget that just because someone doesn't respond or react to words, it doesn't mean they aren't hurt by them.

I'd got her caught up in my process, collateral damage on my crusade to finding happiness.

But there was a silver lining – it had brought us closer, able to rise above our Britishness and share more sacred mother and son moments together.

But surely, I'd gone too far?

I felt bad for being harsh on my parents, but I didn't regret trying to understand how my upbringing shaped me psychologically and taking steps to change the things that I thought weren't doing me any favours.

I knew that I needed to break free from old influences and live life on my own terms. But I also knew that I wanted my parents in my life, their unconditional love, their unrelenting support. I never want to lose the meaning we bring to each other's lives, and I want to be there for them, support them, encourage them and look out for them.

I thought Philippa Perry puts it rather elegantly in the introduction of her bestseller *The Book You Wish Your Parents Had Read (and Your Children Will be Glad That You Did)*: 'I encourage you to look at your own babyhood and childhood experiences so that you can pass on the good that was done to you by your own upbringing and hold back on the less helpful aspects of it.'

There's zero blame. It's just important to find answers.

So, what to do?

It's a delicate dance…

Get clarity.

Connect the dots.

Communicate with love.

Be grateful for what they did.

Take responsibility and be who YOU want to be.

'You don't need to blame your parents
for teaching you to be like them.
What else could they teach you but
what they know? ... They had no control
over the programming they received,
so they couldn't have behaved any differently.
It is time to be free from the role of the victim.'

DON RUIZ MIGUEL, *THE FOUR AGREEMENTS*

MY DATE WITH DESTINY

I'm sitting at home by the fire with Mimi and we're trawling through Netflix for something to watch when *I Am Not Your Guru* pops up.

'Mimi, look, this is all about the event I'm going to; it's a behind the scenes take – shall we watch it?'

I'd seen it a while ago but thought it would help her understand what the hell I was up to – and of course tickle my anticipation. The two of us kicked back on the sofa eager for what was to come.

I'd known about Tony Robbins – the guru of changing people's lives – for a while, read his books, watched his videos. I knew this was his most immersive event held only once a year. Five thousand people for five days in the Palm Beach Convention Center. I was excited, he brought the razzmatazz, he was a big deal, he had coached and brought his celebrity friends to this event, the likes of Oprah, Bill Clinton and DiCaprio. Flying to Florida for a conference where tickets started at $1,500 sounded excessive on paper, but if anything, Landmark had taught me that I was on the right track; I needed to trust my instinct – this was something I had to do. Formerly Anthony J. Mahavoric,

Robbins had gleaned the best bits from his Eastern European heritage and Southern California upbringing: six foot seven, chiselled, tanned, the perfectly white, perfectly straight American smile, the star quarterback physique. A double take and you could mistake him for former American footballer Tom Brady.

I'd forgotten quite how intense the documentary was. I suddenly became so aware of my mother sitting next to me. The narrator started reeling off a bunch of attendees; their father abandoned them, their childhood trauma. I could feel her thinking: *and this is what you're going there for? To be cured from my bad parenting?* I felt guilty as hell, embarrassed, ashamed, like I was watching a sex scene and she had walked in. Thankfully it moved on and started to paint a more eclectic picture: relationship day, goal-setting day, the crowds, the music, the production, the electricity – it was like a rock concert. Tony explained how he could create 'lasting change in minutes'. I had been sceptical about that promise at Landmark, but I had then experienced a genuine lasting shift in perspective. Tony's philosophy was grounded in the same principles, but rather than helping me tackle one big obstacle I expected to dive deeper than ever before.

I resisted giving in to my mother's judgement. Our relationship was different now; it had developed to the stage where I felt I could say things to her that she might not agree with, that might not even make her feel good – but I knew she respected me. This maturity had brought us closer.

Just as I was starting to relax again, scenes of thousands of people began chanting to the chime of Tony's oratory up on the stage, like a congregation worshipping their leader. Oh gosh, she already thought I was off to some weird culty American self-help seminar and this wasn't helping! It didn't matter though; my mind was made up and I knew that I was on the right track.

It's hard to explain. Despite everything I'd done, all the progress I'd made, there was still something missing. I felt there were still things living inside me holding me back from feeling complete, having fun, getting a girlfriend, going to the next level, winning at life. I might be more present, healthier, more forgiving of myself, less narcissistic, less depressed, but that didn't mean I had replaced all that negativity with something amazing. What was happening inside wouldn't necessarily change what was happening on the outside.

I needed something to catapult me to the other side – across the Rubicon and finally end this crusade to feeling truly happy and at peace.

I knew Tony Robbins was the right man for the job. It was in his book, *Awaken the Giant Within*, that he spoke about the science of neuro-associative conditioning. 'What you must do is reorganise your neural pathways so that they consistently guide you in the direction of your desires rather than your frustrations and fears.' He spoke about how our beliefs, values and rules control how we think, feel and behave, and how we can have major breakthroughs to create this lasting change in minutes.

I knew these breakthroughs were possible from Landmark, I knew Date With Destiny was founded on similar principles, and I knew that across the five-day deep dive it was likely I'd have more of those aha moments that could literally change my entire perspective for me.

I packed my bags that night and by the following evening I was checking in to the Best Western in Palm Beach Lakes.

But nothing could have prepared me for what was to come.

—

Palm Beach Convention Center, Florida

'When I say go, I want you all to turn to the person you're drawn to, the person you just instinctively feel will be a good partner for you over the next five days.'

Shit, no pressure. *Team Limitless*, our group of thirty or so stood there huddled around our leader, Thor, standing on a chair. We were in one corner of the gigantic arena. Only an hour or so earlier I'd walked into an electric energy – thousands of people pumped with enthusiasm and anticipation. Tony Robbins veterans or virgins, you could feel the energy in everyone. It didn't feel like a self-help seminar at all – this place was full of business leaders, alpha males and cute couples.

Shit, I'm going to spend the next five days with this person and I need to get it right, but what if I turn to him and he turns to them? What if I turn to her and she thinks I fancy her?

'OK, on three; one, two, three.'

I looked straight up over the top of a few heads at this big, bearded, friendly but trendy giant of a guy. He looked right back at me and smiled – nailed it. Phew.

Reno was from Portland, Oregon – he was a film producer living in LA and had been to a few of Tony's events before but never this one – 'Dude, this one is the holy grail,' he kept saying, towering over me.

Day one was mainly about familiarisation. Your team, your buddy, the schedule of the days to come, some housekeeping and what to expect. We were each given our 'DWD' (*Date With Destiny*) handbook and there was a letter on the third page from Tony that summed up nicely what we had in store. This was the first paragraph:

> Dear Friend,
> Welcome to Date With Destiny and congratulations for making the decision to take your life to the next level. At its core, this program is about understanding why you feel and behave the way you do as well as giving you strategies and tools that will allow you to align with these forces to create the happiness, joy, love, passion success, and fulfilment you desire and deserve...

It went on...

> Most important, this is not a process that requires any of us to change who we are; rather the lessons I have learned all stem from having the courage to be myself, no matter what the context...

He signed off,

> Love & respect,
> Tony Robbins

As absurd and far away from my life back home – I knew I was in the right place.

They'd warned me about the sub-zero temperatures in the convention centre – some people were dressed in adult onesies, others armed with blankets and sleeping bags because it was so cold. But seriously, how cold could it get?

Bloody freezing.

By the afternoon I even exhaled like you do on a frosty winter's morning trying to see my breath in the air. We never really got to the bottom of why, but the rumour was it was to do with keeping us alert and awake through the long hours. We'd often still be in our seats at 1 a.m. wondering how much longer it was going to run – 'Tony Time' they called it.

But most people stuck it out. The content was too good to miss. The entire production made Landmark look poor by comparison. I'd gone from a beige corporate office space with halogen strip lights and Gerry in his off-the-shelf three-piece suit, to rock concert entertainment, Hollywood A-listers, Tony Robbins in his signature blue polo shirt and baseball cap with the four-leaf clover bringing Superbowl energy.

Today I got to see him close up for the first time – he liked to walk up and down the aisles, captivating us with his presence, searching for his next subject to work with. The security detail never far behind either. Shoulders were popping out of their sockets and bums squatting off the seats as people raised their arm to catch his attention, but he picked a young lady just one block in front of me – close enough now to see his grey stubble, his tired eyes, the sweat darkening his navy shirt around his chest. His voice was hoarse, it was as if the decades of these events were catching up with him as he approached his sixtieth birthday. The young enthusiastic locker-room Tony Robbins from all those online videos had matured, he'd collected the pain and joy from all the stories and breakthroughs over the years, and now had softened into an even more compassionate and humbled human being. I got the feeling we were witnessing vintage Tony Robbins and it made him all the more attractive.

CHANGE YOUR STORY
CHANGE YOUR LIFE

Was projected up on the big screens and the title of today's section in the handbook.

We'd covered this at Landmark (where it was rumoured Tony once attended) and it felt good to know some of the content already. My parents did this, he did that, poor me, I deserve this. That was my old story but now I'd learnt to change, and I was creating my new story. (Mis)interpretation, changing those beliefs we have about ourselves, taking responsibility. I was on the right track.

He explained his formula for happiness being when:

$$\text{Life Conditions} = \text{Blueprint}$$

Meaning that when our life is turning out the way we hoped then we feel good.

Conversely, unhappiness comes along when:

$$\text{Life Conditions} \neq \text{Blueprint}$$

Meaning that when our life is *not* turning out how we had envisaged, it can make us feel like shit.

I'd read about something similar in a lot of my self-development books, the 'expectation gap'. This idea that when the gap between where we are and where we want to be is too far apart, we're miserable. The answer Tony gave was so sublime and typical of his rhymey, easy-to-remember sayings, packed with meaning:

'Trade your expectations for appreciation and it's a whole new world instantly.'

And it was true. I'd gone from being Carlos Ley; always in a hurry, stressed, never present, needing the model and the Maserati to feel good about myself, to appreciating the smaller, everyday things. A cup of tea, the view of the Sussex Downs from my bedroom window, my morning meditation, my family and close friends, my health, that feeling after a great workout. I still had the goals, but I was so much more grounded, content and calm along the way.

The wellness trade stands littered around the entrance hall and the random chats in the queue for coffee were all part of the event. The energy was infectious; there were people from all around the world here unashamedly wanting to make change and reach their full potential – I'd found my tribe.

SUPERBOWL ENERGY

Day two

'Listen up, today is what most of you have come here for, this is what can transform you – so don't miss a beat.'

Music, lights and dancers erupted into action – 5,000 people were up out of their seats spilling into the aisles, dancing, going crazy to 'Life' by Haddaway.

The room was electric.

Tony jogged out onto the stage, he was just as pumped as we were, jumping around to the music, pumping his hands in the air, egging us all on. It was like a music concert. Eventually he spanned his arms out wide and looked to the sky like Usain Bolt before pounding his palms together in his trademark style – signalling us to all settle down into our seats.

We were buzzing.

He began by saying that our lives are constantly guided by the emotional state we find ourselves in.

STATE. That's exactly what I've been wanting to change. I had been writing about it in my journal regularly without ever realising it could be tackled in such a direct way. Here we go, I thought.

He followed up by suggesting that an 'angry' state would create a different response to a 'playful' state – and that it is learning how to change from one to another that is crucial to learn.

Yes, Tony – this is what I'm after... tell me how to change my STATE.

As he spoke about his travels and the patterns he'd noticed, he explained that across cultures, the same six human needs seemed to show up time and again.

Yes, yes, I've heard you say this before; the need for **Certainty** *(avoid pain, enough stability and comfort),* **Uncertainty** *(enough adventure, risk and variety), the need for* **Significance** *(to feel unique and special), and the need for* **Love & Connection**. **Growth and Contribution** *as well but they're the bonus ones. The six human needs... And?*

He explained that the real key was to identify which two of those needs sat at the top of your list – because those were the ones that ultimately dictated your life. For most people, he said, the driving forces tended to be significance and certainty.

I pondered what he had said for a second. *Significance and certainty...*

I reflected on the person I knew I was – the perfectionist guy, not wanting to take too many risks, afraid of what people might think, always needing to please, thinking I was special and better than everyone else.

Bloody hell – he's right. Behind pretty much everything I do is significance and certainty. They were my focus, I'd been forgetting about connection and uncertainty.

He went on to explain that suffering could take many forms – worry, anger, frustration – essentially anything that pulls you out of a positive state. The key, he suggested, was that the way out often came from shifting your focus beyond yourself. Whether that meant turning your attention to your children, your partner, or a mission greater than your own needs, that change in perspective could break the cycle instantly.

That was it, that was the sort of immediate mindset shift I was after – the seven years of therapy in seven minutes they all talk about – just decide and know what to focus on. This was gold dust.

It wasn't about needing to change; it was about rebalancing the portfolio, switching up my priorities and giving far more attention to Uncertainty and Love & Connection – it was so simple.

Reno and I turned to each other instinctively and raised our eyebrows in awe.

'Dude, that is some real shit.'

I just smiled back. I knew this was transformational for me.

At this point I'd have happily called it a day, called it a week, I'd already got my money's worth, but it kept coming. Next, Tony told us to think deeply about our 'primary question', our dominant, subconscious question that pretty much drives the reason behind everything we do. After a lot of deliberation, mine became painfully obvious.

How can I be admired?

I realised that pretty much everything I ever did had been designed to get more admiration. From how I looked, to how charming I was, to being a workaholic and trying to be successful, to the girls I dated, to the clothes I wore, to Instagram, to the parties I hosted. It was ruling my life as I constantly tried to feed my deep insecurity that I wasn't good enough.

It was another one of *those* moments, it was a 'breakthrough'. It confirmed that I had been addicted to admiration ever since I could remember.

This was my driving force, Robbins was right, it had been controlling my life – it was determining what I felt, said, did and the life I'd created around myself. It had all been a relentless crusade for more admiration, certainty and significance, and I'd ignored my other essential needs as a human being. No wonder I didn't feel balanced, fulfilled, at peace, light and happy.

And that's when the mother of all pennies dropped.

Something else hit me between the eyes.

I realised that ever since it had all gone Pete Tong (wrong), I had been trying to get back on track – feeling good again, *all through the lens of significance and certainty.*

A smoking hot girlfriend so I can be admired again – *Significance.*

To being successful again – *Significance.*

To being in control so I couldn't be criticised – *Certainty.*

To feeling happy and like having fun so people will love me again – *Certainty*.

But knowing what I knew now, I could see how I'd been getting it SO wrong, that this was never going to work – I was never going to get to where I wanted to be along the same path of significance and certainty I'd walked before (that way was flawed). Instead I needed to choose a new way, a path that prioritised love, connection and uncertainty.

It was a total gamechanger.

My primary question went from *How can I be admired?* to *How can I serve with love and grace?*

This was transformational. One primary question, one line, flip the script, flip the life experience.

RELATIONSHIP DAY

Day three – Relationship Day

The day that everyone had been looking forward to the most, especially me. I was eager to find out where I'd been going wrong with relationships in particular and how to land the girl of my dreams. Reno wanted to get clarity and answers to take home to his on/off girlfriend back in Portland.

Team Limitless seemed more jovial and light-hearted today, there was a giddiness in the air.

Maybe it was all collective breakthroughs, the aha moments, unlocking answers and knowing our lives had changed forever.

Thor warmed us up before Tony was due to come out on stage around midday. 'Turn to page one hundred and seventeen, guys – familiarise yourselves with the questions, ask your buddy about where they're at and what they want.'

Page 117 was aptly blood red with black writing. It stood out – as it should.

Tony purred through the afternoon, lighting up the crowd with golden nuggets – he didn't disappoint, he gave us exactly what it said on page 117 of our textbook:

'The Key to Lasting Passion, Love, & Fulfilment'

I scribbled notes into my book in excitement – knowing, seeing for the first time where I'd been going wrong and what I needed to do to find the girl I could truly build a life with.

My top five takeaways were:

1. **Selection**

- 95 per cent of our success comes down to selection.
- Most people end up in a relationship because of chance and chemistry.
- Chemistry alone is not enough for a long-term relationship.
- Compatibility + chemistry is vital.

Yup, I'd been going all in on chemistry.

2. **Clarity**

- Get clear on your own needs, values and priorities in life.
- Describe your ideal relationship and highlight the top priorities.
- A lot of men need to feel freedom and love.

I'd been pandering to their needs, I'd been pretending to agree, never wanting to upset, disagree or stand up for what I actually thought. How unattractive must that have been.

3. **Attract**

- Become the kind of person you want to attract in your relationship.

It reminded me of Charlie Munger – 'Be worthy of a worthy mate.' I'd been needy and pitiful.

4. **Give**

- Know what they really want and need, then give it.
- Don't live in fear and shame – love with courage.

I'd been operating through fear of saying the wrong thing and losing them.

5. **Polarity**

- Strong masculine and feminine energies create intimacy and passion.
- But if women become too insecure to relax the charge is depleted.
- If men lose freedom or purpose, their charge can be depleted.
- Loss of attraction can be caused by this depolarisation.
- A woman could go from tight and controlling to free and radiant once her husband makes her feel appreciated, needed and loved.
- A guy could go from frustrated, trapped and reserved to masculine and powerful once his wife lets him feel free and empowers his purpose.

No girlfriend yet but I could definitely relate to being more feminine and less masculine as I lacked purpose and direction. I needed to regain my masculine charge again.

Jesus Christ. I'd been getting it all wrong.

Now my eyes were open. Finally, I had a game plan. It felt empowering.

———

It was 1.20 a.m. Exhausted and ready for bed, we had one last exercise. Thor stood up on one of the chairs, clapping to get our attention. The room was growing louder with everyone becoming restless and people leaving.

'Guys, I need you for just five more minutes. Don't cut the corners here, you'll thank me after.' (He was right.) 'Mary is going around handing out letter paper and envelopes. I want you to write a letter to your future partner. Girlfriend, boyfriend, husband, wife.'

'What if we already have a partner?' Reno piped up.

Thor didn't make eye contact, he just continued to his next instruction with a hint of agitation. (Everyone was tired...)

'This can be to someone you have not met yet or to your existing partner, about how you visualise your relationship developing and thriving in the future. Be specific. How they look, how they are, what you enjoy doing together, think about the words you use to describe your relationship and life together.'

Reno sighed. 'Dude, I'll see you tomorrow – I'm done with this.'

I really wanted to bail too but I needed to get this done. I didn't want to half-arse it. I trusted this guy Robbins and I could already see the massive value in getting specific and knowing what I wanted. I got down on my knees to face my chair, leant the paper on the back of my textbook and began writing...

To my future girlfriend...

THE EXORCISM

Final Day

I remembered watching *I am Not Your Guru* and seeing attendees creating their 'Ultimate Destiny' posters, intently synthesising all the work they'd done over the past few days.

White A2 posters, black markers and highlighter pens galore. People were scattered all over the floor like children colouring in at school.

Now it was my turn, and I now knew exactly why all those attendees had looked so enthralled in the process...

They were literally writing down the new rules to live their life by. The principles, goals and visions that were going to keep driving their transformation.

They were designing their own *destiny*.

They weren't relying on fate.

They weren't resigned to 'what will be will be' or 'life's just happening to me'.

They were becoming the 'masters of their fate and captains of their souls', as William Ernest Henley would put it.

They were taking control of their lives.

Here is a copy of my poster (although I know you won't be able to see the colours and words – it should just give you a feel for it).

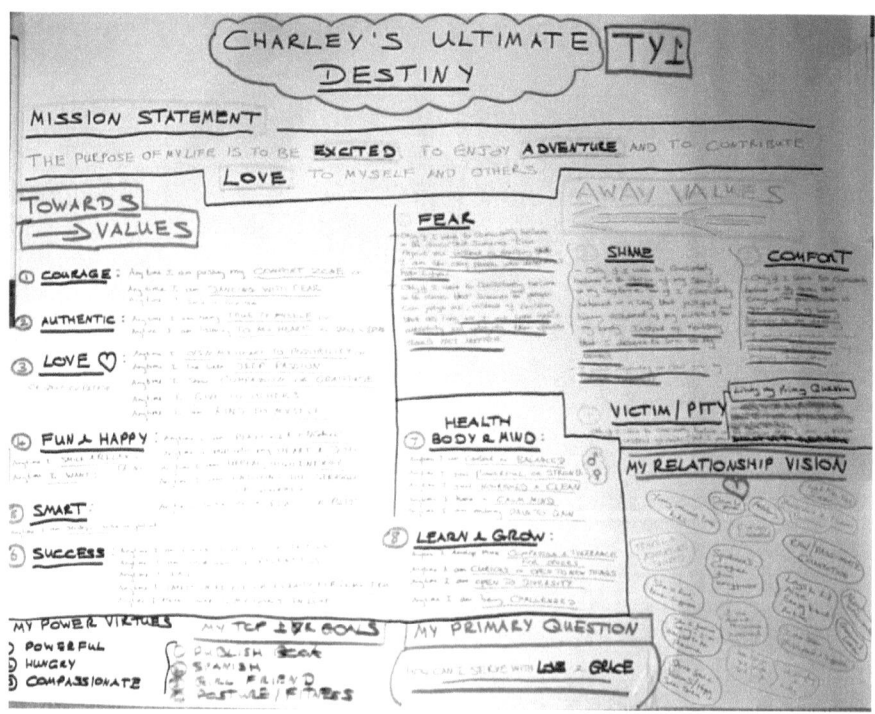

I thought the final day was just about big posters and big goodbyes, but I should have known better.

There was one more exercise.

'Integration: Conditioning Your Magnificent Future'

It was time to rip out the weeds and plant new seeds...

We'd all created a list of our top four values that had been holding us back. The types of emotional states we now knew we had to avoid if we wanted to make real change. Here are mine:

1. **FEAR** – caring what people think and avoiding criticism at all costs
2. **SHAME** – thinking I'm not good enough and depending on other people's opinions for my happiness
3. **COMFORT** – procrastination, perfectionism and wanting to play safe
4. **VICTIM** – feeling pity for myself and blaming other people

We also had our individual list of the top four values that were going to pull us towards our ultimate destiny. The emotional states that signified the type of life we really wanted to create. Here are mine:

1. **COURAGE** – getting out of my comfort zone
2. **AUTHENTIC** – listening to my heart and being true to myself
3. **LOVE** – opening my heart to possibility, living with passion, being kind to myself and others
4. **FUN** – being playful and engaged, upbeat and high energy

You'll notice my positive values are mostly the inversion of my negative ones.

It was now time to do some gardening.

Robbins explained that we needed to consciously plant the seeds we want in the gardens of our minds, and for it to work, we must do it with real emotional intensity. The same sort of intensity that causes a life moment to be embossed in our nervous system – fused into our memory banks.

We split up into groups of four. I remember it like it was yesterday...

'OK, guys – ready?'

The room was peppered with worker bee huddles – spread out into every corner in search of white space and a buffer from their neighbours calling out their lines. Groups were spilling out into the hallways, the emergency exits and bathroom corridors. It looked like the *Guinness Book of Records* for the most acting role plays in one room. Scripts in hand, flamboyant body language and passionate gestures.

Ivana, Nancy and I held Reno in our arms just after he finished – he was emotional and exhausted. He had given it everything. I was up next.

The pressure was mounting – it felt like match point. Everything had led to this moment: going broke, not knowing who I was anymore, unhappiness, heartbreaks, the people I'd met along the way, the seminars, the therapy, the books, and the will to find answers. I knew this was my best chance to finally close the loop on my journey – to find peace and feel good again.

'Come on, dude, you got this, Charley boy.'

Reno, Ivana and Nancy stood together opposite me with their arms interlocked, willing me on. It was like I was about to give the motivational speech to my team before the big match. Everything was primed, they were waiting for me to begin. I looked down at my script one last time and took a few seconds to psych myself up – this was my moment, the intensity was building, I was trying to focus among the piercing chaos, surrounded by drama.

'Come on, Charley, let's go, buddy.'

Something wasn't right. I wasn't ready. Tony said this had to be deeply emotional – I needed to feel the words in every synapse of my body, but I was more worried about remembering what to say.

I only had one shot – I couldn't screw it up. The time and opportunity was running away and I could sense the guys getting impatient.

'Sorry, guys – can you just give me a second?'

I turned away from them, crouched down onto my haunches and shut off the noise. This was it – I only had a few seconds. I ran through my script one last time, reciting the lines under my breath. I couldn't think the words out of my mouth – they had to flow so I could concentrate on what they meant and embody the emotions.

The pressure was mounting everywhere – everything conspiring to get me to pull rank, flinch, fire my arrow.

Still on my haunches, I began to conjure up the emotions inside of me. I felt like a method actor priming himself in the green room. I dug deep and grabbed hold of all the remnants of frustration, anger and sadness inside me.

I revved myself up, entertaining the thought of this not working, the consequences of losing the match point and having to endure more years of frustration.

My quads were beginning to numb.

My boyhood self glided back into the frame, his big dreams, his tender heart, his lone wolf crusade to feel whole, loved and at ease. I could feel the oxytocin being injected into my blood and compassion starting to dance with the dark and fill the back of my eyes. I needed to do this for him.

I was ready. I was primed.

'OK, guys – let's go.'

I stood up to face the team and like an explosion I ripped into the script...

'I, Charley Law, *see*, *hear* and *know*...'

The roar came from the depth of my soul.

'... that I will no longer indulge in the stupid, destructive, debilitating emotions of fear and shame...'

I tore into it and yelled using every fibre of myself as I confronted the words like an enemy who'd wronged me.

'... because the people pleasing, the insecurity, the not feeling good enough, the being afraid of what people think, all destroys the fire burning inside of me and ultimately it will cost me my happiness.'

I began to tremble as I lost my temper – ripping out those weeds. I was a man possessed. I saw looks of shock on the guys' faces but I carried on, unstoppable.

'Who I really am is a man of courage, authenticity and love – to be vulnerable, honest, brave and compassionate to myself and others.'

I slowed down now to make sure I absorbed each and every word and looked into their eyes with conviction and raw belief. Convincing them and convincing myself. There was no doubt – I was insisting my new truth. The bass in my voice momentarily broke into a high-pitched squeak as my vocal cords malfunctioned. They looked at me as if to say, *OK OK we believe you – take it easy!*

'All I really have to do is remember and know to dance with fear, dance in the rain, be bold and be myself, and my life will ultimately become abundant, passionate, exciting and full of love.'

I felt myself move into a quieter, more sacred inward-looking state as I reeled off my new commitments, and as my body spoke the words I felt passion, and love and joy begin to tingle through me.

I repeated it two more times and then moved on to the next incantation. It was taking everything out of me but I stayed focused.

'I, Charley Law, *see*, *hear* and *know*...'

I spoke now with less hatred and more compassion – like a tired long-suffering parent pleading with their child to just stop.

'... that I will no longer indulge in the stupid, destructive, debilitating emotions of victimhood, self-pity and comfort... The blame, the negative energy, the playing it safe, it destroys optimism, hope and positivity and it will cost me my happiness and joy.'

It was like I was speaking to my former self – persuading with confidence. I was stating facts now – the new rules.

'Who I really am is a man that takes responsibility and is fun and happy, and my life will ultimately be full of connection, success and positivity, and that's how I'm committed to living my life!'

I repeated this also another two times and then it was all over.

Silence.

The first thing I felt was relief and peace wash over me. Their faces were of shock, awe and delight. I knew I'd nailed it – they did too. It was too convincing to be anything but real. We fell into a group hug and in that moment, I knew that I'd reached a new milestone on my journey. I had crested a certain peak and there was no going back now.

DANCE LIKE NOBODY IS WATCHING

I'd landed back in London on my birthday. I hadn't slept and I'd lost my voice. I'd invited a bunch of friends to the pub in Notting Hill. Usually I'd be panicking – *what if not enough people come? Am I looking good enough?* But this time I knew how to be myself, relax, have some fun and welcome anyone that did come. I'd made the shift. That night I ended up going out with a handful of my pals and I really did dance like nobody was watching – I had the courage to do it, to be me and to just have some fun.

I felt like Charley again. I had well and truly understood how to feel free and it was damn liberating to be able to feel the fear (old fears and new ones) and do it anyway.

Two weeks later I was back at home sitting by the log fire where my mother and I had sat awkwardly watching Netflix before my trip. Now it was just a few days before Christmas and my brother Matthew was home and began quizzing me.

'So what did you *actually* do, Charley? Did it *really* help?'

I tried my best to do it justice, to give him the elevator pitch. But Matthew wasn't convinced.

'Sounds like a load of old mumbo jumbo if you ask me,' he said.

'Yup.'

'But, Charley, come on. All this stuff hasn't *really* paid off, has it?'

I knew what he was getting at. But he couldn't see what had changed inside of me.

I smiled to myself because I knew that if I could just keep feeding the new values I'd committed to, they would become automatic, habits, part of my personality and this would set me on a new trajectory.

I would meditate, journal and chant my new incantations every morning, reinforcing the new patterns. I had ripped out the weeds and planted new seeds, but needed to keep watering them to ensure they took root, sprouted, became something I could harvest. New incantations reinforced new changes.

And sure enough, after a few weeks, then months, I began to notice more change; being more thoughtful and less selfish, not needing so much admiration, having more fun – it all started to bed in, the stabilisers slowly came off, the old habits started to loosen their grip, and I was able to run on my new feet.

It was remarkable. Tony was right – he could create lasting change in a short space of time.

I thought back to that day at Goodwood Racecourse where I felt naked and not really sure how to be. I'd been looking for my new clothes and now I'd found them.

Now I'd found my new perspective, new values – I was a new person. The well-known Ryan Holiday quote rang true in my ears – *confidence is earned, ego is stolen.*

I had made change actually happen.

And although I couldn't find the words to explain to my brother that evening – I knew it was just a matter of time before things on the outside started to change too.

> The seeds you water grow.
> The seeds you neglect wither.
> Keep reinforcing the new patterns
> until they become automatic.

STEP 5 – RESPONSIBILITY IN ACTION

Are you still talking about what happened?

How it's their fault?

Thinking and talking about problems will etch them deeper into your mind.

Of course it's important to first try to *process, heal and let go* of as much as you can, and that bit can be slow, delicate and requires empathy. But unless you want to be stuck feeling sorry for yourself, hard done by or pitiful – then the only way is for you to take responsibility and move on.

Go back, have a look, make peace and then crack on.

Those nice sympathetic chats with your psychologist, your best friend, your partner or your mother about what happened can be really quite soothing but do that too long and it becomes unhealthy – you're pursuing the comfort of being soothed rather than the challenge of doing the work. I know it's not what you want to hear but you need to be mindful of what you're actually getting out of these chats. Instead seek truth, which you will often only get from someone who isn't really concerned with telling you what you don't necessarily want to hear.

Be willing to hear what you don't want to. Encourage those same friends, family, or colleagues to give you honest feedback about where they think you might be getting it wrong. It won't be easy for them either – we're naturally social and agreeable animals, we're wired to want to get along (for our ancestors it was a matter of life and death). For anyone to tell you what they *really* think to your face is uncomfortable for them too, so you need to be brave and coax it out of them.

Your ego will likely jump up and down – it will go APE! But now you are wise to the powerful Chimp Mind antics. You know how much your ego and pride love to cling onto your identity, and you begin to separate your *self* from those impulses.

Shun the ego. Don't soothe it.

Truth will set you free.

And what about those lingering emotions like bitterness, resentment, guilt or hurt you can't seem to shake off?

Responsibility in Action.

You might need to have a difficult conversation with a friend, your boss, or one of your parents to be able to move past an emotion within you.

- *Address past differences.*
- *Apologise for your part.*
- *Tell them how it made you feel.*
- *Explain what you will not tolerate in the future.*

Communicate with compassion. They may never understand. But you'll be amazed what it will do for you. Hard conversations are one of the most powerful ways to change how you feel quickly.

Remember that life starts at the edge of your comfort zone.

If you're interested in other techniques that can shift your mindset and emotional state quickly, you might explore approaches such as Neurolinguistic Programming (NLP), hypnotherapy, or Gestalt therapy. In some jurisdictions, assisted therapy with substances like MDMA, ayahuasca, or psilocybin has also been studied for its potential to support healing from anxiety, depression, addiction and PTSD – but only where this can be done legally, safely and under the supervision of qualified health professionals.

All these methods are designed to influence your subconscious and change your habits quickly. Breakthroughs are real.

And don't forget the mother of all insights.

If there's something about you that's getting in the way...

You *can* change your personality.

You *can* change the meaning you gave to things that happened.

You *can* change what you (mis)interpreted.

If *you* created old beliefs then, you *can* create new beliefs today.

The power lies within you, my friend.

Once you've ripped out the old weeds and planted the new seeds into your subconscious, you just need to keep watering them. You need to keep reinforcing the new values, emotional states and mindset you've committed to until those roots take hold. It gets a lot easier then.

Remember that you are what you repeatedly think, feel, say and do.

The name of the game is: *being intentional.*

- *Be intentional* about what you think about.
- *Be intentional* about who you spend time with.
- *Be intentional* about what you meditate or journal about.
- *Be intentional* about how you conduct yourself.

You might need to make brave life choices about work, relationships, your environment and lifestyle.

Be intentional.

Be brave.

Have the courage to take a stand and be disliked.

When trying to change and move forward you must adopt a two-pronged attack:

1. **Immediate Action Commitments**
   Doing uncomfortable stuff in life you've been putting off.

2. **Mindset Exercises**
   Internally reinforcing new ways of being *(meditation, journaling, affirmations)*.

You can't only think your way to a better life. It requires action. Work on the internal and the external together – they complement each other, and you will move faster. This is seldom spoken about.

Caution #1

Double-check you're not trying to get back to being how you used to be by being how you used to be (like I was).

Maybe there's a reason why the old way was the wrong way, and you need to find a new way.

Are you trying to get back on track by being more significant and certain again?

If you want to feel happy, energised, light, fulfilled and complete then maybe you need to walk a new path. Could connection and uncertainty be your new gateway to feeling how you want to feel?

Caution #2

It's one thing sitting in a cosy room with a therapist riffing about how your issues might be connected to your upbringing, but it's another thing altogether talking to your parents about it. These sorts of conversations can be extremely delicate and can go wrong if not managed correctly.

Try to avoid harsh-sounding, one-size-fits-all psychological words like *pain*, *suffering*, *trauma*, *abandonment* and *abuse*. They might technically describe what happened, but instead think of less antagonising words like *difficult*, *lonely*, *controlling* or *in shock*.

Words matter.

Timing is important too. Try to wait until you have made sufficient progress, have understood things fully and are emotionally mature enough to communicate with grace. Jumping the gun and confronting loved ones can be damaging.

Caution #3

Beware of no man's land.

It can be one of the hardest things to do all this work, be brave and make giant leaps only to be left slightly on your own. You've moved away from your old world, but you haven't arrived at your new world yet.

Whatever you do, don't let the inertia pull you back to your old ways of being.

Resist at all costs. Choose wisely who you spend time with.

It can pay to temporarily limit time spent with people you love but who have influenced your old ways of thinking. Wait until the seeds of change have bedded in and your external world has gained momentum and traction. Then you are less susceptible to their influences, and you will be able to stand stronger in your new clothes.

Gratitude. That's the antidote to the never enough, always wanting more.

Being present. That's the antidote to worry, stress and anxiety.

Forgiveness. That's the antidote to anger, resentment and bitterness.

Self-love. That's the antidote to insecurity and needing to matter.

Humility. That's the antidote to grandiosity and ego.

Positive thought. That's the antidote to magnified negativity.

STEP 6
CLARITY

> 'There is one quality which one must possess to win, and that is definiteness of purpose, the knowledge of what one wants, and a burning desire to possess it.'
>
> NAPOLEON HILL, *THINK AND GROW RICH*

PIGS IN BLANKETS

'Can I top you up, Father Christopher?'

'Thank you so much, Charley – doesn't the house always look so wonderful this time of year. So, tell me, what are you up to at the moment?'

The family Christmas drinks party. My mother doing her bit.

I'd previously imagined myself spending Christmas in Cartagena, Colombia. Maybe slipping on my black silk shirt, a dust of Dunhill aftershave and a tingle of excitement before an evening of salsa, sangria and señoritas.

Instead, I found myself having small talk with the local vicar; magnum of Charlemagne Fizz from the cash and carry in one hand and a tray of pigs in blankets made by Mrs Ligget in the other.

The Colombia business didn't work out.

After eighteen months of work – the research, the partner, the pipeline of deals, the investment deck – the first deal fell through on terms I couldn't accept. We could have pushed on to the second opportunity, but my gut told me to walk away.

So I did.

But that was okay.

I was learning to see these ventures differently now. Not as 'failures' but as data points. Each one teaching me something, narrowing the field, getting me closer to my actual sweet spot.

The old me would have forced it. Taken more risk. Proven I could make it happen. The new me trusted my instincts.

But now I was back at square one. No job. No business. No clear path forward.

And yet – I wasn't panicking. I'd built something more valuable than a business plan: I'd built the internal architecture to navigate uncertainty. The pressure was there, but so was the trust that I'd figure it out.

The Tudor farmhouse did really come alive at Christmas: the wood panelling, the open fires, festive cards scattered among family photos and ornaments, the subtle holly tacked around the picture frames and along the beams.

I shuffled on into the sitting room trying to navigate my way to a safe haven.

'Charley!'

Oh gosh, who is it now?

I turned around – ah, phew, it was George. His daughter Olivia rents the barn on our farm to run her livery business from, and she hired my sister Nina to work for her part time. They are a lovely family.

I knew George was an executive coach. He stood there smiling at me with his kind face. Late fifties, grey, smart tweed jacket and tie. He was always still and curious – none of that bravado malarkey. One of my favourite sayings is *empty vessels make lots of noise* – probably because this used to be me, but George was quite the opposite. He was quiet, unassuming and full of wisdom.

'How's the new business going, Charley?'

'As a matter of fact, George, it's no longer.'

'Oh really?' He looked surprised.

'Yes, it's a shame... We had everything set up, I had a great Colombian business partner, some ideal target acquisitions, committed capital from investors to do the first deal, but the title holder for the land just wouldn't agree to enough of our terms so we couldn't go ahead with the transaction – we were gutted, after all that work. We looked at the second deal in our pipeline but that was a full buyout, double the capital and a lot more risk. And you know what, George, all that momentum stopped, and it made me take a long hard look at what we were doing.'

He nodded sympathetically.

'I was like, are we a private equity company or an operating company? Was I really going to live in Colombia? I sensed more of the risk too; I was reticent to put the little money I had left into this deal and so I wasn't prepared to put investors' money in either. So, you know what?

I decided to walk away from the whole thing, George. It wasn't easy! Eighteen months of graft, but my gut told me it was too risky. And guess what, a month or so later there was a landslide and that second mine got cut off from the local market and we'd have gone bust.'

'Wow, Charley, sounds like you dodged a bullet there. Good on you, though, it's not easy to walk away from something like that, but you failed fast and I bet the investors were grateful.'

'They were. And it actually felt quite empowering to make that call and not worry what people were going to think. The whole thing gave me a lot of confidence – and now I'm like, shit, if I could do that then I could do pretty much anything.'

'So what's next?'

'That's a good question! I think I'm done with mining and commodities. Too many complicated countries, too much risk, hard to build your own business. Other than that, I'm not sure – maybe I need to come and speak to you!'

'Very happy to help if you need, Charley. And the book? How's that going?'

'Making good progress, thanks… You know, step by step.'

'Well, if you ever need another pair of eyes.'

'Thanks, George – I will.'

We moved on.

'I have a question – where do you draw the line between therapy and coaching, George? You must get drawn into psychology with a lot of your corporate clients, you can't have one without the other, can you?'

'Interesting. Well, I'm not a psychologist – us coaches tend to look forward and therapists tend to look back – but you're right, it can get a bit muddied.'

I had Sabine in my mind and knew what a game changer the therapy had been; connecting the dots, understanding how my mind worked. I couldn't imagine having coaching, chatting about the future, mindset, strategy, goals without having laid the groundwork first.

'Isn't it crazy to think how many of us are chasing after something, getting coached even on how to obtain something, when that thing after all, might not be what we really need or want deep down?'

'Go on,' George nudged, dipping his head to look over the top of his specs with a knowing grin.

'You know... it might just be what our parents want for us or what we think will impress our mates, or what we've always been told we should do. Does that make sense? There must be so many people out there chasing after things before they've got really clear about what it is *they* really want. Look at me, I'd be trying to figure everything out through the lens of Carlos Ley, my alter ego – a recipe for disaster!

'What's that American coach called? You know, "The Ultimate Coach", the one that charges $200k and you have to fly to Arizona to see him in person. Hardison, that's it, Steve Hardison. I read his book and remember him saying something like, creating goals and affirmations without first examining your underlying beliefs is like "putting frosting on dog poop"!'

He gave me a look of acknowledgement – as if I knew what I was talking about.

'You're spot on, Charley. And for folks to spend a bit of time really getting clear on their own priorities, their own dreams, desires – as you say, what *they* really want, it can be transformational. What aligns with them, their natural abilities, their interests and what energises them, rather than carrying on with situations they might have just ended up in quite randomly. It's powerful, to design a life congruent with who you are and living that life on your own terms... Well, Charley, if you ever want any help then just shout.'

We exchanged a few book recommendations and bid each other farewell.

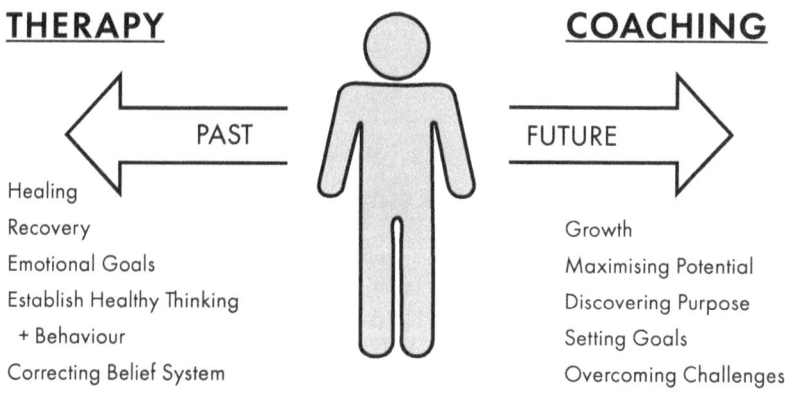

THE MICHELIN MAN

Fast forward a few weeks, and fate stepped into my life in the form of the Michelin Man.

It's a bitterly cold, frosty morning. I'm standing on the station platform – visiting a mate for the weekend – waiting for the 7:48 a.m. train back to London.

I walked into the warm air of the carriage and found a free four-seater immediately on the right and sat down next to the window. Ahh – fifty minutes of quiet. I reached for my ear pods to crack on with *Attached* by Amir Levine and Rachel SF Heller on Audible. Relationships decoded, I was deep into it. The book distilled all relationships into these three 'attachment types': secure, anxious and avoidant.

'Basically, *secure* people feel comfortable with intimacy and are usually warm and loving; *anxious* people crave intimacy, are often preoccupied with their relationships, and tend to worry about their partner's ability to love them back; *avoidant* people equate intimacy with loss of independence and constantly try to minimise closeness.'

The book piqued my attention from page one. There was no denying it, I was a combo between *anxious* and *avoidant*. A classic, apparently!

My myriad of past failures all started to make sense. The irony of me panicking about whether they were going to text me back, versus me wanting to back off as soon as anyone was remotely keen.

'Remember, an activated attachment system is not passionate love. Next time you date someone and find yourself feeling anxious, insecure, and obsessive, only to feel elated every once in a while, tell yourself this is most likely an activated attachment system and not love!'

I thought back to all those love addictions that caused me so much misery.

Attached! Where had you been all my life?!

'True love, in the evolutionary sense, means peace of mind. "Still waters run deep" is a good way of characterising it.'

That line really struck a chord with me. 'Still waters run deep.'

I'd been operating in the shallow choppy waters of insecurity, anxiety and lust, thinking it was chemistry.

The book was packed full of great actionable advice about dating.

Why someone who was anxious shouldn't date someone with an avoidant personality, but should date someone who is secure. This was where I had been going wrong. If I got a message from a woman it made me feel happy and calm. But if she didn't reply, perhaps for several days, I became a nervous wreck. I was never able to relax into a relationship. It was exhausting for me, so I can only imagine what it would be like for someone I was holding to those kinds of standards.

Now I knew that, I had a better idea of what to look out for.

The hiss of the hydraulic airlock caught my attention and I looked up. Who would have believed it, but there was George, looking like the Michelin Man with a pair of rosy cheeks and a wet nose drop barely clinging on.

Bugger, I'm now going to have to chat to him again all the way up to London.

'George!' I faked the enthusiasm. 'Have a seat.'

'Hello, Charley. Are you sure? I don't want to disturb.'

'Of course – here, I'll move my bag.'

The inconvenience quickly dissolved, and we immersed into a deep conversation. It was one of those moments where the minutes disappeared into a time warp.

He listened intently to what I had to say, and that encouraged me to keep talking. I could tell he was quietly observing my entire demeanour – like any good coach would. From how shallow I was breathing, to my eye contact, to my mannerisms, to the story I was telling myself.

'George, I feel like I'm starting to run out of time. I'm 36 and feel like I'm falling behind. I'm done with the mining and commodities, but I just can't make up my mind what to do next. Or where I should even be living.'

'Charley, do you know what the three most important questions one needs to answer in life are?'

I shrugged.

'It's very simple. The three most important questions one needs to answer in life are: What to do. Where to live. Who to be with.

'All three sorted feels great. Just two, depending on who you are, can feel unsettling. But not knowing what to do, where to live or who to be with, or worse, not having a job, one's own place and being alone… well, that's enough to make anyone have a wobble.'

The train shot through a tunnel and shuddered a little from side to side in the dark. When the sunlight re-entered the carriage, George was still observing me with the same neutral, kind, searching demeanour as when we went in. The guy seemed so at ease. I felt like I had to fill the silence…

'That makes a lot of sense, but my problem is I can't decide what to do. I've got these high standards, I'm ambitious, believe in myself – I want to live my best life.'

Battersea Power Station appeared out the window after what seemed like five minutes. We could have carried on and on.

I was trying to figure out what to do with my life – George did this for a living. He signed me up for some coaching there and then and I couldn't wait to get started.

PANNING FOR GOLD

Knock knock... George pitched up at my apartment – he was immediately distracted by the walls littered with flow charts, goals, vision boards and inspirational quotes. He pulled up a chair. I was sceptical at first. What else could he teach me? I'd read all the books, listened to all the podcasts. He was a self-awareness coach. I was becoming an expert on self-awareness myself. But I needed to cover all the bases.

I'd signed up to three two-hour sessions spread over three weeks. I wanted to do it faster, but he said we needed big enough gaps to digest, think and let my subconscious do its stuff – he was right.

'Today, Charley, we're going to do a timeline of your life.'

Really?

I tried to push back a bit – show with my body language I didn't think much of the idea. I'd spent the last year or so with Sabine delving into my past – I'd dissected it to the nth degree. But George wasn't interested how my childhood influenced me psychologically, he just wanted to pick up clues for what turned me on so we could plan my future.

Panning for gold through the rivers of our past.

I didn't realise that this would turn out to be one of THE most useful exercises.

Just thinking about it isn't enough – having a coach there, talking out loud and writing it down – it throws things up, the process. I documented the highs and lows of the past thirty-six years. We assessed the peaks and troughs. Why so great? Why a disaster? Why so happy? Why frustrated? Why so motivated? Why so energised? We began to plot some common themes that brought the best out in me. The comradery, the competitiveness, the countryside, the space, the travel, the growth.

Then he pushed me more, he went deeper. Was I leading or following? Was there structure or freedom?

We triangulated and flex tested what we threw up and ended up with nine words that described my ideal environment:

- Adventure.
- High-performance.
- Growth.
- International.
- Entrepreneurship.
- Movement.
- Recognition.
- Responsibility.
- Leadership.

I didn't know it at the time, but these golden nuggets would turn out to be vital in paving the way for my future.

THE ALGO

'Take your time, Charley, it may sound obvious but what you put in you get out. Really try to answer the questions honestly – the type of person you are, not who you would like to be. Hope that makes sense.'

George's instructions did make sense. I completed reams of multiple-choice questions and I couldn't wait to see what the results would say about *me*, not Carlos Ley.

What was my personality type? What would the algorithm say about me? Would it give me more answers?

But forty-eight hours later, my inbox was still empty.

I was in the gym with my sister – she was visiting.

'That's it, Nina... just three more minutes to go. Keep pumping those legs!'

'I am, Charley, stop being bossy.'

Nina and I are side by side on the spin bikes.

Not a drop of sweat despite the thick red Mickey Mouse hoodie.

'Come on, Nina, you won't get that ten-pound note if you don't keep pushing until the end... Five minutes to go... Come on, keep pushing... That's it!'

'I know, I know, Charley, leave me alone.'

She dipped her head and leaned forward out the saddle to give it a bit more oomph.

I flicked away Spotify and refreshed my email inbox.

Ping!

'George Lepine. Psychometric results and feedback'

At last.

I scrolled down to the attachments and began scrambling through the information.

'Come on, Charley... You've stopped peddling! Don't be a lazy bones now, haha.' She burst out laughing...

'All right, Nina. OK, look I'm peddling... Give me a sec, something important has just come in.'

'Oooh, important, hey?'

'Yes, it's my personality test. Sshh, just give me a sec.'

'Don't have much of a personality, do you? HAHAHA,' she roared.

'All right, all right – how come you're so full of beans today?'

All right here we go... 'The Type Dynamics Indicator Test (TDI)':

I was 'The Guide' – innovating, generating ideas, deeply intuitive, harmonizing, building rapport.

The Hogan Development Survey revealed my dark side: Excitable (enthusiastic but hard to please and gives up easily). Sceptical (hard to fool but cynical and suspicious). Leisurely (appearing friendly but quietly resistant. Saying 'yes' but meaning 'no').

Ouch. Busted. The algorithm had me figured out.

A Richard Feynman quote popped into my head: 'The first principle is that you must not fool yourself – and you are the easiest person to fool.'

These truths were exactly what I needed to hear. Another piece to the puzzle.

A FRAMEWORK OF PATIENCE

'How are you getting on with George?'

My mother was checking in, curious to know if I'd finally figured out what to do next.

I guess some people can just go and get any job. But I'd realised I wasn't wired that way. I needed my work to align with something – to feel purposeful, to energise me, to make sense with where I was heading. Otherwise, I was just going through the motions. Dead man walking.

I'd met Simon Sinek, author of *Find Your Why*, at an event in New York – the guy that became famous after his TED Talk, *How great leaders inspire action*, went viral. His golden circle diagram essentially illustrated the simple but powerful idea:

'People don't buy <u>what</u> you do, they buy <u>why</u> you do it.'

I remembered Simon saying in his Q&A, when trying to figure out what to do or what we're good at, to always ask close friends and family what they really think about us – invite them to be totally truthful.

'It's amazing what you can learn,' he said, 'what they can see but we can't.'

Cue my mother.

'That's easy, Charley – you're very persuasive. You could sell coals to Newcastle.'

Another piece to the puzzle.

The pressure was mounting, that feeling of panic was starting to creep in – I needed to decide. Analysis paralysis was real – I could see it, but at the same time I wanted to get it right.

Tomorrow would be my last session with George. I sat down at my desk to make some notes.

A3 paper, highlighters, black markers, George's notes, my personality test results, Napoleon Hill's *Think and Grow Rich* and Naval Ravikant's famous Tweet Storm: *How to get rich (without getting lucky)*, two of my favourite wealth creation resources.

This was the rest of my life – I wanted to commit to the right thing and focus on that for the next few decades.

Think and Grow Rich is the godfather of all the self-development books – everyone else's work seemed to stem from this original classic. Andrew Carnegie, the steel and railroad tycoon of the nineteenth century, one of the richest Americans in history, commissioned Napoleon Hill to study the secrets of how the wealthiest people in the world made their fortunes. It took him twenty years and his findings were consolidated into these *Thirteen Steps to Riches*. It sounds corny, but the book has stood the test of time, with enduring wealth creation wisdom from the likes of Henry Ford, John D. Rockefeller and Charles M. Schwab.

What I loved about it was the blueprint, like a mentor telling you – just do this, follow these steps. Naturally I think a lot of us are aware of some of these principles for success; focus – consistency – sacrifice – discipline, but seeing these critical ingredients inked onto the pages, bold and systematically, made it feel definitive.

Not, dabble and see what happens.

Do this and you *will* be successful.

It made me believe the juice would be worth the squeeze.

Hill's trademark writing style was persuasive and inspiring – each chapter another call to arms littered with CAPS trying to hit home the key points. The BURNING DESIRE, the DEFINITE PURPOSE, the BELIEF, the SPECIALISED KNOWLEDGE, the ORGANISED PLAN, the MASTERMINDS, the PERSISTENCE and and and.

But *The Seventh Step to Riches* was playing on my mind: DECISION. 'CAREFUL ANALYSIS of thousands of men and women who had experienced failure revealed that LACK OF DECISION was near the head of the list of the Thirty Major Causes of Failure. This is no mere statement of a theory – *it is fact.*'

I got it – I had the blueprint; I knew what I needed to do but how could I make the DECISION without first getting clear on – *what – to – do*? I couldn't create a BURNING DESIRE around just anything. I was going around in circles.

Maybe my friend Naval Ravikant's more contemporary, viral Twitter storm might help me shed some light. *How to get rich (without getting lucky)*.

Thirty-nine bite-size bits of brilliance. Modern wealth creation wisdom. But it was more than that, there was far more overlap between self-help and wealth-building than I ever appreciated. You could even use wealth as a metaphor for anything you want in life. To get it you need to be mindful enough to be clear about your ambitions, understand your underlying motivations, spot opportunities wherever they present themselves, and reframe your thinking if necessary to be able to take advantage of them. And knowing yourself is the first and most important tool.

Here are a few of my favourite lines from Naval's famous tweet storm:

1. Seek wealth, not money or status. Wealth is having assets that earn while you sleep. Money is how we transfer time and wealth. Status is your place in the social hierarchy.
2. Ignore people playing status games. They gain status by attacking people playing wealth creation games.
3. You will get rich by giving society what it wants but does not yet know how to get. At scale.
4. Pick an industry where you can play long-term games with long-term people.
5. Play iterated games. All the returns in life, whether in wealth, relationships or knowledge, come from compound interest.
6. Pick business partners with high intelligence, energy, and, above all, integrity.
7. Learn to sell. Learn to build. If you can do both, you will be unstoppable.
8. Arm yourself with specific knowledge, accountability and leverage.
9. Specific knowledge is found by pursuing your genuine curiosity and passion rather than whatever is hot right now.
10. Building specific knowledge will feel like play to you but will look like work to others.

I tried to figure out which of my options ticked the most boxes.

Was it the book? Writing feels like play.

Was it coaching? I could just focus on this, do it forever and become great at it.

Was it going into tech sales? That industry wasn't going away – I could definitely play long-term games.

Was it venture capital? That also felt like play, and I'd build wealth by having equity in many companies.

Was it joining a climate tech start-up? I'd be following my genuine curiosity.

The truth was – I couldn't decide. More analysis paralysis. I was getting caught up being too idealistic. (My personality test had warned me about that.)

I took another look at my overdrawn bank balance, reminded myself I was 36, and felt a toxic shot of panic-infused adrenalin seep into my blood. Flustered and frustrated, I took my phone to bed and began to escape into mindless Instagram reels – doomscrolling through the endless content, dazzling my dopamine receptors. But I had no idea that the fast-talking New Yorker, one of my digital mentors, Gary V, was about to come to my rescue.

A moment caught my attention…

This graduate kid, Ryan, was on the pavement leaning down, peering through the car window where Gary was sitting in the back seat. He was asking advice on how to prioritise what he was doing with his job vs his side hustle.

Gary answered the kid instinctively – he knew exactly what he needed to do. I felt like he was talking to me – like I was the young kid getting worked up about how to figure it all out right now.

'By building a framework of patience.'

What? I hadn't heard that one before. 'Have patience and execute' I thought was the motto. This was new.

'Like if you think you need it tomorrow – you're gonna burn out. And you're gonna put too much pressure on yourself. Once you have a framework of patience then you can pull it off. And I think where everyone gets caught up – everyone wants it so fast that it fucks them up – does that make sense?'

Shit, he was totally right. My situation was creating panic, not patience.

'Take some of the pressure away, that will really help you, Ryan – like it really will... because then it's not about being frantic and manic, you're NOT beating yourself up on one night where you're just gonna fuckin play *Fortnight* and drink a beer, because you're thinking in fifty-year terms not in fifty-day terms.'

Create a framework of patience. It just made so much sense. Where to live, what to do and who to be with. I was never going to figure it all out like this – stressed and under pressure.

Now I knew what I had to do – *huh*, my conversation with George in the morning was easy.

- Get a job, a nine-to-five, anything.
- Write my book mornings and evenings.
- Create a framework of patience.

- Figure things out from there.

Generally, I was starting to make better decisions in life. It went back to Naval's adage 'life's not about conditions it's about decisions.' The work was starting to pay off and I was responding to life situations better.

More at ease, less insecure, not needing to prove so much, thinking more long term. Clive Woodward, the England Rugby World Cup-winning coach, is known for his mantra of needing 'to build a score' in test rugby. I'd been the one in life chancing my luck kicking for the corner – hoping I'd win the line out and score a try. High stakes, wanting to impress, taking the shortcut. But now I was thinking differently. I was happier within myself – and that meant that it was easier to go slower, be patient and make better long-term choices.

Easy Choices = Hard Life

Hard Choices = Easy Life

I was less affected now by the external, I could see a lot of it for what it was.

As the famous quote from the cult classic movie and novel *Fight Club* by Chuck Palahniuk goes: 'We buy things we don't need, with money we don't have, to impress people we don't like.'

On paper, taking a nine-to-five felt like I was going backwards, but although I didn't realise it at the time, these sorts of decisions were paving the way for ultimate fulfilment and for me to create my dream life – on my own terms.

A RED-LETTER DAY

She lay on my bed, her hands trembling as she raced through the pages. I stood in the doorway, helpless and exposed. *How was she going to react?*

Months earlier I'd invited my South African friend Nicole down from London to my new apartment in Sussex. The same Nicole who gave me that nudge to explore therapy, the inner workings of my mind, and launchpad to becoming a better version of myself.

I'd got myself a job working at a well-known sporting estate, selling sponsorship for their international events.

'Hello!' she said, climbing out of her Mini Cooper.

She looked like a pro tennis player who had slipped on a summery red dress. Athletic, bronzed, long toned legs glistening in the June sun, delicate gold jewellery kissing her skin, barely any make-up – she was a picture of radiance and confidence. She was secure in her own skin. It was damn attractive. I grabbed her bag in the car park, and we headed to my apartment. I was excited, I'd missed our frequent meetups – she brought some London colour, edge and energy down to the green countryside.

'Charley, you guys are great together! She's amazing!'

I probably heard it three or four times that weekend, a few local friends dipping in and out of our flow – they knew I had a 'lady friend' down from town, eager to know what was going on.

'Ah, Nicole and I are just friends; we've known each other for years – but yes she's awesome, isn't she.'

'Thanks so much for coming, see you soon!' I hollered to her as she drove off, tyres scrunching the gravel. We'd had the best weekend, I knew she liked me, I liked her too, but it didn't take long for my old ways to kick into gear. Avoidant. Afraid of commitment. Wanting to keep my options open. I didn't speak to Nicole for weeks; I was well versed in back-pedalling into the friend zone. Well versed in sweeping the guilt of raising her expectations under the carpet.

—

Chicken Kievs, potato waffles and peas – I was reaching for my bachelor's dinner out of the microwave when I heard the familiar message alert on my phone – *ping!*

A mini hit of dopamine. Maybe it was one of the girls on Hinge I'd sent messages to.

I couldn't have been more wrong.

The message stopped me in my tracks.

It was about to change everything.

It was from Nicole.

'Hey. How are you? Just wanted to say it is obvious that we have something, Charley. I've felt frustrated that after such a nice time together at yours, we haven't made plans to see each other again and to maybe just allow something very casual to happen ... because why not? I hope you aren't allowing yourself to be too protective of your heart, Charley. You are a gem. Take me out of the picture; please promise me that you aren't searching for something too prescribed or perfect. It feels like that at times if I am honest. Don't always fight this world alone. Time flies by so fast and I just think that you could be sharing more of your life with someone close to you.'

I choked up. She knew me better than anyone. But I knew myself by now and I knew she was right – I was missing out on life.

Previously I was drawn to a relationship type which kept me guessing, I never knew where I stood, which meant I overanalysed and felt I always needed to chase. But Nicole was different. Her self-assurance and inner security meant I knew where I stood. And that left space for my avoidant tendencies to surface – the side of me that wanted to stay in control. But I knew my tendencies now. I knew I was being a perfectionist and avoidant. And I knew I needed to take a chance.

And so thats when I decided – right, I'm going to let go, open my heart, and give this a try.

And that's exactly what I did.

Nicole and I spent more time together and I gave myself permission to just experience and explore. I was able to create space away from worry or consequence. My avoidant, anxious tendencies contrasted with her secure and mature nature. I let go more and more and trusted more and more... and then there was more laughter, more passion, more intimacy and before long a deep sense of wholeness crept in, like she was part of me, and I was part of her. We'd fallen in love.

I remembered that phrase I loved in the book *Attached*: 'Still waters run deep.'

It was true. And the only reason this happened was because I'd done the work. I was self-aware. I could catch my self-sabotaging tendencies and chose a new way that changed my life. This wasn't mumbo jumbo – it was tangible life changing stuff.

It wasn't until a few months later though that the real significance of it all actually hit. We were lying in bed chatting and I remembered the letter I wrote on Relationship Day with Tony Robbins – *To my future girlfriend...*

Leaping out of bed I went to fetch it, tingling with excitement.

'You're not going to believe this, Nicole.'

She looked confused as I passed her the envelope without even thinking.

'Here, this is for you.'

I stood in the doorway as she sat on my bed and opened the envelope inquisitively – her light-hearted energy quickly turning to something more intense and focused.

Shit – hang on, what had I written?

It was over a year ago – she might be offended – what if I was describing someone else? I tried to recall what I'd written as she flipped over the first page.

Shit – this could backfire massively.

> To my future girlfriend...
>
> You're going to think I'm crazy...
>
> I put my faith in people I respect and Tony told me to write you a letter because what you focus your attention on in life you get – so here goes!
>
> Honestly you are everything that I have been searching for and I'm glad that every single past mistiming, rejection, my ability to be totally avoidant, whatever – has all meant that I was available to meet you, I'm glad I was so stubborn and didn't settle for less.
>
> I mean let's start with how smoking hot you are – not that I'm superficial haha – you have the most amazing body, legs, long legs – you are so natural – your face, complexion and eyes are so youthful and vibrant – full of energy and fire and kindness.
>
> You make me feel like I can be completely myself; I'm so proud to have you by my side and I never want to stop sitting next to you...

The room was silent. I didn't know what to do with my hands. I had to wait for her to absorb the words and give me her verdict. I was petrified she would turn around and say – *you prick, go find some other girl that matches your messed-up perfect criteria.*

But she didn't. She kept reading – captivated.

I mean some of your friends are quite annoying, but we can't have it all! Plus, we're going to have to teach you to ride properly.

It's exciting to find someone who really wants to build a life full to the brim with adventure, compassion, deep relationships and always exploring and growing.

You inspire me to be better and keep striving.

I know my life will never be the same as I have found you.

All my love,
Charley x

By now I was sitting next to her on the bed; she flipped over the final page to check there was nothing on the back. She turned to me and paused – she held the moment like it had been choreographed for the movies... her eyes glistening with emotion.

'It's me, it's completely me. But how?'

She was totally overwhelmed, I was too; she couldn't believe it. We read through it again together and it was a perfect match.

You couldn't make it up.

I knew in that moment my life would never be the same.

As cheesy as it sounds, I'd trusted the process, I knew that it had all been worth it – I had found the girl of my dreams.

All because of three things... I'd identified the tendencies that were holding me back, the framework of patience I'd created, and learning to embrace uncertainty.

If I hadn't made these shifts I would never have started seriously dating Nicole. I would have been too stressed, and my mind would have been too busy to properly connect with her. I wouldn't have given it a go because I wasn't 100 per cent sure how it would turn out.

Know your tendencies.

Framework of patience.

Embrace uncertainty.

Theory was turning into reality.

Your mindset is like a lens into your reality.
It is framing your world and how you interpret things.
Change your lens, change your interpretation
of what is happening to you.

THE SPRINGBOKS

'Goodbye – enjoy Cape Town.' The air stewardess smiled as we disembarked into the sunshine.

The humidity hit me as I stepped out into the tunnel – I breathed it into my lungs and soaked it all up. Ahh, South Africa – it was good to be back. I hung back to let a few people past; Nicole was stuck behind. Then I remembered, *shit*, I'm about to meet the parents.

Before I knew it, we were all piled into their Lexus saloon cruising towards Stellenbosch. Nicole and her mother were chatting like excited school kids in the back. Her father Kevin and I sat up front in silence.

It was a strangely empowering feeling. Nicole had told me so much about her father. His sensitivity, being an entrepreneur, his work ethic, the early mornings, his keenness for learning and reading, and how much he loved his daughters. I knew we were going to get on, but I didn't feel the need to talk or prove – I felt calm, secure and excited to just let things unfold.

A few days later Nicole and I made the four-hour journey along the coast and arrived at the enchanting beachside resort of Infanta. A posse of families came here for the long summers – it was their little secret, rich with memories.

We were here for Kyle and Kate's wedding, great friends of Nicole. I was the plus-one boyfriend – we've all been there.

The Friday night dinner – always steals the show. We rocked up at this bar-cum-den-cum-magical mystery tour oasis. Off a dirt track, tumble weed, in the middle of nowhere. Think Burning Man meets Bali beach shack.

I felt a bit self-conscious. *Ah, that's Nicole's new boyfriend*, I could feel them all thinking.

The guests were all glammed up in their 'Infanta Flare' costumes – I missed the memo and was just wearing a suede jacket and jeans.

But just like with Kevin in the car – I didn't feel the need to compensate and fill the space with bravado like Carlos Ley would have done. I just watched that mild anxiety come and go and then eased into being more comfortable and in the end, it turned into a magical evening.

'Bru – you're all right you know.' One of the okes slung me another shot.

'Nicole, this one's a keeper!'

I always used to rate any encounter with – *did they like me?*

Dr Carol S. Dweck talks about this in her bestseller *Mindset*. 'Every comment, every look was meaningful – it registered on my intelligence scorecard, my attractiveness scorecard, my likeability scorecard. If a day went well, I could bask in high numbers.'

That used to be me – always measuring myself against external validation.

If we're fixed on our identity – and our daily scorecard can't validate that identity anymore – our self-worth and self-esteem hits a low and we feel like shit, depressed even.

Identity + Scorecard = Self-Worth

> '...lurking behind that self-esteem of the
> fixed mindset is a simple question:
> If you're *somebody* when you're successful,
> what are you when you're unsuccessful?'
>
> CAROL DWECK

Dweck introduced me to this idea of a *fixed mindset* vs a *growth mindset*.

Fixed = Believing our abilities are fixed and cannot be changed.

Avoiding challenges, criticism, failure and giving up easily.

Growth = Believing our abilities can be developed through effort and learning.

Embracing challenges and criticism as opportunities to learn and grow.

Not 'I'm a failure', just 'I failed'. Small difference, big impact.

Fixed Mindset = Fixed Identity

But by now I knew I was on the right track. I knew I'd started to develop a growth mindset.

I was embracing Charley 2.0. I wasn't fixed on the past, needing to be how certain people expected me to be – I'd let go of that and was confident enough to be myself.

I could see first-hand how I could create whatever I wanted. I felt liberated and at ease – I'd found my new clothes, but I knew they could still change also.

'Kevin, are you guys up for watching another episode?'

Hungover and tired after the four-hour drive back to Stellenbosch, all we wanted was to crash on the sofa.

We were deep into *Chasing The Sun* docu-series about the South African Springboks run-up to the Rugby World Cup in Japan and how they managed to turn their fate around. The four of us lounged around the TV gripped by Rassie Erasmus, the head coach, delivering yet another awe-inspiring speech.

'Don't smile at them. Please don't smile at them. Siya, when you go and toss [the coin] – let him get the idea I'm here to fuck you up.'

His words were ruthless and bloodthirsty, his calm, business-like delivery gave it extra venom.

Flashback to Yokohama. The Rugby World Cup Final. Sixty-five minutes in. England trailing South Africa 12–18. The tension was electric.

From a scrum just past halfway, all eyes on Faf de Klerk's drenched long blonde locks as he whips the ball left to Am, who zips it wide to Mapimpi. Suddenly, space opens up. He breaks through, chips ahead and Am tears after it. A perfect bounce, a slick offload and Mapimpi scores. Poetry in motion. The music swells. His face lights up. The commentator erupts...

'It's a beautiful thing.'

'The bottles are popping.'

'Champagne.'

'Shampompo!'

'Shampizi!'

'There are bubbles flowing everywhere.'

Images of crowds around the stadium, across South Africa, Rassie in the box – it was euphoria, a nation lit up. The hairs stood up on the back of my neck, Nicole's father's eyes glistened with tears. It was the first try South Africa had ever scored in a Rugby World Cup Final.

It was magical, and in that moment – it all made sense.

Everything we'd seen in this team and the way Rassie coached them to victory over the four years was all the same ideas and principles that I'd been learning on my own journey towards change. The psychology, the philosophies, honest conversations, the core motivators, the belief, the focus, the habits, the goals, the cause. It was all self-awareness and all the ingredients to creating a winning high-performance team.

It resonated with me. I started reading autobiographies of world-class sports coaches – Eddie Jones, Pep Guardiola, Arsene Wenger, Clive Woodward and Ric Charlesworth were my favourites. They all spoke about it, they all championed self-awareness as being a key to unlocking high performance and our best selves.

Ric Charlesworth, one of the best hockey coaches in the world, goes on and on about it in his book – *World's Best:*

> 'Self-awareness is an indispensable accompaniment to any successful performer whatever the activity.'

> 'Few athletes can fulfil their potential without knowing themselves well and understanding their inner drives.'

> 'We would be foolish to allow our biases and preconceptions to influence our judgement and decision making.'

> 'Noticing, naming and acknowledging these complex and

conflicted emotions was the first step in creating the bedrock for a culture of excellence.'

'A culture of excellence is about creating an environment in which we can be our best selves.'

Emotions. Self-awareness. Inner drives. Decision-making. 'Mumbo jumbo' was legit!

All these elite athletes were at it. It was getting them results. It was helping them win at sport, but it was also the ingredients to a better life.

Joe Marler, the England rugby player, wrote this little extract about their coach, Eddie Jones, in *The Guardian*. It sums up so nicely our British nature.

> Eddie said: 'You are all fucking cowards, mate, you're too scared, you're too fucking nice. You're almost too English, afraid to offend anyone, including your teammates.' If you're not prepared to turn round in training to Jamie George and say, 'Mate, that throw wasn't good enough', you'll never make progress. He shook the niceties out of us and showed us you can still be a tight-knit group, and unbelievable friends, but also with the ability to give and receive feedback that's going to improve you and the team.

Carol Dweck would be giving the nod – that's precisely what she means by having a growth mindset.

I used to be a coward. At home, with my friends, at work. Too eager to please, eager for attention, eager not to be rejected or to upset anyone. Now I could see how different life was by being frank, real and having a growth mindset. I was ready to double down.

FIXED

'Either I'm good or I'm not'
'Feedback + criticism are personal'
'My potential is predetermined'
'I don't like to be challenged'

GROWTH

'Failure is an opportunity to grow'
'I can learn to do anything I want'
'Challenges help me to grow'
'Feedback is constructive'

A LOADED GUN

Nicole and I were married, and we had a baby on the way.

'Oh, hey!' They'd heard the familiar squelch of the rubber seal separate from the wooden door frame as I appeared into the apartment. Nicole sat up from the sofa with excitement and Popsey's little paws trotted towards me – her claws clipping against the wooden floor with eagerness to greet me.

'Welcome home!' She was waiting patiently while I lifted our whippet up towards me and kissed her velvety cheeks.

'Hello, Hubby! How was your day?'

I gave Nicole a squeeze and bathed in her affection – her pregnant belly pressed against me. It felt good.

Cosy candles and a whiff of roast chicken.

A *framework of patience* and just over a year later this is where I'd arrived.

It reminded me of a quote by Naval Ravikant: 'A fit body, a calm mind, a house full of love. These things cannot be bought – they must be earnt.'

I knew what he meant.

I was about to quit my job at the sporting estate. It had served its purpose – given me the stability I needed while golden things happened in my life. Nicole. The baby on the way. Finishing the book.

It had also given me something unexpected: perspective. Working in a corporate environment, being part of a team, being led rather than leading. I learned about culture, about winning hearts and minds, about what motivates people. I saw what worked and what didn't. I was taking mental notes on everything – how I'd do things differently one day when building my own business, or helping others build theirs.

But now it felt like a cage. I was ready. The urge to make my move was eating me up inside – to commit to a path and go all in.

I'd narrowed it down to two options:

1. Starting a coaching business (I was coaching informally already).

2. Climate tech (I was also consulting for a waste-to-energy start-up).

'What's up? You've been quiet today.' My wife's intuition was in total harmony.

I looked down at the butter melting into my green beans.

'Ah, I don't know; I'm definitely leaning towards coaching but I think it's a combination of being afraid of actually pulling the trigger and really wanting to make absolutely sure I'm making the right call – sometimes I just wonder whether there's more for me to do, another chapter, not just teaching self-development.'

'Well... I have been saying that I don't think there's any harm in still applying for a job in climate tech – you may as well.'

'NO. THAT'S NOT THE POINT,' I snapped. 'I can't just do a bit of this and a bit of that – I have to decide, this is it now. I'm either all in or not at all. You can't dabble.'

The pressure was getting to me – I was at a major life crossroads.

'You know I've pretty much finished part six. Just one more section and I'll be able to get that off to Jemima [my editor] …

'Spoke to Ed earlier today – he's really struggling at the moment; Chris is too after his divorce – these guys… I wish I could just give them my book – it's all in there you know – I've just got to get it done.'

It was easy to get frustrated about my career, the feeling of having fallen behind, and forget about the chaos and stress in my life only a few years ago. I needed to remind myself daily how much had changed – now when I open my eyes in the morning instead of panic, there's mostly a feeling of peace, love and calm. It's priceless.

'I know we're not exactly flush at the moment, but you have no idea how grateful I am that you don't put me under pressure. It's weird, even though we are where we are – I feel this sense of inevitability that if we keep making the right decisions, if we keep thinking long term, then things will work out.'

'I can feel that too.' She said.

'You know what I love though? This process I've been through writing the book. It's the first time in my life I've really dedicated myself to something. Five years, two hours a day – I was average at writing and look how much I've improved. I know what it takes now, I know what dedication looks like and so I can apply this formula to anything and get really good at it. The problem though is going to be deciding *what* to choose – I wouldn't have managed to keep going if it didn't mean so much to me. Napoleon Hill's right – I have the BURNING DESIRE.

'You will – you're so close.'

'I've put so much into this book – it's painful to think that I won't be able to give it 100 per cent of my attention and promote it. Maybe I should just focus on that – it could be a bestseller... It's what I'm passionate about... I solved my own problems and now I can help other people solve theirs, right?'

I paused. Waiting for Nicole to endorse my yarn.

'I'm sorry, but I don't think that's a good idea. We don't have much savings and if you're going to put all our hopes on this book then that's not a good idea. What about when I go on maternity leave?'

It was the sobering reality I needed to hear. I was conflicted, passionate about the book but realistic about my career and finances.

'I'm sorry to say it like that.'

'No, you're right, I know you are. I just need to make up my mind what to do.'

I walked into our guest room and sat down at my desk to gather my thoughts.

David Goggins, Warren Buffet, Tony Robbins, Tim Draper and Naval Ravikant were all there Blu-Tacked to my wall – scattered around my two favourite quotes:

HAVE PATIENCE AND EXECUTE – *Gary Vee*
BE SO GOOD THEY CAN'T IGNORE YOU – *Steve Martin*

I looked up at my ten-year goals, my one-year goals, my monthly, weekly, daily habit tracker – pulling me in the right direction, one step at a time.

It helped me re-group.

Think about the big picture:

Perspective.

Ten years.

Patience.

Process.

I knew that I just needed to keep doing what I was doing and *trust the process*.

I tidied my desk – made my to-do list for tomorrow and visualised waking up at 5 a.m. the next morning to stretch, meditate and write.

The angst eased and I felt grounded again.

Nicole walked in.

'Look, I think it's just worth you going to see a couple of your mentors and talking it through with them before making the final call, don't you think?'

More talking, more thinking, more deliberating, it was driving me mad, but I knew she was right – I'd come this far.

'That's a good idea. This is the rest of my life, I'm 37 – I've got to get it right now.'

Within a week I had meetings lined up.

I felt like a loaded gun. Primed. Coiled. Ready to fire. But what was the target?

I was inspired to think big and be bold.

Theodore Roosevelt's famous quote was framed on my desk: 'Far better it is to dare mighty things, to win glorious triumphs, even though chequered by failure, than to rank with those poor spirits who neither enjoy much nor suffer much, because they live in that grey twilight that knows neither victory nor defeat.'

Jeff Bezos's words from a panel were at the forefront of my mind: 'You can choose a life of ease and comfort, or you can choose a life of service and adventure.'

I hadn't come all this way to think small – I was inspired.

Then there were the *beliefs*.

Beliefs, beliefs, beliefs.

Like I have already said, if there was one central piece of advice from all my books, gurus and mentors about making change and creating success, it was that everything boils down to our *beliefs*.

> 'The mind is its own place and in itself can make a heaven of hell or a hell of heaven'
> MILTON, *PARADISE LOST*

We can create, interpret and believe whatever we choose to. I knew that whatever I put my mind to, and if I applied enough focus, enough persistence, and enough discipline, over a long enough period of time, I would succeed.

After *I love you*, I think that the next best thing a parent can say to a child is, *you can do anything you set your mind to*. The power of just one person telling us 'you can do it', again and again is life-changing. My mother gifted me this belief.

As Kobe Bryant said, 'The most important thing is to try and inspire people so that they can be great in whatever they want to do.'

'Don't worry about this – I'll finish up, you go and write.'

'You sure?'

'Yes – honestly. But just before you go... I wanted to say... about everything we've just been speaking about, remember your tendency to wait until things are too perfect, don't fall into that trap, just start.'

It was a sensitive spot, but I knew she was right. The personality tests had already exposed my idealistic and perfectionist nature. If I couldn't do something in a big or complete way, I often didn't even bother. It wasn't so much 'go big or go home', it was 'go big or don't even leave the house'. Like with riding – I love horses but didn't go riding because going every now and again wouldn't satisfy the part of me that insisted I needed to spend a lot of time and money doing it to be the best. Nicole had recognised I had done the same in relationships – not wanting to commit unless everything was perfect – and in my career, waiting for the perfect job, the perfect opportunity, the perfect moment... and then doing nothing about it in the meantime.

That morning also I'd heard the insurance tycoon Patrick Bet-David offering a chilling piece of advice that hit me where it hurt: 'The most dangerous unhappy people I've met are those who are both extremely ambitious and extremely lazy. What this combination produces is envy... These are the people who think big and want to do something big, but they're not willing to put in the work to earn it.'

Maybe not that lazy but certainly a procrastinating perfectionist – which has the same effect. His words haunted me, he was right – I did tend to feel envious and jealous of other people's success. I was guilty.

I knew what was needed:

Trade envy for inspiration.

Then action, action, action.

In David Schwartz's book, *The Magic of Thinking Big*, he talks about needing to be an 'activationalist' – the importance of taking massive action.

'... action cures fear. Indecision, postponement, on the other hand, fertilise fear.'

I knew I was on the right track.

I was being objective, zeroing in on the target but trying to hold my nerve...

> Pull the tigger too soon – wrong direction.
> Pull the trigger too late – regret and lost opportunity.

I knew I needed to zero in more before making my final move. I needed to wait until the target came into my sights like a big fat watermelon hanging still from a tree in the warm afternoon sun – just like in Frederick Forsyth's epic 1973 movie *The Day of the Jackal* when Edward Fox, the blonde debonair film star, is lining up his 22-calibre sniper rifle – cold, calculating and meticulously planning the assassination of President Charles De Gaulle. Three practice shots to zero the sights and then he pulls out a single polished brass bullet, slots it into the chamber, squints into the telescopic sights and squeezes the trigger. THUD. The watermelon obliterates into a shower of red, pink. Clinical. Deadly.

The clock was ticking. I desperately wanted to pull the trigger but I couldn't see the watermelon just yet. And if you have no idea what I'm on about with the watermelon analogy – I was waiting for more clarity on exactly what I wanted to do before pulling the trigger!

'There is no heavier burden than unfulfilled potential.'

CHARLES SCHULTZ

OLD EMBERS

'Hey, Nick – thanks so much for making the time.'

He'd made close to $100 million three times in his career. First in carbon credits, then in gas and most recently in uranium. Nick knew how to make money. He knew me too. We used to work together. I valued his opinion.

'Come and have a seat over here...'

He pointed to the sofa in the corner of his private gym.

Late fifties, fit, energetic and wearing his green gilet and baseball cap. I was ready to plug in to his high twitch, stimulating mind – you had to keep up – conversations with Nick were always animated.

'Sasha, hold fire on the massage – I'm going to have a quick chat with Charley.'

'OK-ay,' he said in his thick Russian accent, while smiling at us. White towel around his waist stepping out of the sauna. Fresh beads of sweat sliding down his tanned leathery skin like a waterproof anorak.

I brought Nick up to speed with where I was at.

'Look – I can see you're really passionate about the self-development stuff, I can see you doing it, you'd be great at it – I just think you might struggle to build the sort of life you want – I thought you wanted to play polo?'

'That's funny – Louis [another mentor] said exactly the same thing.'

'Let's just put the self-development to one side and think about your other options. I remember you sending me that report you commissioned a few years ago – *materials of the future*, you know a lot about these new age technology materials – it's what the world needs. You'd be great at it.'

His words stunned me – like I'd seen a flying pig sail across the skyline.

I'm sorry, what?

It was like I'd completely forgotten that the world of commodities even existed. I'd written it off – an industry of crisis and cortisol. But it woke something up inside of me – it blew fresh oxygen onto some old embers.

'Charley, you've got nothing to lose – you may as well just go and chat to a few people in the industry and at least get a feel for what you'd be walking away from.'

'Shit, Nick – you're right. I've been down in Sussex, out of the game, just thinking about my book and… maybe climate tech – it's like I've been in the echo chamber of self-development. It makes a lot of sense to get options on the table and then decide. Thanks for this.'

'Oh, and, Charley – just remember something else... when I was your age, I hadn't made my money yet; you've got time.'

I was excited driving home – the conversation sparked possibility and reminded me of my interest in geopolitics, international trade and natural resources.

I hadn't quite connected the dots yet, but Nick had just helped me rediscover some *gold from the rivers of my past.*

I couldn't help feeling frustrated though. Was I back to square one? Hadn't I put that world behind me?

AN EXOTIC COCKTAIL

I was used to seeing her in *Tatler* magazine, *Hello* or maybe spotting her across the room at a drinks party with her model mate, Amber Le Bon, operating at the epicentre of the buzz and attention.

Now the socialite turned human potential coach Sabrina Percy was sitting opposite yours truly in the cold, empty basement of Jak's restaurant, just off the Kings Road at 4 p.m. on a Tuesday afternoon in November. And not for the first time. Her arms were crossed, we kept our thick winter coats on. She leant back in her tan leather throne-like armchair and I leant forward eagerly on the sofa like one of her subjects.

'I've had a bit of a wobble, Sabrina – I need your help with something...'

Her eyes brightened with anticipation and glee – she thought she was there to mentor me on how to become a better coach, but this was far more interesting.

No more tutorials on how to use the weaponry – she was sharpening her blades.

I gave her the spiel... 'I'm just torn really; I don't know whether to go back into commodities, I thought I was done with that, or whether to bite the bullet and try to build this self-development business... I know I'm passionate about it, but you know... I've been doing a lot more coaching, it energises me, I know I'm passionate about it, but I'm worried I'll get bored and frustrated doing it all day. I just think...'

'OK, fine – got it,' she interrupted, gesturing me to stop – she'd heard enough. 'Let me just ask you this...'

She sat even taller on her throne. Delivering the words like a surgeon – with knowing confidence... 'And I want you to be totally honest – don't overthink it...'

Yes, fine – come on then. I'm ready for anything. I'm the self-development guy.

'Charley, where do you *really* want to be in ten years' time? What do you want your life to look like?'

'That's easy,' I said. 'I want to have a happy and healthy family, I want to have peace and love in my heart, I want to be successful, I want to help people live better lives, to be financially free, to be able to travel with my family and put them through great education.'

'Yes, yes, I know all that,' she said dismissively. 'But what else is it YOU want. What have you always dreamed of? What are you going to regret not having done when you're on your deathbed at ninety-five?'

I paused. I looked away at the floor. I expected to reel something else off the tongue – show her that I had all bases covered, but it wasn't that easy.

'Well, I think, probably... to be honest – um.'

Squirming around it eventually came out... 'I've always wanted my own polo team, Sabrina.'

I felt like I'd admitted something I shouldn't. Exposed.

I paused – waiting for a gesture of approval.

There was an awkward silence. She was expressionless. Waiting for my next move.

Had I just embarrassed myself? What must she think of me? Was I sure?

It was like a mother watching a toddler struggling to swim – resisting the urge to reach out and help.

I could either back-pedal or keep going.

I checked in with myself. *Was this really what I wanted?*

It was.

'Yes – a polo team. It's what I've dreamt about since I was young – playing with my father.' I said, looking her in the eye with deadpan conviction.

Sabrina grinned knowingly. She asked a direct question, and she eventually got a direct answer. 'That's interesting, Charley – you didn't say that you wanted to be speaking to thousands of people on stage like Tony Robbins, did you?'

No – I suppose not.

She let it sink in. The power of pure coaching playing out in real time.

Helping me see things that I couldn't, opening me up to hardcore truth.

'Now imagine you have a clone – there are two of you. One of you starts a self-development business; coaching, podcasting, writing books and doing online courses, and the other goes into commodities. Which of you is most likely to get the desired outcome in ten years? Who would you rather be? The coach? Or the commodities pro, but building a business founded on your newfound principles, sourcing commodities for corporations around the word, on a trajectory towards your financial goals, with the resources to employ someone to run your passion project alongside?'

I gave her a defeatist smirk. 'I mean, obviously when you put it like that...'

'Get mathematical about it – what's going to get you to where you want to be?'

It all made a lot of sense. She introduced me to the idea of creating an *Everest Goal*. The ultimate goal, achievement, accomplishment sitting at the top of the mountain and then you reverse engineer all the steps along the way that will ensure that you have the very best chance of achieving that goal. It helps to get really strategic.

What skills? What experience? What type of environment? What habits? Which people? What practice do I need?

'Charley, this is why you don't waste any time with anything that isn't going to be working towards your ultimate goals. Time is your scarcest resource – you have to be ruthless and strategic with it. I don't think it needs to be this binary decision either – one or the other – why not make an exotic cocktail? Work in commodities but be known for your skills and knowledge around self-development too?'

An exotic cocktail – I liked the sound of that. It sounded different from splitting my time, which obviously she had advised against. It was about ensuring I didn't become so focused on one thing that it became my entire identity again. Being able to wear different hats would both differentiate and elevate me.

'Wow – thanks for this, Sabrina, you have no idea how much you have helped... We're talking about the rest of my life here.'

That's what great coaches do:

- Shine a light.
- See the blind spots.
- Get clarity.

I left with my mind dancing with possibility. Everything she said had made sense. *Surely, I'd figured it out now?*

I was zeroing in on the watermelon. The target was coming into focus. All I wanted to do was just pull that trigger... hear the thud, see the splatter of pink juices and get on with my life.

But all of a sudden doubt began to hijack my mind again.

Was this my watermelon or was it Sabrina's?

What if I'd answered her questions slightly differently?

What if she knew more about the potential to make money online through leveraging media?

Did I let myself get influenced by her?

Fuck.

I realised how easy it was for me to spin up whatever story I needed to, how good I was at persuading myself and everyone around me of whatever I wanted.

But what was the *truth*?

What was *real*?

What did *I* really want?

I knew that we all give *meaning* to different things. I knew that the *meaning* we give things often comes from our *beliefs*. And I knew now that we could change our *beliefs*. Didn't that mean I could create meaning for whatever I wanted?

Christ. I was going crazy, going around in circles. I realised that there was no right answer, and I was at risk of pulling away too many layers of the onion.

I needed to get back to basics. Facts. First principles. I needed to get hyper-objective. Hyper-acute to bias, to opinion, to influence.

Who's writing the book? Why? What do they know?

Who's giving the advice? What filter do they see the world through?

Listen. Read. Question. Challenge. Consider. Ignore.

I remembered Naval Ravikant saying that 'the average of everyone's opinion comes to zero'. It was time for me to make up my own mind.

I visualised myself waking up every day – podcasting, coaching, running workshops, masterminds, trying to come up with new content ideas to build my brand. Who my peers would be, who my clients would be, would it be enough?

I listened individually to my head, my heart and then my gut. I tried to notice if there was a feeling of expansion or contraction.

Then I switched it up.

The commodities pro: Travel. Adventure. Africa. South America. Pressure. The tricky characters, the cultural challenges, the conferences, the suits, the competition, the numbers. I imagined myself operating in that world as Charley 2.0, wanting to serve, wanting to inspire, working with great people, forever learning. Carlos Ley wouldn't put in a reappearance. Things would be different this time, I told myself.

Again, did I expand or contract?

Again, I scanned my head, heart and gut.

What grains of insight did each give me?

I tried to invert the visualisation: *How would I feel if I never did it?*

I even tried to imagine: *What would I do if I couldn't fail?*

I remember Rumi's quote as much as possible: 'The quieter you become, the more you are able to hear.'

Truth hides in the nuance, the intuition, the gut. But it takes time and concentration. Always for a few minutes at the end of my meditation I used the time to ponder these different life scenarios and what that path would actually feel like – it's the time when I felt the quietest and I could sink deeper and get closer to the truth.

I knew I needed to lean into the hard choices, the uncomfortable, scary choices – I was looking for the same feeling I had when I took the scary leap of faith to open my heart to Nicole and see what happens. That feeling of jumping in without a lifejacket.

Equally though, I didn't want to overlook what might feel easy, that thing that feels like play to me and work to everyone else – completely congruent with who I am and what I love doing.

I was thinking hard about it all – really hard. I was thinking about it all until it hurt. It was the rest of my life – I wasn't going to put it down to chance, to someone else's opinion, to a whim. I was looking for an informed, analytical and intuitive decision based on the evidence.

'The real truth inside you
will be remembered
not discovered.'

DR ZACH BUSH

THE SWEET SPOT

'Charley, you should check out James King's book, *Accelerating Excellence*.'

I always listened to any advice my friend Henry gave me.

He knew I was at a life crossroads. He got my situation better than most. Henry had worked in Africa, and in commodities, he's an entrepreneur, he knows about taking risk, he's a similar age, he has a young family, he's the founder of the Christian Meditation App called *Glorify* – so gets a lot of the stuff I was into also. He knows me, my journey, my challenges, my failures.

He got me.

So why had Henry recommended this book?

The first six pages were littered with endorsements from high profile advocates across elite sports, business and government, praising James King's work in high performance.

The anonymous testimonial from Command Sergeant Major, UK Special Mission Units, was enough for me – 'I've watched and admired how James designs and builds sustainable human performance programmes that deliver results. *Accelerating Excellence* is a long overdue manifesto for elite performance and James King is the ideal ambassador.'

Sounded legit to me.

Even GQ were jumping on the band wagon, 'He has cracked the algorithm for excellence.'

But what did it have to do with me?

The book was dense and textbook-like. I flicked through the chapters to get a feel for what it was all about – or more truthfully, check that James didn't know a whole load of stuff that I didn't.

Habit stacking, routines, beliefs, emotional control, failure, the importance of environment. Most of it was familiar territory – I was relieved.

Scanning the contents pages though – something did pique my attention...

'Chapter 3 – Finding your Sweet Spot.'

I dived in.

He began explaining the importance of something I'd never heard of – something called *concordance*.

'Concordance: When a person's nature, the qualities that make one unique, are in agreement/harmony.'

He used the professional footballer Gareth Bale as an example to explain the idea of concordance. How Bale used to get ridiculed by the Tottenham Hotspur fans when he used to play left-back and let goals in willy-nilly with little to no defensive awareness. But despite Bale's shocking performances, the manager, Harry Redknapp, stuck by him and praised his technical and physical abilities until one day he realised 'Bale's defensive role was suffocating his greatest psychological strength: to attack! He was playing in the wrong position.'

After moving him to an attacking winger – Bale began scoring goals for fun, becomes Tottenham's star player and signs to Real Madrid for a record £85.3m. 'No longer fighting resistance, he was performing in harmony with the qualities that make him unique, smack bang in his sweet spot.'

It made so much sense. This reiterated to me how critical it was to find *my* sweet spot.

It's all very well believing one can become great at anything given the right formula, but James was right, good maybe, but unlikely great. Unlikely world class.

He puts it very simply:

To become the very best we must identify goals where we have the strengths required to excel. He uses this diagram to illustrate how our sweet spot is at the intersection of our strengths, values and interests.

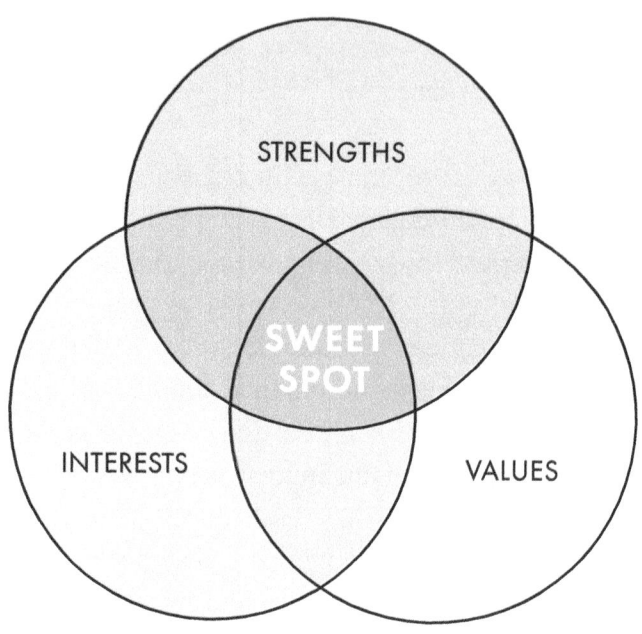

Strengths: *What are you naturally good at?*

Interests: *What are you passionate about, drawn to, like reading about?*

Values: *What's important to you, what drives you? What does the world need?*

It was a real reminder how important it is to actually enjoy what we're doing too. I thought this sentence of his was pure genius: 'The reward of the interest is the interest itself, it disguises repetition, like an anaesthetic to the pain of unrelenting immersion in one single area.'

'... it disguises repetition, like an anaesthetic to pain...' *Drop the mic, James.*

I remember hearing one of Cristiano Ronaldo's teammates talking about just how many more hours Ronaldo puts in during training than anyone else, and in the end, he put it down to Ronaldo probably just enjoying it more than everyone else – it was less of a chore. His interest is so great it dissolves any pain of the daily grind and so no one is ever going to keep up.

It had become clear to me that I'd done the right thing in taking just that little bit more time to make my decision. The difference between striking a ball with a golf club or a baseball bat in the sweet spot and not is like night and day. So, if I could just find my sweet spot, I knew I'd propel myself faster and further than I could imagine.

I filled out my own diagram:

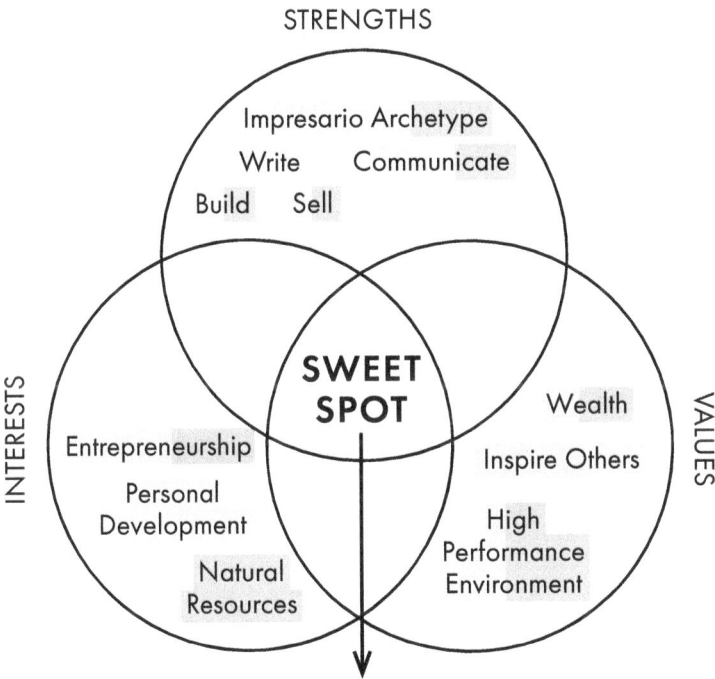

Build a personal development biz + Stay open to opportunities in natural resources

Personal Development vs Natural Resources. The conflict was still real.

You can see that both options covered all three circles extensively.

But this simple diagram gave me what I needed – answers.

Laying it out like this I could see that coaching and personal development had a stronger presence and, if I'm honest, out of the two it was the thing BURNING strongest within me.

Finally I knew the path I needed to follow.

There's another very similar and effective exercise I also used during this process called *Ikigai*. It's a Japanese concept that translates loosely to 'a reason for being' or 'reason to get up in the morning.' This one focuses on the intersection where your passions, talents, values and what the world needs all meet. Essentially, your personal sweet spot of purpose. It's very similar to James's *Sweet Spot* diagram.

I knew which direction to take now, but that didn't mean it was easy to kiss goodbye to my old work. The pull of commodities was still there – it was still part of my identity, but by going deep – by pushing aside my ego, not caring what people might think, and getting really honest about what I believe I was born to do, I knew I'd finally arrived to the right answer.

I remembered Graham Weaver, the Stanford professor and private equity investor, saying: 'Ask yourself: what would you do if you couldn't fail? Then do that.' That's exactly what I was doing.

I remembered Steve Jobs talking about the importance of focus, how that often meant saying no to things we liked doing, things we also wanted to do. Focus meant choosing one path. Not hedging. Not keeping options open just in case.

It felt risky, it felt uncomfortable, it was precisely the feeling I was looking for. Jumping without a life jacket – the same feeling that led to changing my life with Nicole.

It was a sign I was moving in the right direction, that these impulses were normal.

At first, I couldn't visualize what this coaching and personal development business would actually look like. The book, sure. But beyond that? It was foggy. Uncertain.

But I knew the direction. As Rumi said, 'As you start to walk on the way, the way appears.'

And slowly, it did.

Maybe Sabrina was right. Maybe one day I'd become that exotic cocktail – coaching AND something more. Sure, I was taking more risk this way, but I was backing myself.

I remembered something Richard Branson once said about how he managed so many companies: focus on one thing at a time.

Right now, this was what I needed to do. Get the book done. Build the coaching business. Help people. Do it well.

And who knows where that might lead? Zig Ziglar's words came to mind: 'You can have everything in life you want, if you will just help enough other people get what they want.'

I knew the rest would reveal itself.

And I can't tell you how much of a relief it was – to have the clarity. Not every detail mapped out. But directional clarity.

Knowing what my purpose was.

Knowing that I wouldn't have any regrets.

I had found one of the most precious things in life…

Clarity.

And it was this same clarity, (that now sat deep within me), that gave me the courage and conviction to take the leap.

As Warren Buffet says, 'You get chances to do things that just shout at you. And the thing you have to do is, when that happens, you have to take a big swing.'

The sweet spot.

'Have courage to follow your heart and intuition.
They somehow already know what you want to become.'

STEVE JOBS

STEP 6 – CLARITY

Can you see how clarity is a superpower?

It makes sense, right... to achieve anything you must first be clear on what you want.

Maybe it's not the first time you've heard this – *get clear*. But shit, it's not necessarily that straightforward. And I don't know about you, but I couldn't find anyone to show me *how* to think through it all.

Can you see how important it is to first know the difference between what's important to YOU rather than your parents, your friends, society and even your conditioned self?

Remember how we spoke about separating your *self* from your thoughts, ideas and beliefs. That means you can separate your *self* from any fixed identity too. You can help loosen the grip of your ego and move towards a growth mindset – seeing your identity as always evolving – less attached to the *self*. Your identity is not who you are, it's something that can be created by you, therefore it's not you.

Can you see the power of using all the different pieces of the puzzle to get as much clarity as possible?

Too often we're hit with over-simplistic advice that just doesn't consider the complex and nuanced reality of figuring out YOUR path. Without the right guidance it can be the single hardest thing to figure out, especially in a fast-changing world. Too many people gloss over how important it is, claim it can be solved in one quick conversation or exercise. And in my experience, that's just not the case.

Can you also see how important it is to be careful who you listen to?

This is a skill that can take time to hone. Which advice to take and which to discard. Figuring out what to do – it's an art. Who's giving the advice? What are their values, ambitions and intentions? Does it align with your vision? Be objective and filter the advice against your own criteria.

Charley, what's one hack that will help me fast-track my way to figuring out what I want?

If you could see my face you'd see a smile. Because the answer to that is counterintuitive. The hack is knowing that there is no hack (that it's not meant to be easy), and by knowing this you will arrive at the answer faster. Instead of casually deliberating, you will give it the time and attention that is required. You know it's not straightforward to find, but once you have it, it's a superpower. A lot of stress comes from thinking it's meant to be easy, thinking that answers will just come to you and then they don't. But just a few months of focused attention could save you years of indecision, missed opportunity and regret.

But will I ever know for sure which is the right path to take?

Honestly, maybe not. But this is why I encourage you to use these methods to narrow things down as much as possible and then sometimes you just have to choose, make a committed decision and make damn sure that whatever you do choose becomes the right call in retrospect. It's not necessarily about making the right choice, it's about making the right choice work.

Is thinking about business models and wealth really necessary in personal development?

Personally, I'm into all this because I want to live the best life possible; wealth, health and happiness. One of my favourite quotes by Naval is: 'The true mark of intelligence is getting what you want out of life.' That has two parts: first, figuring out what to want, wanting the right things that will actually bring you fulfilment. Then, working out how to get them. If things like wealth, security, stability and a meaningful career are important pieces of the puzzle for you, then yes, it's worth thinking critically about your options. The question is: how are you best going to reach your destination?

If it's just clarity I'm after, can I skip to Step 6?

Unfortunately, no. Step 6 is only effective if you've done the work to get there.

Clarity isn't found in chaos; it's found in the calm.

By the time you arrive here at 'Step 6 – Clarity', you'll be primed. You'll have offloaded the baggage, stress and tension. You'll be self-aware. You'll have created a framework of patience. You'll be calmer, clearer and more in tune with your intuition and emotions. You won't be clinging on to an old identity, you won't feel that you need to be a certain way to stay attached to certain people in your life. You'll have adopted a growth mindset, and know that you can become whoever you want to be.

You know that you can do anything, but you can't do everything.

You know that finding your sweet spot can mean catapulting you much faster towards what you want in life.

Tools to Clarity:

- Pan for gold through rivers of your past.
- Ask close friends and family what you're great at.
- Know who to listen to and what advice to discard.
- Take personality tests.
- Be really honest with yourself about what *you* want.
- Study business models and blueprints to success.
- Start dabbling – collect more data points.
- Speak to mentors and people in the respective industries.

- Run the Sweet Spot or IKIGAI exercise.
- Think about being on your deathbed. What really matters.
- Ask yourself: What would you do if you knew you couldn't fail?

Use these tools to open your mind to possibility and collect more data, but then know that the final answer lies within you. Know that the answer lies in the nuance, in your intuition.

You're going to have to quieten your mind and navigate those conflicting forces deep within you.

Often if you're presented with two options the right option is the harder one.

But maybe the easier one is easier because it's more congruent and just feels like play.

Or maybe the easier option is actually the lazier more comfortable option.

Can you see? The answers lie in the nuance.

Why aren't you convinced? What's stopping you from committing? Do you lack belief? Are you afraid? Or is it something else? Maybe it's just not the right thing.

You have to be a detective.

- Trust your gut.
- Follow that whisper.
- Don't settle for ordinary.
- **And make the call.**

You'll likely never be 100 per cent sure, but choose the thing that burns brightest inside you.

You'll likely not have a clear path or vision yet. Take the steps and it will reveal itself.

You'll likely have to say goodbye to other things you like doing – but remember that's focus.

Gareth Bale was lucky enough to have Harry Redknapp help him figure out his sweet spot, his correct position. But imagine if that never happened, he might have forever remained mediocre, average – imagine the unfulfilled potential.

I don't want you to have any regrets.

I promise you it will be SO worth it. Just as Marianne Williamson said in her book, *A Return to Love*, 'It takes courage to endure the sharp pains of self-discovery rather than choose to take the dull pain of unconsciousness that would last the rest of our lives.'

And remember that clarity can give you this courage and conviction you need to go and conquer your dreams.

Clarity, Courage, Conquer.

Manifesting, The Law of Attraction, raising your vibration, energy, the quantum field, whatever 'mumbo jumbo' you want to call it.

If you can see it, believe it, feel it and speak it, it can become a reality.

Work hard, stay focused, trust the process and have faith.

CLARITY IS A SUPERPOWER.

'I think it's very important not to do
what your peers think you should do,
not what your parents think you should do,
or your teachers or even your culture.
Do what's inside of you.'

GEORGE LUCAS (BILLIONAIRE ENTREPRENEUR AND
CREATOR OF *STAR WARS* AND *INDIANA JONES*)

STEP 7
CONSISTENCY

> Clarity shows you the destination. Consistency is your vehicle to get there.

MOMENTUM

I was clear now on my vision, values, purpose and strategy. Big decisions became easier. We decided to move to Cape Town – lifestyle, young family, Nicole's parents, outdoors, lower cost base to build a business.

'Walk me through it, Charley – what are people actually getting?'

I was on a call with Christian, one of my coaching mentors.

'I've been thinking about this. I never felt like the odd session here and there with a coach did enough. Back when I was feeling stuck it certainly wasn't the answer.'

'So, what would have actually helped you back then?'

'Well, this is it Christian. I'm thinking it has to be a programme. What's transformed my life is not one thing – it's a combination of things – it's multidimensional – it's all the different pieces to the puzzle – everything is connected.'

'That's exactly what I would have wanted. I had no idea what I needed

– so finding someone I could trust or relate to, and committing to a process – in the right sequence to get this outcome would have been priceless. Imagine how much time, money and heartache it would have saved me!'

Christian smiled. 'I like it. This isn't coaching spun up in a weekend – this is deep work – it will be unique to you, and I have no doubt Charley that you will change lives.'

From then the business plan was straightforward: podcast and book for awareness, speaking engagements for companies, a small group of private coaching clients and my proprietary programme.

It definitely wasn't plain sailing to start with.

There were lulls. People asking, 'What are you doing? How long are you going to give this?' There were definitely moments when doubts crept into my mind.

But the deep clarity I'd fought for kept me in the game.

Clarity melts the shackles of doubt, distraction, fear and procrastination.

Clarity was my superpower. It gave me the courage and conviction to keep going.

And it turned out the sweet spot effect was real too.

Big names started coming on the podcast. Ben Earl, the England and British Lions rugby star. Tim Draper, the billionaire VC. Eduardo Della Maggiora, unicorn founder. And they were all saying similar things: talking about the same challenges, the same inner work. I thought, *Wow. I really am on the right path.*

The early clients who went through the programme were my proof of concept.

Founders who'd built successful companies but felt empty. Corporate leaders stuck in toxic cultures, questioning everything. A hedge fund manager who'd lost his spark. A headmaster re-building after a divorce. A commodity trader (ironically) at a top firm – burnt out, spiralling and struggling with indecision. A management consultant, navigating change, at a crossroads and searching for clarity.

They became raving fans.

'This changed my life.'

'It's like a bible for transformation.'

'I made a life-changing decision because of this work.'

It gave me such a high.

Helping these high achievers get back on track, figure out their path, their purpose – what they were going to do with their one precious life.

It turned out that the combination of my deep personal development work and hard-won business experience was in demand too. CEOs dealing with conflict, navigating challenges – I had the war wounds. I'd been there. I could help them strategically AND emotionally.

Social events had gone from: 'Charley pipe down about all that "mumbo jumbo" and have another shandy.' to, 'Hello Charley, I'm Claude, heard you worked with Hugo – he said it was a game changer. Could we speak?'

I'd stuck to my guns, didn't follow trends, and the proof was in the pudding.

And I was just getting started.

UNDER FIRE

Sunday afternoon. Sweltering. I was at the braai (BBQ) with a cold beer, the Springboks about to kick off. Then my phone rang.

It was Mark, one of my private clients. Business owner. We'd been working together for three months on clarity, emotional control and navigating a challenging business dynamic.

'Charley, it's happened. I need your help.'

I could hear it in his voice. Something was off.

'What's going on?'

'He just called. He's been talking to our main investor behind my back. They're siding with him – putting in more capital, but only if I'm diluted down to nothing or bought out completely.'

Fuck.

'How did he deliver it?'

'Cold. Rehearsed. Like he'd been practicing. Said he wants an "independent future". Ten years of partnership and this is how it ends.'

I could hear the adrenaline in his voice. The shock. The betrayal.

'Where are you right now?'

'At home. My wife's furious. I'm furious. I don't know what to do. I just... I want to call him back and—'

'Stop. Don't do anything. Not yet.'

'Mark, listen to me. This is exactly what we've been preparing for. This is the test. You have six weeks of lawyers, negotiations and raw emotions ahead of you. And how you show up will determine not just the outcome of this deal, but how you're going to feel on the other side of it.'

'I know. That's why I called you.'

'Right – so what would the old you do in this situation?'

'Probably rush to make it go away. Throw all my healthy habits out the window. Not tell anyone what's going on. I'd end up being too forgiving – somehow feel bad for him, blame myself then regret things down the line.'

'Right. So we're not doing any of that.'

I walked him through the playbook:

Slow the pace. Don't rush to resolution. Let things unfold. Get comfortable in the discomfort. Study his behaviour. Understand the motives.

Keep the rituals. Double down on exercise, meditation, morning routine. Stay close to nature.

Remind yourself you have a choice. Every email, every call, every response – you get to choose how you show up.

Know your tendencies. You're too forgiving. Too quick to blame yourself. Too easily soothed by silver tongues. When you can't think clearly, lean on your mentors and family.

Let the emotion out in safe places. Don't bottle it. Release the pressure like a steam valve.

―

Over the next six weeks, Mark did exactly that.

And then the call I'd been hoping for came.

'It's done.'

Mark's voice on the other end was composed.

'How did it go? How do you feel?'

'I didn't roll over. I stood my ground – calm, compassionate, but firm. And I walked away with my dignity, and a deal I can live with. Honestly Charley – I'm super proud of how I showed up – the old me would have messed this up.'

'Brilliant. That's exactly what we—'

'But Charley, hang on, there's something else.'

He paused. The pause before uncomfortable honesty – preparing himself to say it, preparing me to hear it.

'I'm still angry with him. I wake up thinking about it. Go to bed thinking about it. Every email, every memory – it's consuming me. And I know I'm supposed to let it go, but I can't.'

'All right, let's step back.'

I took a breath. I knew how important this was.

'Mark, this sort of resentment can be a killer. It can affect your entire future. Let's think about this carefully.'

'What's the payoff for holding onto this?' I asked.

'What do you mean?'

'Why are you holding onto this? What's the benefit to you?'

He paused.

'Because... I'm the victim? Because I need someone to blame?'

'Go on. Why do you need someone to blame?'

'I don't know Charley. He's just wrong. He's behaved so badly.'

'Exactly – so if he's wrong, then what does that make you?'

Another pause. Then he got it.

'Ah. So I can be right.'

'EXACTLY.

'You have every right to feel wronged, but what's more important to you? Being right about what he did? Or feeling free and at peace again?'

The line went quiet. It was sinking in.

'What's it costing you to hold onto this?'

'Everything.' he said quietly.

'You're on the right track – you know what you want in life – don't let your ego and pride derail you now.'

'Huh... I guess you're right.' He said conceding.

I could sense him coming to terms with what that actually meant – letting go of needing to be right. Not needing to prove to his ex-partner and everyone else that he was the good guy. It was hard to swallow.

'So what do I do?'

'You take full responsibility.'

'What? No. That's not fair – he's the one who—'

'Mark, I'm not saying what he did was right. I'm saying you got yourself into that situation. You chose him as a partner. You missed the red flags. You stayed too long. That's on you. And until you own that – really own it – you're going to stay stuck.'

He went quiet.

'Write him a letter,' I said. 'You don't need to send it.'

—

Two days later, he called back.

'It's done. I wrote it. Four pages.'

'What happened?'

'At first the anger really came to the surface – everything he did, everything I wanted to say. But then I shifted. I tried to actually feel what it would be like to forgive him, to let it all go.'

'And?'

'It was terrifying, Charley. Like I was falling. Letting go felt like losing – like I was weak, walked over, insignificant. Like he'd won. But then it dissolved and I realized that wasn't true at all. I landed somewhere completely different – this freeing state. I could see everything so clearly. How my ego had been clutching to this one thing. How much energy it was taking. All to protect some insecurity about myself.'

'THAT'S IT, MARK. THAT'S EXACTLY IT!'

'I can't believe how much it had been consuming me. And once you let go you experience this expansiveness, this abundant feeling – that there's infinite possibility – you realise how insignificant the whole thing was in the grand scheme of things.'

'Love it. So what are you going to do now?'

'Huh? What do you mean? I'm done, Charley – I'm free.'

'You should call him.'

'WTF?!'

'Call him. Tell him you take responsibility for your part. That you're sorry. That it's been consuming you.'

'I can't do that.'

'Why not?'

'Because... because I don't want him to know how much this has been eating me up. I don't want to give him that satisfaction.'

'Then you're not done yet.'

'If you're still worried about how it looks to him, you're still holding on. You're still trying to be right. And you'll end up sacrificing everything – just to protect your pride.'

Another long pause.

'He really hurt me, Charley.'

'I know. And you have every right to feel that. But staying hurt doesn't punish him – it only punishes you. And everyone around you.'

—

A day later.

I called Mark.

'How did it go?'

'Hardest thing I've ever done. He was shocked. Defensive at first. But by the end, we were actually talking like humans again. I doubt we'll ever see each other, but I don't hate him anymore.'

'This takes courage, Mark. Well done. How do you feel?'

'Like a new person. I can't believe how much we can sabotage our lives like that. If I hadn't done this work – if I hadn't seen this – I would have carried that resentment forever. It would have poisoned everything. My business, my relationships, my kids. I'd have been right, but I'd have been miserable.'

'Welcome to the human condition,' I said. 'Most people carry this stuff to the grave. They die with "I was right" written on their tombstone. But you've seen it now. And once you see it, you can choose differently.'

Six weeks later, Mark sent me a message:

Stars aligning. New opportunity, two people I've been wanting to work with for ages. Wife said I'm different: 'actually present now.' Letting go unlocked everything. Thanks, Charley.

—

This story isn't to show you how great I am as a coach.

It's to show you that this work actually makes a difference when life punches you in the face.

Mark had done my programme. He was in a great place. He was self-aware. He'd gained clarity on his values and vision. He'd built the rituals and the support structure. And so when the test came – and it always comes – he was ready.

Can you see how different the experience, the choices, the outcome and the trajectory would have been if he hadn't done the work?

If he'd rushed to a resolution?

If he'd let the stress affect his decision making?

If he'd held onto resentment and needed to be right?

This is what Eckhart Tolle meant when he said, 'One day you may catch yourself smiling at the voice in your head, as you would smile at the antics of a child.'

Mark saw it. He caught himself. And he chose differently.

Consistency isn't just about the meditation streak or the morning routine. It's staying consistent with who you've decided to be, even when the pressure is on. Even when your old patterns are screaming at you.

That's what separates transformation from just having a few good weeks.

Consistency is the compass that keeps you on course to your destination.

How you think.

How you react.

How you show up.

It's about knowing your worth.

It's about mind, body, spirit.

Your support structure.

Embracing the struggle.

Patience and process.

Clarity over vision.

Emotional control.

Self-awareness.

Forgiveness.

Discipline.

Ego.

Staying consistent is multidimensional.

If you're heading into any kind of negotiation, here are twelve hard-won tactics I've learned from over twenty years in business.

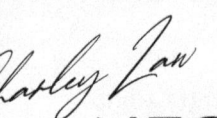

NEGOTIATION TACTICS

12 Hard Won Lessons – Over 20 Years in Business

1. PREPARE AND RESEARCH THOROUGHLY

Know everything about your opponent, the market, and alternative options. Preparation boosts confidence and allows you to anticipate objections, giving you control from the start.

2. ESTABLISH RAPPORT AND BUILD TRUST

People are more likely to agree with those they trust. Use active listening, empathy, and rapport-building early on to create a cooperative atmosphere.

3. ANCHOR WITH A STRONG FIRST OFFER AND DISRUPT THEIR RATIONALE

Set a confident initial number to anchor their expectations, then justify it with solid reasoning. This not only establishes your position but also challenges their logic, especially if they counter with low bids. By questioning their stance, you keep them on the defensive and shape the negotiation in your favour.

4. LEVERAGE TIMING

Never be rushed. Stay calm and patient – resist the urge to react (sleep on it or defer to your inner circle). Do though create urgency for them. Subtly apply urgency to push them towards a decision.

5. PROJECT CALM, DETACHMENT, AND BE WILLING TO WALK AWAY

Confidence to walk away is one of the strongest positions you can have. By appearing relaxed and indifferent to committing, you disarm their pressure tactics, keeping them uncertain about your bottom line and strengthening your negotiating position.

6. MAKE SMALL, CONTROLLED CONCESSIONS

Move minimally in negotiations. Each small concession shows you're willing to be flexible but not desperate, which helps wear them out and signal firmness.

7. DOUBLE DOWN ON ESSENTIALS FOR MENTAL CLARITY

Prioritise habits like journaling, exercise, and meditation to stay grounded, resilient, and patient. Clear thinking and emotional control are your greatest assets under pressure.

8. UNDERSTAND AND ALIGN WITH THEIR CORE MOTIVATIONS

Ask open-ended 'how' or 'what' questions to uncover the other party's needs, motivations, and concerns. This approach not only makes them feel heard but also helps soften their stance. Focus on what truly drives them—whether it's security, recognition, or connection—rather than just their stated demands. By aligning your offer with these core motivators, you create tailored solutions that resonate deeply, offering you both leverage and a strategic advantage.

9. CREATE DECOYS AS BARGAINING CHIPS *

Present demands or points that aren't essential to your position. Use these as concessions later to gain leverage on what truly matters. Emphasize less critical items to divert attention from your true priorities, strengthening your negotiating position.

10. FRAME OFFERS IN TERMS OF VALUE, NOT COST

Emphasise the benefits and value your offer provides, rather than just the cost. This makes it more attractive and reduces haggling over price.

11. CREATE A 'CRISIS' IF NEEDED *

Amplify an external factor beyond your control (e.g., time constraint or limited resources) to gain concessions and strengthen your position.

12. MAINTAIN CALM WITH STRATEGIC UNPREDICTABILITY *

Hold a steady, calm demeanour, but occasionally interject with unexpected emotional reactions. This controlled unpredictability keeps them off balance, making you harder to read and giving you control over the negotiation flow.

* Adapt your approach to fit the situation. In high-conflict scenarios, use firm tactics; with fair counterparts, focus on collaboration. Matching your strategy ensures adaptability and effectiveness.

Use these tools to negotiate with confidence and control. Good luck!

BEHIND ENEMY LINES

Nearly a year had passed since we'd moved to Cape Town. Nicole and I now had two children – Clara and our newborn son, Cruz. The coaching business was growing steadily, clients were getting results, and life had found a rhythm.

But I wasn't done learning.

I'd been invited to join the SAS Leadership Trust Programme in Hereford, UK – a week-long immersion designed to push high-performing leaders beyond their comfort zones. I flew back alone, leaving Nicole with a toddler and a three-month-old, to spend a week at one of the world's most respected leadership programmes.

Many of my clients were senior leaders navigating high-stakes decisions under pressure. If I was going to help them effectively, I needed to keep evolving my own understanding of leadership, resilience and what it takes to perform when everything's on the line.

At the heart of their philosophy was the very real possibility of SAS units having to operate behind enemy lines – cut off from command (especially back in the day). The need to operate under extreme pressure, to make split decisions. The teams rely on autonomy, trust, and the ability to think clearly. They don't need constant direction; they lead themselves through shared purpose and mutual respect.

Bill Walsh, the legendary 49ers coach who won three Super Bowls, wrote in his book *The Score Takes Care of Itself*: 'The trademark of a well-led organization in sports or business is that it's virtually self-sustaining and self-directed – almost autonomous.'

Two completely different worlds, two very similar philosophies.

It was the penultimate day of the week-long onsite. We sat in our familiar horseshoe formation. There was a buzz and banter. The competitions, the comradery, the adversity and the vulnerability had forged connection.

But the mood was about to make a sharp U-turn.

The coach stood motionless beside the whiteboard. Scribbled across it in thick black marker was a simple loop, labelled in block capitals: **LOSER'S LOOP**.

He didn't raise his voice. He didn't need to.

'This,' he said, tapping the board, 'is why some of you – despite being capable, smart, relentless – keep ending up back where you started.'

We leaned in. Not physically, but mentally. Something about the simplicity of the diagram unsettled everyone. A straight line would've implied progress. This loop meant you'd been running hard but going nowhere.

'You try. You fail. You rationalise. You bounce back – but deep down, you don't really believe you deserve to win. So eventually... you sabotage. Or quit just before it happens. And the cycle begins again.'

No one moved.

Then he said something I'll never forget: 'The centre of this loop isn't fear. It's *lack of self-respect*. Not confidence. Not skill. Not bad luck. It's the quiet, invisible belief that you're not enough. And it pulls everything around it – like gravity. You can change the habits, the tactics, the scenery. But if the core hasn't changed, nothing will.'

And that's when it really sank in.

There I was thinking that a lot of it had been a bit of bad luck. The setbacks, the rejections, always thinking 'this time will be different'. I was proud of my resilience, to go again, to keep trying, but the truth was that I'd got more comfortable failing and starting again than actually seeing something through.

It sounds ridiculous to say out loud, but I know that coach was right – it was because deep down I didn't really believe I could do it, or deserved it.

I'd keep going, yes. But I was orbiting the same damn star.

I had been in the Loser's Loop.

It wasn't a mindset issue.

It was self-respect.

Not arrogance. Not bravado. The quiet, inner knowing that *you deserve to win.* That you don't have to prove anything to anyone.

I glanced around the room. Nobody spoke. A few heads were bowed. Others stared blankly at the board. We had just been handed the mirror we didn't know we needed.

Fortunately, by this time, I knew that I was out of the loop – but still, the simplicity, the concept, it gave me something to chew on, seeing so clearly where I had been going wrong.

You could feel the dominos cascading along the horseshoe as individuals had their own moment of realisation – many still stuck in the loop.

The room was despondent. Coach didn't seem surprised – it was part of the process.

Awareness was the key. This little idea packed a punch and resonated with all of us.

Triggering the proverbial, *shit, that's where I've been going wrong.*

Once you became aware of it, you could actually do something about it.

Self-Awareness = Choice to Change.

Got it, Charley, but what does this have to do with consistency?

Everything.

The reason we want to be consistent is because we want to reach our goals.

The reason leadership exists is to guide yourself or a team towards a goal.

Leadership and consistency are close relations. They're inseparable. And you can't reach your goals without them.

Effective consistency and self-leadership will help you maintain the right trajectory towards your objectives. But consistently sabotaging and going around in circles will not. Our self-worth, self-respect, self-image – if not addressed properly – become kryptonite, sabotaging you every step of the way, no matter how many times you get back up.

Leading a team is the same. To maintain trajectory toward a common goal, you must demonstrate self-worth, confidence and clarity. But true leadership goes further – it activates those qualities in others. It empowers from within. Wins hearts and minds, as the SAS would say.

'We are what we repeatedly do. Excellence, then, is not an act but a habit.'

ARISTOTLE

COACH CHARLEY

'Who *is* Charley talking to?' asked my father.

'He's on a coaching call,' replied Nicole.

'Oh right – won't be long, will he?'

'Why don't you come and help with bath time – Clara and Cruz would love that.'

Next door I had my MacBook perched on a pile of books and Zoom was ready to roll. I looked out of the bedroom window at the brilliant blood orange skies growing richer as the sun sank into the ocean and the silhouette of Cape Town's Table Mountain faded into the night skies. It was awe-inspiring.

'Hello, Charley! I'm *so* sorry about that.'

The biotech CEO shuffled around in her Tesla to get comfortable. Her textured woven pale pink Balmain jacket, the thoughtfully paired silk shirt, her dark cropped hair and flawless almond skin, the cream seats and panoramic sunroof, even the Knightsbridge red-brick mansion block in the background, it all spoke success, style and intelligence.

'Just to say I have to leave a few minutes early today because I'm speaking on a panel at 7 p.m.'

'OK, no problem, let's get into this, Dhivya. Congratulations! You've made it to the last day of the programme.'

I can see her sense of accomplishment radiating through my computer screen. She's a doer, it's how she operated – ready to complete my programme. The final piece to the puzzle.

'Let's do it! You know, Charley, I've already got a bunch of friends I want to recommend this to.'

The ultimate accolade – referrals. It was proof this stuff really did work. It wasn't just me.

'All right. So we've covered a lot – Desire, The Body Baseline, The Essentials.

'Next up we deep dived, we went below the surface, into your subconscious – uncovering your traits, tendencies and emotions that were holding you back. Remember how hard you've been on yourself? Your exceptionally high standards? We really did get to *Know Thyself* a lot better, didn't we?!'

She looked down as if to blush.

'So, once we knew what to work on, we came up with your antidotes, and we created your personal "Mindset Manifesto" to change. This was for you to take *Responsibility in Action*. You can see now why there was no point moving onto *Getting Clear* until we addressed these forces holding you back first, right?'

'It's on my kitchen fridge! I'm on it – meeting with our chairman scheduled for next week.'

'Love it – let me know how that goes. OK, so then in the last few sessions we got into the fun stuff, *Clarity*. Remember your doubts around direction, career and priorities? We did a personality test, we looked at your values, we went digging for gold in the rivers of your past to triangulate what really makes you tick, and then we pulled it altogether to build some serious conviction around your sweet spot.'

'Charley – you have no idea; this was a total gamechanger, it's what I needed.'

'And with that renewed sense of purpose we got all excited – you created the vision of your future. I told you to really go for it, THINK BIG, get it all down, think about all the areas of your life. Your dreams, goals and desires, and that's what you did! But then I ruined the party, didn't I!'

She nodded knowingly.

'This was tough for you, but I think one of the most impactful exercises. I challenged you hard, encouraged you to get super realistic. *You can do anything, but you can't do everything.* We talked about the pain of regret – you imagined yourself on your death bed and it forced you to reflect, go deep within yourself and really think hard about what actually matters and what your priorities are. Remember your ideal guy? How we went from so many non-negotiables to only a handful?' I said it with my knowing look this time – a nod to her own perfectionism.

She conceded and smiled.

'With all that in mind you were able to refresh your goals and we spread them out into a seven-year planner so you could start to think more long term, get perspective and slow down. And that, Dhivya, brings us all the way up to today!'

She puffed out her cheeks with a smile.

She had come so far in just a few weeks.

'Charley – this has been incredible. You know I'm way less stressed, I even met someone the other night, and – get this – we're speaking to the Gates Foundation about possible investment. It's all happening!'

'What! That's amazing. Well, I did tell you this stuff is life-changing – haha! OK, but seriously, come on, we've got to get this wrapped up for you now.'

I was eager for her to have the last hit of the programme.

'You're now in this rare position of having real clarity around what you want and what your priorities are in life. But more than that, because of how we got here, everything is soaked in real meaning and gravitas, Dhivya, it's coming from a place deep within you – there's a real why and conviction attached to this clarity you now have. And so, this clarity becomes your superpower.

'In this modern world we're bombarded by temptation, invitation, options and distractions. Now you know exactly where you're going and how you want to spend your time.

'Now you have a strong reason to guard your time.

'Now you have a good reason to say "*no*".

'Unless it's a *hell yes!* It's a *no*.

'But here's the catch.

'There's one last thing. The final step. And without it, all this work we've done together is going to be meaningless. The often forgotten one: *Step 7 – Consistency*.

'I'm sure you've heard it all before, discipline and self-control are the keys to staying consistent. Motivation only gets you so far...

'*But how to be more disciplined?*

'*How to develop better self-control?*

'*How to stay on track?*

'*How do you build the* architecture *that makes sustained performance inevitable?*'

She leaned forward slightly.

'There's one thing that ties all this together, one thing that helps to sharpen the blade of discipline, one thing that is going to help you stay consistent, stick to your commitments and help you build confidence by doing what you say you will. And that's HABITS. As James Clear said in his hit book, *Atomic Habits*, "Your outcomes are a lagging measure of your habits."'

'Great book, isn't it?'

Of course she'd already read it. She was a doer. She didn't need help with discipline – she was already up at 5 a.m. doing her Vinyasa Yoga. Was I wasting her time?

'His principles and tactics are brilliant, but they're not that helpful unless you have the right inputs to support them. You'll see what I mean in a second. I've read pretty much every book out there on building good habits and I've synthesised all the most important ideas into these six golden nuggets.'

She reached for her workbook like a diligent student.

'Here goes: First up, the **Habit Loop**, a term coined by Charles Duhigg in his book, *The Power of Habit*.

Cue, routine, reward.

Think of McDonald's: golden arches (cue), the meal (routine), the engineered hit of sugar, salt and fat (reward). They've cracked the loop perfectly. So if you want to create a new habit, hack this loop. Create an obvious cue – like putting your running shoes by the door. Define the reward – whether it's a coffee or guilt-free TV time. Control the loop, and you control the habit.

I could hear her thinking – fine, next.

'Next is **Willpower**. You'll love this, by far the biggest hack for me. Have you heard about the radish experiment?'

She shook her head.

'In the nineties, the psychologist Roy Baumeister and his colleagues invited a group of hungry, fasted college students into a room with tempting freshly baked chocolate cookies and some unappealing radishes. The students were split into two groups. One group were allowed to tuck into the cookies, while the others could only eat the radishes and had to resist the temptation of the cookies.

'The "radish group" found it hard, many apparently gazed longingly at the warm cookies, some even picked them up, admired them, flirted with the idea, but nobody actually bit into the forbidden food – the temptation was always resisted.

'Afterwards, both groups were taken to another room and given geometry puzzles to work on. They thought they were being tested for IQ but actually they were being tested to see how long it would take for them to give up. What they didn't know either was that the puzzles were unsolvable.'

Dhivya was well and truly dialled back in.

'And here's the bombshell… The students that had been allowed to eat the cookies worked on the puzzles for an average of twenty minutes, but the radish eaters, the ones that had to resist the cookies, gave up after just eight minutes on average. Can you see? The radish group successfully resisted the temptation of the cookies, but that effort had left them with less energy to solve the puzzles.

'And that was it – that was the eureka moment: <u>willpower is like a muscle, it gets depleted</u>. Our effort to resist something uses up energy and that diminishes willpower. It runs down like a Duracell battery. Healthy habits require self-control and self-control requires willpower.'

'Gosh, I like it, I'd never thought about willpower like that. So, being selective about what we want to use our daily finite resource of willpower for can be a powerful strategy? Where is our self-control best put to use? Which habit? What time of day?'

'Exactly. Do you remember me telling you about meta habits? Like waking up at 5 a.m., going to the gym or not drinking alcohol, habits that have a big impact on other habits. That's why it's a good idea to just choose a couple of key habits to focus on, channel your willpower and master them. The big habits should take care of the little ones. A rising tide lifts all boats as they say.'

I caught sight of the clock – time was running out. I needed to crack on.

'Next up, it's all about the **Process**. Have you heard that Desmond Tutu quote, "There is only one way to eat an elephant: a bite at a time"? I'm sure it's nothing new to you, but it's worth reminding ourselves that it's not about trying to eat the whole thing in one go – it's about breaking it down into achievable and sustainable bite-size pieces.

'A common mistake is trying to go too hard too fast and then not being able to stick to a new habit. It's counterintuitive but the best way to start a new habit is to make it super-easy.'

'I can relate entirely, Charley. I've been trying to explain this to one of my guy friends. He's been talking about doing this six-week, six-pack challenge for nearly two years now but never gets around to it. I keep telling him he doesn't do it because it requires so much effort – hardcore exercise and an intense diet – I told him he's got it the wrong way around.'

'Precisely, he'd have been better off just committing to five minutes or five sit-ups a day – make it super-easy and then build. Think where he'd be now if he started that two years ago! Make it easy and low friction, get traction, and then build. Find joy in the work itself, and the outcomes will follow.

'OK, Dhivya, next up – the fourth nugget – and this one's critical. **Identity**. Here's what separates the people who transform from the people who plateau: they stop thinking about habits as actions and start thinking about them as identity.'

'You're not someone trying to meditate – you're a person who meditates. You're not working towards becoming a runner – you are a runner. The behavioral change follows the identity shift, not the other way around.'

'Own it. Embody it. Because identity conflict is real. The tighter you cling to an old identity, the harder it becomes to make change. Don't stand on the sidelines of your own life.'

I waited for her to finish scribbling notes and pop her head up.

'Last two nuggets. Number five, a clear and definite **Purpose**. You'll have no problem with this one. Friedrich Nietzsche said: "He who has a why to live, can bear almost any how."

Finding the cure for dementia drives you. Five years, two hours a day drove me to finish my book. Without a clear reason why, life's distractions will pull you off course.

'Why is it really important? What does it really mean to us? Even fitness goals. Why are you really doing it? To look good on the beach? Or to be able to run around with your kids? The stronger the *why*, the stronger the outcome.

'And finally, Dhivya, – stay with me! Last but not least, number six, change your **Environment**, change your life.

'The "social contagion of health" was a study where researchers observed the health of dogs living in a kennel environment and found that when a healthy dog was placed in a kennel with sick dogs, the healthy dog's immune system was suppressed, and it eventually became sick. But when a sick dog was placed in a kennel with healthy dogs, its immune system was strengthened, and it eventually recovered. The study proved that the immune system could be influenced by social cues like the presence of others. Crazy to think that the internal biology of a dog can be influenced by others dogs it's surrounded by, right?'

She was itching to flex her biology and neuroscience knowledge, but I could see she was more interested in not being late for her panel. I wrapped things up.

'We've all heard the saying, *we're the average of the five people that we surround ourselves with* – it seems obvious from a cultural perspective, but this experiment shows just how much more is really going on beneath the surface when we're in close quarters with friends, colleagues, or family. The way we're wired physiologically and mentally is literally changing without us knowing.

'Healthy, unhealthy.

'Positive, negative.

'Ambitious, lazy.

'I honestly believe that the single most powerful thing one can do to make change is to change our environment.

'"... experts agree also that the person you *will be* one, five, ten, twenty years from now depends almost entirely on your future environment."'

That's from David Schwartz, *The Magic of Thinking Big*.

'I couldn't agree more,' Dhivya said. 'I've got some of the smartest people in the world on my team, they push me to be a better leader. And the rich diversity gives us different perspectives, which is super important in what we do. I can see how people working from home can struggle for motivation though. Especially entrepreneurs. You might have to go in search of the right people, your tribe, the people who are going to challenge, help and inspire you. It's not easy to find the right people, is it?' She paused. 'Is this where you invite me to join your mastermind, Charley, haha?!'

I stayed shtum and smiled. Obviously having someone of her calibre was exactly the sort of person I wanted to attract to my mastermind (mentoring a highly vetted group of entrepreneurs and business leaders all supporting one another).

'Well, you know my favourite saying, Dhivya: "Change your environment, change your Life!"

'And that's it – the six golden nuggets to build good habits and stay consistent in life.'

1. *Hack the Habit Loop* – cue, routine, reward.
2. *Willpower* – it gets depleted.
3. *Process* – fall in love with it.
4. *Identity* – let go of the old and embrace the new.
5. *Purpose* – know your why.
6. *Environment* – the invisible force shaping your future.

'But can you see how without having done the work leading up to this – knowing yourself, knowing what matters, knowing what you want and why, having a clear vision of your future across ALL areas of life – these six nuggets would be like having the weapons but no ammunition?'

It was the perfect place to end. 'Got to run – let's catch up soon.'

And we were done. The final piece to the puzzle – consistency.

I closed my laptop and went next door.

—

'Brush! There you are.'

Nicole and my father were leaning over the side of the bath playing with the kids.

'How did it go?' Nicole mouthed subtly.

I gave her a nod, a wink and a thumbs up.

'Come in, these three are having a whale of a time.'

'Look, Dada is here now – shall we show him our trick?'

Cruz squeaks and splashes the water with excitement as he lowers his face into the water to blow bubbles. 'AH brrrrrrr. AH brrrrrrrrr.' Clara erupts with laughter; her giggling was infectious – they loved it!

I perched on the loo. Nicole looked up at me with that loving, motherly glow as if to say – *let's remember this*. My father was captivated and so in love with his grandchildren – it was a moment of pure joy.

'Here, pass me the towel, I'll do this. You two go next door and check on dinner,' she said.

FULL CIRCLE, OPEN DOOR

We shuffled outside onto the patio where the sun was setting behind Table Mountain – his face was animated and youthful even though he was in his early eighties. He took in the spectacle. Breathed it in.

'God's own country this is. Charley, I must say, I'm terribly proud of you, you know.' He put his hand on my shoulder.

'Thanks, Daddy – that means a lot, we're getting there.'

There was a pause. I could hear Nicole inside, kids laughing.

He was flying back to the UK the next day. We'd made some special memories during his visit; it had meant everything to him, and he'd been on great form. But I wanted to tell him something, and I didn't know when I might get another chance.

'Daddy.'

'Yes, Brush?'

'I want you to know how grateful I am for everything you've done for me over the years – I really do appreciate it and I'm sorry for being so hard on you at times. I think I just get hung up on the negative stuff sometimes and forget a lot of the good.'

'Huh. You were a bit.' Smiling, surprised and verging on the satirical. As if to say, *finally some recognition!* 'Well, that's very kind. I know I wasn't perfect... but we gave it a good shot, your mother and I.'

'You did,' I said. 'You gave us a brilliant childhood. The opportunities, the support, the love. You know, I think it takes having your own child to fully understand what you and Mimi did to raise us lot. I really am grateful – thank you for everything, Daddy.'

My words eased something inside me, just as I felt they did inside him.

'I've realised it's not about trying to change you. That would be madness.'

He chuckled. 'You'd be wasting your time there. I'm a bit of a dinosaur, Charley.' He looked down into his glass of Chenin Blanc. 'I know I can be a bit much sometimes. But I do mean well.'

'I know you do,' I said. 'And that's why I'll always stick by you.'

He looked out again toward the sea and I could see his eyes starting to glisten. 'You're doing a bloody good job of it, this life you've built. Makes me proud.'

We hugged it out. A moment I'll never forget.

That was it. That was enough.

There was no big resolution. No sudden healing or cinematic breakthrough.

That's the work. Not changing him. Not needing him to validate me or suddenly become someone else. Just holding the door open. Just being the son I want to be. And letting the rest be. Not every story ends with a perfect bow. But some end with truth, and that's more than enough.

That evening, I reflected on the journey. Miami. Jelena. Sabine. Landmark. Tony Robbins. Naval Ravikant. George. Sabrina. Nicole. Chats with my parents, and everything in between.

It had all lead me to this moment.

I had changed on the inside and my life had transformed on the outside.

I was happy, fulfilled, motivated, building a successful coaching business and surrounded by the people who I love and who love me. They were always there – but I didn't recognise them, or if I did, I shut them out.

I'd gone from being insecure, in a rush, cutting corners, people pleasing, needing to prove, addicted to admiration, and needing to conform, to living a life on my own terms, feeling complete, thinking long term, at ease and self-assured. I used to be trapped and now I was free. I was proud of the person I had become. I'd recalibrated myself from the inside out, sculpted my own identity while building deeper connections with my brother, sister, mother, father and close friends.

Nicole's father, Kevin, once said to me:

'Like who you are.

'Like what you do.

'And like how you do it.'

I felt like I'd finally got there.

I could see society for what it was with so many of us being driven by our subconscious needs and fears to please, to matter, to compare, to not fail, to feel loved, to seek validation and status. All driving so much of our behaviour and decisions. I'd escaped the trap of that hollow, anxious and never-ending existence.

I could see so clearly now how much self-doubt had held me back in life. But I'd broken through that. Built real self-worth – not the borrowed kind from external validation, but the earned kind that comes from integrity. From doing what I said I would do. From keeping promises to myself. From following through when it was hard and no one was watching. I didn't need to convince myself anymore. I had proof. And proof doesn't lie.

I thought about what the future might hold. How we wanted to raise our children. How hard it would be not to want to overprotect them. I knew the greatest gift I could give them was a whole heart and healthy self-esteem.

I needed to do my best to keep a happy and loving home.

I want them to learn how to think, not what to think.

I want to encourage them to make their own decisions and overcome their own struggles.

For them to learn to love and be loved fully.

Of course, I knew it would be easier said than done, but I wanted to do my upmost to give them roots to grow and wings to fly. I thought back to a line from Kalil Gibran's *The Prophet* that always stuck in my mind: *You may house their bodies but not their souls.*

I want to live by that.

I was excited about what the future held for myself, my family and my business.

How things might turn out approaching life with this new mindset.

Thinking long term.

Thinking big.

Wanting to serve.

Wanting to inspire.

Wanting to work with great people.

Wanting to forever learn.

How different might that be?

STEP 7 – CONSISTENCY

Hey – you made it. Thanks for sticking with me.

Here's a quick recap of this step for you – it's the final piece of the puzzle.

It's like placing the final shape at the centre of all the other shapes – it lights up, infiltrates and draws on all the other pieces to unlock your future.

Clarity shows you the destination.

Consistency is your vehicle to get there.

1. Know your why.
2. Know your worth.
3. Have a clear vision of your future.
4. Adopt a long-term mindset (think in four-to-ten-year cycles).
5. Extrapolate back to create long-, medium- and short-term goals.
6. Decide on your daily meta habits that quietly propel you towards your goals.
7. Agree on the sacrifices required with yourself and people around you.
8. Let go of the outcome, fall in love with the process.
9. Simplify, guard your time, focus (even saying no to things you like).
10. Curate your environment for less temptation and more inspiration.
11. Utilise fresh willpower – do the hardest thing at the start of the day.
12. Break it down into small, easy bite-size pieces then build.
13. Track progress – tick it off. Get old school.
14. Don't outsource discipline – a coach can support you, but the hard yards are on you.
15. When you're knocked off track, get back as quickly as possible.

Consistency is a multidimensional game.

If you think you might be in 'loser's loop' or be struggling with low self-respect or self-worth, here are the five steps to building back your worth.

1. Your cup is empty.

Acknowledge this is where you are.

2. Know you can fill your cup.

Know that despite what might have happened in your past, you created these ideas and beliefs about yourself, so know that you can also change them now.

3. Make it rain proof.

The surest way to change a belief about yourself is to create proof. Think about if you believe in ghosts. Most people would only really believe in ghosts if they actually saw one – they had proof. So, to fill your cup up, you need to make it rain proof. Speak up, push back, say no, have a go, be brave, get uncomfortable, do what you say you're going to do – follow through. Create undeniable proof that you are who you say you are.

4. Draw from the well.

Go inward and start nurturing the beliefs that matter – compassion, worthiness, enoughness. Re-educate your soul. Remind yourself, daily, of your value. Talk to yourself like someone you care about. Use meditation, journaling, affirmations – whatever helps you embody the truth. Be kind. Be respectful. Choose self-love over people pleasing, proving, or chasing validation. You are already enough, right now, as you are. This is the mindset shift where the rot stops and self-worth begins to grow.

5. Let the water in.

When you start making progress, don't dismiss the acknowledgement or the wins. Absorb the progress and watch your inner confidence rise.

Be brave and dance in the rain.

'Bet on yourself. Move like it is already yours.
Because sometimes that mix of belief and being bold
is the only gap between staying stuck and making history.'

EDUARDO DELLA MAGGIORA, CEO AND FOUNDER OF BETTERFLY

FINAL THOUGHTS

Brené Brown once famously said, 'Vulnerability is the last thing I want you to see in me, but the first thing I look for in you.'

If she were in the cut-throat business environment of the kind where I used to operate, that might almost sound like a threat. But Brown is a social psychologist who became famous for her TED Talk on shame and vulnerability and how they impact human connections at every level.

She is just one of the many people who cast a glorious light over this book. Her TED Talk is one of the top five most viewed ever, precisely because it has cut through all the noise and helped so many people navigate the minefield of self-help.

I hope my story has shown you what's possible, and will help you get closer to how you want to feel and where you want to be. I was incredibly privileged – I had the time, resources and access to figure this out. I've distilled it into this book so you can get there faster and without spending a fortune.

It doesn't have to take years. With the right structure, a clear, step-by-step path to transformation, you could change your life in a matter of weeks. From scattered and stressed, to calm, clear and fulfilled.

And self-awareness is the foundation to meaningful change, being vulnerable with ourselves before we can be vulnerable with anyone else, drilling down into exactly why we all think, feel and behave a certain way. Once you know yourself, you can begin to change yourself.

I wanted to give you the full story so you can see all the steps that I took along the way. And with any luck, you can see that in order to really make change – to change your life – it's never just one piece of the puzzle that will do it, but multiple pieces.

Change is a multidimensional game. At times it might feel like a lot, a minefield, an overwhelm of information. But the reality – what I came to see – is that it's just a lot of the same stuff dressed up in different ways.

If you stick to my steps, then you won't go far wrong. Whether you're at the beginning, middle or end, this perspective of what you might have missed or what lies ahead should keep you on the right track.

Step 1 – Desire (You must first want to change)

Step 2 – The Body Baseline (Strong body, strong mind)

Step 3 – The Essentials (Your guiding lanterns)

Step 4 – Know Thyself (Introspection, awareness)

Step 5 – Responsibility in Action (Take ownership, get uncomfortable)

Step 6 – Clarity (Your superpower)

Step 7 – Consistency (Staying on your path)

You'll always come across more cool stuff out there – ice baths, breathing exercises, inner child work, psychedelics, to name a few – but whatever it is, it should fit into one of these steps. You'll not only know where you are – but it should dial down the overwhelm, help you make a call on your next move and know the juice is worth the squeeze.

For me, sequence was the key to it all too.

Can you imagine trying to build new habits before actually getting clear on what you want?

Can you imagine trying to get clear without really knowing yourself first?

Can you imagine trying to go deep and know yourself better while you're stressed as hell?

Try to avoid being like I was early on – the narcissist with a Green Goddess juice and a yoga mat, only focusing on the superficial, thinking I had all the answers.

Have the courage to slow down and look inwards.

Eddie Rickenbacker, a World War I hero, said, 'Courage is doing what you're afraid to do. There can be no courage unless you're scared.'

It sounds obvious, but I like this because I think it's easy to forget that doing something courageous is meant to feel scary and uncomfortable.

The number one regret people have before they die is that they wished they had the courage to live a life that is true to themselves and not the life others expected of them.

I don't want you to have this regret.

But where to start?

At the beginning. *Step 1 – Desire.*

Stoke the fire of desire:

Be honest.

Believe (I believe in you).

Know your why.

Follow a path.

If you want real actionable guidance, this is where I can help. My programme, *Beyond Mumbo Jumbo,* is the practical implementation of these seven steps – a framework I've lived myself and refined with leaders, entrepreneurs and driven individuals who demanded more from life. It's immersive, efficient and it works, saving you years of trial and error.

If you're stuck, at a crossroads, care deeply about not having regrets, and are serious about fulfilling your potential – this is the path. The sooner you start, the sooner everything changes.

So, my friend, I hope you can see why the juice is worth the squeeze. Trust me, it is so worth it in the end.

And if there are just three things you take from this book, remember...

1. It all starts with a dream – *believe.*
2. Embrace the discomfort – *lean into the struggle.*
3. And never settle – *reach for the stars and keep going.*

This is the book I wish someone gave me at the start of my journey when I was confused, unhappy, needing to get back on track and knowing there must be another way but not knowing how.

Enjoy the journey. I did. And I have never regretted taking that first step.

NEXT STEPS
⬇

1.

Sign up for **the Compass**

A concise newsletter every few weeks – your guide to clearer thinking, deeper meaning and forward momentum. You'll also get first access to my latest podcast episodes and updates.
www.charleylaw.com.

2.

explore the programme: Beyond mumbo jumbo

Fast-track your transformation with the 7-step framework. Claim 30% off with coupon code: ACTIVATE at www.charleylaw.com.

3.

Share the journey

If this book spoke to you, pass it on to someone who needs it. You never know whose life you might change, and together we can build a movement of people living their best lives.

YouTube: @CharleyLawOfficial
Instagram: @charley_law
Facebook: Charley Law
LinkedIn: Charley Law

RESOURCES & BIBLIOGRAPHY

BOOKS

Here are some of my favourites, including most of those mentioned in this book.

I have tried to group them into which of the seven steps they fell into for me.

Step 1 – Desire
The Lion Tracker's Guide To Life, Boyd Varty

Step 2 – The Body Baseline
Serve to Win, Novak Djokovic
The TB12 Method: How to Achieve a Lifetime of Sustained Peak Performance, Tom Brady
How to Die Young at Ninety, Dr Jan de Winter

Step 3 – The Essentials
The Five-Minute Journal

21-Days of Inspiration, The Chopra Center
The Power of Now, Eckhart Tolle
The Untethered Soul, Michael A. Singer
Awareness, Anthony De Mello
The Almanack of Naval Ravikant, Eric Jorgenson
Can't Hurt Me, David Goggins
The Prophet, Kahlil Gibran
How to Live a Good Life, Jonathan Fields
Principles, Ray Dalio

Step 4 – Know Thyself
The Chimp Paradox, Professor Steve Peters
Ego is the Enemy, Ryan Holiday
Daring Greatly, Brené Brown
What Are You Doing With Your Life?, J Krishnamurti
Healing the Shame That Binds You, John Bradshaw
The Four Agreements, Don Miguel Ruiz
Psycho-Cybernetics, Maxwell Maltz
The Mask of Masculinity, Lewis Howes
Reinventing Your Life, Jeffrey E. Young and Janet S. Klosko
Breaking Negative Thinking Patterns, Gitta Jacob
Positive Intelligence, Shirzad Chamine
Boarding School Syndrome, Joy Schaverien

Step 5 – Responsibility in Action
EST, Playing the Game the New Way, Carl Frederick
Awaken The Giant Within, Anthony Robbins
How To Change Your Mind, Michael Pollan
The Courage to Be Disliked, Fumitake Koga and Ichiro Kishimi
Attached, Amir Levine and Rachel Heller
The Book You Wish Your Parents Had Read (and Your Children Will Be Glad That You Did), Philippa Perry

Step 6 – Clarity
Enneagram, Tina Madison
Think and Grow Rich, Napoleon Hill
Find Your Why, Simon Sinek
Accelerating Excellence, James A. King
The Magic of Thinking Big, David J. Schwartz
Mindset, Dr Carol S. Dweck
World's Best, Ric Charlesworth

Step 7 – Consistency
Winning Hearts and Minds, David S. Gilbert-Smith
Atomic Habits, James Clear
The Power of Habit, Charles Duhigg
Discipline Equals Freedom, Jocko Willink
High Performance Habits, Brendon Burchard
The Score Takes Care of Itself, Bill Walsh
Wooden on Leadership, John Wooden and Steve Jamison
Winning, Clive Woodward

PODCASTS

A few favourite episodes and shows.

Episodes:
 'Diary of a CEO Podcast Episode 209 with Dr Tim Spector'
 'On Purpose Podcast Episode with Dr Zach Bush'
 'The Knowledge Project #18 Naval Ravikant: The Angel Philosopher'
 'The Joe Rogan Experience #1309 – Naval Ravikant'
 'The School of Greatness Ep. 679 with Joe Dispenza "Heal Your Body with Your Mind"'

Shows:
 The High-Performance Podcast with Jake Humphrey & Damian Hughes
 Impact Theory with Tom Bilyeu
 The Knowledge Project with Shane Parrish
 Modern Wisdom with Chris Williamson
 The School of Greatness with Lewis Howes
 The Tim Ferriss Show
 The Ed Mylett Show

RESOURCES

The Paleo Diet – thepaleodiet.com
Dr Jelena Petkovic – drjelenapetkovic.com
Brené Brown: The Power of Vulnerability – TED Talk
The Chopra Center and Deepak Chopra – deepakchopra.com
The Art of Meditation – theartofmeditation.org
Summit Series – Summit.co
The Magic of Human Connection – themagic.love
Dr Joe Dispenza – drjoedispenza.com
British Association of Behavioural and Cognitive Psychotherapies – babcp.com
Mind – mind.org.uk
James' Place – jamesplace.org.uk
Principles You, personality test – principlesyou.com
The Myers-Briggs Type Indicator assessment – eu.themyersbriggs.com
Hogan Development Survey – hoganassessments.com
The Enneagram – enneagraminstitute.com
Landmark Forum – landmarkworldwide.com
Date With Destiny Event – tr.tonyrobbins.com
Sadhguru – isha.sadhguru.org/uk/en
Sabrina Percy – centien.co.uk
George Lepine – galconsulting.co.uk
Leadership Trust – leadershiptrust.co

ACKNOWLEDGEMENTS

Thank you to Bella Forbes, Jemima Hunt, George Pickford, Dhivya Venkat and Jonathan Eyers for your invaluable guidance as I wrote this book. Thank you to John Bond and the Whitefox team for your patience, support and utmost professionalism through the publishing journey.

Thank you to my parents, Carola and Victor, for your blessing in sharing such intimate parts of our lives. Your selflessness and encouragement for me to speak our truth and share for the service of others is truly inspiring.

Thank you to my brother Matthew for always standing by my side.

Thank you to my sister Nina for the moments of joy you bring to our lives.

And finally. Thank you to my wife Nicole. I could never have written this book without you – I would never be the man I am today without you. Thank you for our two angelic children, Clara and Cruz.

Charley Law is an executive coach, author and speaker who works with business leaders, entrepreneurs and high-performing teams to build the internal architecture for sustained performance and fulfillment.

Through his programme *Beyond Mumbo Jumbo*, private coaching and keynote speaking, he helps clients navigate transition, move beyond burnout and align success with how they actually want to live.

His approach is holistic – integrating mental, physical, strategic and spiritual foundations to deliver transformation that lasts.

Charley lives in Cape Town with his wife Nicole and their two children, Clara and Cruz.

All enquiries: team@charleylaw.com

www.ingramcontent.com/pod-product-compliance
Lightning Source LLC
LaVergne TN
LVHW041957060526
838200LV00002B/53